THE HUMAN EXPERIENCE: THE EARLY YEARS

for Stephen Green

'For now we see through a glass darkly; but then face to face: now I know in part, but then shall know even as I am known.'   *1 Cor. 13. 12.*

The Human Experience:
The Early Years

CEDRIC CULLINGFORD

Ashgate

Aldershot • Brookfield USA • Singapore • Sydney

Published by
Ashgate Publishing Limited
Gower House
Croft Road
Aldershot
Hampshire GU11 3HR
England

Ashgate Publishing Company
Old Post Road
Brookfield
Vermont 05036
USA

Ashgate website: http://www.ashgate.com

British Library Cataloguing in Publication Data
Cullingford, Cedric
    The human experience : the early years
    1.Child development 2.Experience in children 3.Child
    psychology
    I.Title
    305.2'31

Library of Congress Catalog Card Number: 99-76357

ISBN 0 7546 1156 6

Printed and bound in Great Britain by MPG Books Ltd, Bodmin, Cornwall

Contents

Foreword by Kieran Egan

Cedric Cullingford's aim is to represent the mental world of the child with unprecedented clarity. He aims to show that this world, in its normal experience by children, is significantly unlike what we typically assume it to be, and significantly unlike anything exposed by the most prominent research programs.

The book is structured logically, beginning with an outline of children's understanding that emphasizes its range and complexity. He develops compactly a picture of children's extensive intellectual competencies. He supports this picture with extensive reference to empirical research, but this is largely left to footnotes and intrudes on the text very little. The picture he presents conflicts at many points with common assumptions about children's thinking.

Chapter 2 addresses the mythology of children's intellectual incapacity, and discusses the reasons for and history of the unjust patronizing of children's minds that has been common in western cultures. He looks in some detail at various developmental theories and their representations of childhood intelligence - particularly Piaget's - showing how they illegitimately defend, and further propagate, the view of children as intellectual incompetents.

Chapter 3 prepares us for the approach he is to take in the remaining chapters in detailing children's construction of a sense of their world. It might be described as a methodological justification for what follows, except that it also continues the substantive argument. In particular, he argues for a form of discussion with children as a source of reliable data about their thinking and feelings.

The following four chapters build a description of how children come to make sense of their world. They begin with how they construct a theory of mind, then how their social relationships further that theory of mind, of self, and of the world in which it exists. He focuses on the family, the school, and then the wider social world. In all cases he shows the sanity of children, their realistic sense of the world they encounter (as distinct from their supposed ignorance and fantasy about the world), and their eschewing of the kinds of suppressions and evasions that are common in adults. These chapters are built around quotations, sometimes quite extensive, from children, following the methodology of interview and analysis that he justifies in Chapter 2.

Chapter 8 elaborates his general argument that we have not often taken childhood seriously - even those who purport to study it. To do that we must first clear away the kinds of assumptions and presuppositions that prevent us from seeing major features of childhood experience. Only by performing this difficult task will we have an ability to sort out what we should do in the school, in the family, and in society to enlarge our experience generally. He argues that we should not suppress so much of childhood experience and work to preserve and fulfil capacities that are evident in childhood and too often atrophy thereafter.

This is an unusual book. On the one hand it overlaps with some of the "romantic" books about the wonder of childhood - but is much tougher-minded and uses extensive empirical support. On the other hand it overlaps with the psychological and educational literature on children's thinking and development - but is more daring in its construction of a distinctive view of children's experience. It has more in common with Angel's Ashes than with the typical educational or psychological research study.

Central to the book is its view of childhood experience. It must be said that Cedric Cullingford's view is unusual in my reading of education and psychology books. The reference to Angel's Ashes above is appropriate also in that the image one comes away with is of considerable trauma as the lot of every child in adapting to the world they find themselves in. The central chapters make for some uncomfortable reading. Cedric Cullingford presents a stark picture, but one that has the uncomfortable ring of truths we might prefer not to acknowledge. As he concludes: "How do we survive all this?" And his answer is the remarkable mental capacities demonstrated, if only we see them straight, by young children.

The constant image Cullingford uses is of the child's gaze, addressed to the world they are new to. That gaze, he emphasizes, and supports, is not the innocent and ignorant eye commonly suggested, but is critical and intelligent. The youngest child, he argues, is not simply responsive, but is active and critical in interrogating the world.

I think this book achieves a vividness and intensity that I haven't seen elsewhere.

Preface and acknowledgements

This is an ambitious book, written over a long period and drawing on a mass of evidence which has gradually emerged from complexity into a coherent whole. It is this mixture of respect for the material in all its richness and the realisation that it all carries a significant message that makes the book so important. The message it carries should enable us to change first the way we think about the young and then to act towards them and their education radically differently.

Every piece of evidence, and every quotation used to illuminate and flesh out the individual draws attention to the uniqueness of each person's experience. But we are all human and we all share and understand other peoples as well as our own, some of the pleasures and traumas, hopes, disappointments and ambiguities. Just as each experience is unique, so it is common to us all and we are only diminished if we do not acknowledge the shared human experience.

This gives us a problem in terms of tone There are some important and over-reaching themes which emerge from the individual pieces of evidence. These are not mere generalisations. Each individual voice stands for a whole mass of corroborating evidence. Whilst each individual is unique, this is a book about their collective gaze. It is about the underlying truths beneath the cultural distinctions, the unstable and chaotic environment of which each child is trying to make sense. When we therefore write that 'the children say' this is not a sweeping statement but one that is meant to give dignity and respect both to the individuals and to their shared experience.

This study is part of the discipline I would call 'education' which means to others that it draws on a number of disciplines. One day, I trust, the battles for the hegemony of individual subjects and the academic demarcation lines will be over. Meanwhile, trying to look in a new and open-minded way at evidence rather than trying to make it fit into an 'a priori' hypothesis it might well raise some academic suspicions. The research community, after all, relies on closed networks.

Perhaps this is one reason why we haven't really listened to the voices of children and how their experiences affect them. Afterwards, as we get older, we learn better how to control and limit what happens to us and the information we receive. But for young children the human experience is still raw and immediate. When we say 'children' we imply the universality of the human experience.

I have tried to listen carefully to the voices of the children in these studies, but I have also listened to many others. Some of these will be found in the references which indicate how much good research has taken place, even if the implications have not been fully understood. But there are also a number of individual friends and colleagues who, over the years, have supported and challenged and help in their different ways. Again, I can only draw out a representative sample: David Winkley, Kieran Egan, Lew Owen, Susan Smith and Susan Ellis. And as well as all those I am aware of omitting, teachers in particular, are many others who have influenced me inadvertently and importantly, just as children are influenced in their early years.

Introduction

We are coming to the end of a century of violent conflict and violent changes. As we approach the Millennium we do so not so much in a spirit of hope as in a spirit of anxiety. When we look back at the global conflicts of this century and the rise in crime, we can be forgiven for wondering to what extent the rapid developments in technology have distracted us from paying attention to the understanding of human nature since they have also contributed to the growing sophistication of violence.[1] We have witnessed Nation States building crime into the centrepiece of their administrations and such new extremes of violence against the innocent, that they have not yet lost their power to shock.

One image of our times is of two boys leading a toddler off to his death, captured on video.[2] That image synthesises the two characteristics of our age, the ability of technology to record man's inhumanity to man. The changes in information technology and its applications is disturbing in its rapidity. But the failure to understand why people behave as they do and what to do about it is the more disturbing. It sometimes seems as if people do not actually wish to know the causes of behaviour, as if all they want to be distracted.

One of the most significant applications of the new technology is in entertainment. There are more and more sophisticated forms of distraction, simulations in films, new physical extremes of rides in theme parks and more and more 'realistic' recreations of speed and violence. Nothing could be less real than 'virtual reality' where with great technical sophistication and attention to gory and explicit detail people are placed in the extremes of fantasy. Whatever the form of entertainment people find themselves placed in strange simulated worlds, full of violence, in films or electronic games shooting people mercilessly and without effect. All is action, rather than thought, and all thought geared to the action, distracted from distraction by distraction.

There is nothing sadder (to those on the outside looking in) than the sight of people chained to the instruments of entertainment, buffeted by the throbbing lights and throbbing sounds, finger on the trigger or foot on the accelerator, as if they were in the purgatory of simulated pleasure from which they could not escape. For those who are addicted to distraction it is

xi

hard to break away. It is an effort to face reality. Facing things as they are demands greater courage than escape.[3]

The desire to escape, to be 'bored', is understood much better by children than by adults. This is because they have not learned how to dilute experience or to re-formulate it in such a way that it is no longer challenging. To them the world is unstable and uncertain. 'Chaos' is no theory. The challenges they face is understanding *why* things should be as they are accumulated, are still raw and unmitigated by previous experience of how to deal with and deflect reality. Finding a way to avoid the unpleasant or to escape from it is more apparent for it's not yet becoming an automatic and undetected habit.

The emphasis on distraction by machinery serves to contrast the intelligent effort put into creating entertainment, and the lack of commensurate attention paid to understanding the individual and shared human experience. It is because people have to be entertained *rather* than understand. Yet we need to understand the sources and motivation of the extremes of behaviour and its connection to the ordinary and the everyday. We also need to understand why some people can enter a school gymnasium or a café and shoot at random. These are the extremes. We also need to understand the experience of childhood - not as we nostalgically recreate it, but as it really is, so that we understand why people, all people, are as they are. This book is not about the psychopathology of the minority, but about the common conditions and influences that affect us all and which can lead to such different outcomes.

The shared experience of all human beings is complex, which itself explains why we are all so individual. The ways in which young children, from their very beginnings, scrutinise the world have a number of different layers. They do not gaze at the world purely in terms of the physical, what is seen and felt, or what is gratifying. Their discriminations of sight and sound includes refinements of categories and responses in terms of fairness and consistency. They rely on their interpretation of concepts such as shape and perspective. And they also make moral judgements, about truth and falsehood. All this happens at the same time rather than in a series of stages. This book explores how this happens and the implications.

This book also explores why distractions are so attractive and the ways in which people put up sometimes necessary barriers between themselves and the truth. In trying to explain, it challenges some long held notions about the human experience in the early years. Some of the very features it describes - resistance to change, and the desire to fit anything new into existing habits of thought will apply to reactions to the book. The unfreezing of the mind, and the reconsideration of beliefs can be disturbing processes and, for reasons the book describes, are usually initially resisted. When George Eliot sympathetically describes people as 'well-wadded with stupidity'[4] she points to the need to find an exclusive protection against thought, sometimes in a cult or a religion, sometimes in astrology or in some form of mental oblivion. This book attempts to explain why this is so.

One of the reasons that people try to learn to protect themselves is because so much that happens is inadvertent. We are concerned here with the real, inner personal experiences of human beings - not what is meant to happen to them but what does and how it affects them. So much work is done on measures to raise standards, to make a difference to the individual through systems and policies. Little that is done has an immediate effect. Here we are concerned not with measuring the inputs but with the experience, the outcomes, the realities of the individual's life. We are not concerned with intentions - however well meant - but by their results. The two can be very different. David was one of three brothers. One day his mother said to him, after he had done a kind act, "Ah David; you're the thoughtful one. Stephen is the handsome one, and Peter the clever one, but you are the kind one". The mother meant to pay a compliment. She had perfectly good intentions. But to this day David remembers feeling and thinking "That means I'm ugly and stupid". Examples of the inadvertent and the unintentional abound. It is one of the reasons we are trying to explore the human experience from within.

This implies that the book is ambitious. Any book that tries to communicate rather than display the cleverness of the author should be so. It is based on the reconsideration of a mass of empirical evidence. Whilst it is a story, and an account which is an individual interpretation, it is not only a 'story'. It is grounded in the belief in validity and reliability. The subject matter has too much significance not to demand a search for truth.[5]

All the experiences of the twentieth century are well documented, from the terrible events of the holocaust to the burgeoning technical achievements. We know what happened and what is happening. We need to be able to ask not only what but why? We need to do so not seeking an instant solution or whom to blame but with an insight into the nature of the human experience at the formative stage and at a time we tend to have forgotten and suppressed. Sometimes people cling to the myths of innocence or genetic inevitability because they do not believe that anyone *can* understand. Sometimes they do so because they do not wish to understand since this would make them responsible for taking some action.

Acknowledging the power of young minds is a challenge few seem to want to face. Perhaps it has too many implications both to systems and, more significantly, to the sense of personal coherence. When we learn, for example, that children just a few days old have already learned a preference for one language rather than another, are we to dismiss this as a mere genetic pecularity?[6] Is language genetic? When we learn that babies not only cannot understand logic but prefer puzzles to everyday and banal reality - the pleasure of seeing tricks played with the numbers or figures seen and ostensibly taken away and returned far outweighs the already logically understandable - we realise how active are their minds.[7]

This book tries to reinterpret and encapsulate the essential experience of young children. No space could be large enough truly to sum up such a mass of complex evidence. But the evidence in its abundance is like the evidence of history. To make sense of it we need to choose those parts which illuminate the larger themes, those individual experiences that give insight into the whole.

At the heart of this endeavour is to explore the young mind's 'gaze', what he or she observes and experiences of the world, the people in it and the many forms of communication and meaning. If we endeavour to listen to the experiences of children and reconsider the complex way in which they attempt to make sense of their environment we are forced to reconsider many of those notions that have become a kind of academic folk-lore. Whilst acknowledging individual differences and idiosyncrasies, this book tries to explore what human beings have in common, so that we can deal more successfully in helping others through their experience of life.

> We that acquaint ourselves with every zone,
> And pass both tropics and beyond the poles
> When we come home, are to ourselves unknown
> And unacquainted still with our own souls.
>
>   (Sir John Davies, 1599)

Notes

1. Every history of the 20th Century draws attention to the conflict. Eric Hobsbaum's *Age of Extremes*. London, M Joseph 1994, carries a comparatively mild title for such a phenomenon.

2. Smith, D. *The Sleep of Reason*. London, Century. 1994.

3. There is a parable in the Bible when Christ is confronted by a 'drop-out' who cries out to be saved. He is questioned firmly and to the point. "Do you *really* want to be saved?" The answer is probably not; it would mean too much effort.

4. Eliot, G. *Middlemarch*.

5. Perhaps like Karl Popper's notion of testing an idea.

6. Mehler, J; Jusczyk, P; Lambertz, G; Halstead, N; Bertoncini, J and Amcel-Tison, C. A Precursor to Language Acquisition in Young Infants. *Cognition*, Vol.29, 1988, pp.143-178.

7. Wynn, K. Addition and Subtraction in Human Infants. *Nature*, No.358, 1992, pp.749-750.

1 Through a glass darkly? The abilities of young children

In many ways we take ourselves for granted. Fixing a gaze at all that happens around us, curious about all that is being communicated, we seem to lack a curiosity about the way we are and the way we came about. This is not to suggest that we are not interested in ourselves. On the contrary, we are each of us the only real subjects of interest in the Universe. Our senses, our gratifications, our understandings and how they are received by others are of such intense concern that we almost forget how peripheral we might be in other people's schemes of things. Self-absorption is not the same as self study, or rather the study of the human experience, the analysis of how individuals come to consciousness and become as we are. In fact the subject of the greatest fascination for all - the essential human experience that we have in common rather than seeking to define differences according to gender, 'race' or socio-economic circumstances - is the subject of comparatively little academic investigation.

There are many books which seek to give comfort to the individual's sense of worth, books which explain what to do, as well as courses in self-assertion and regimens to promote happiness. There are religions, psychologies, astrology and sects who seek to explain everything. But these are all concerned with the individual self, from the self's point of view. The subject of human growth and development, of learning and education does not elicit the same curiosity or wonder. Whilst there is an abundance of literature on how to teach, and what to teach, there is relatively little even on the learning process, and almost nothing at all about the experience of those who undergo it. The energy of endeavour is put into finding solutions rather than exploring the need for them, in measuring activity rather than exploring its reasons.

If people do stop to marvel, or accept surprise, about human development, it is as likely to be about the progress made in the field of communications as in any other matter. Every day seems to accelerate the pace of change, with new systems and new facilities that mean that all kinds of manner of things can be learned, and infinitely more ignored. Excitement at the development of neural circuits in computers, and the application of chaos theories to technology seem to replace curiosity about the most sophisticated intelligence system of all, the brain. But then technologies, however complicated, are much easier to study. They do not have the same arbitrary inspirations, the emotional drives, the moral senses and the self-awareness that makes the individual being what he or she is.

The rapid development of communication systems is symbolic of two important insights into the human condition. The first is the acknowledgement of ability and power. The means to control the environment, no longer to have a sense of physical frailty or loneliness suggests an application of intelligence that is always outward looking and which should suggest not only power but growing responsibility. The mastery over information technology symbolises the capacity and the potential of thought about ourselves.

The development of communication systems, however, also begs a question. What is it that we are so busy communicating? Does the quality of our dialogues match the means by which we can extend them? In so far as there is concern with the quality of what is being communicated by electronic means, it focuses on the misuse of the system, on appropriate or disturbing messages. There is, indeed, a rift between the means of communication and what is being communicated.

If the proper study of mankind is "man", turning from self-absorption to an analysis of the human condition, then it is perhaps surprising how 'improper' we have been. For every empirical study of people as they are how they are affected by their conditions and how they react with them there are any number of research projects and policies concerned with how people *should* be and either how to make them so or how to punish them for not being so. The human gaze is outwards, at what is immediately visible rather than what appears hidden. We argue about what should be learned, and about teaching styles, about the management of the education system and about the assessment of skills. But how often do we explore the effects of all these on the learner? We discuss different personality inventories and create new psychological categories to see how people fit into them. But how often do we explore the individual experiences of learners?

Just as strong as the capacity to learn is the refusal to do so. Not knowing is part of the defence mechanism of everyday life. For it is well understood that to change someone's style or habit of thought and action is very difficult. Most of the individual energy devoted to learning is devoted to fitting anything new into the structures of attitude which already exist. It is as if people would be afraid of what they might find out.

The lack of curiosity about evidence derives partly from fear. People seek evidence to support them in their set of beliefs, even if they are contradictory. They do not want them - at a personal or at an academic level - challenged. If politicians, for example, actually listened to the many studies consistent with each other about the importance of early learning, they would need to act quite differently. But the fear of responsibility and the burden of dealing with it is only part of the explanation. In itself such awareness of what is being avoided would itself be a burden so it remains unacknowledged. The other symptom of avoiding such curiosity is that people feel they already know all the answers.

The explanations given are always simple. It is as if all the conflicts of human nature were already accounted for. Explanations are simple and also complex defence mechanisms. Do we really understand the deepest motivations for love and hate? Do we really understand the ways in which people create prejudices against and stereotypes of each other? If we look at a typical 'tribal' conflict such as that in the former Yugoslavia, can we really say that we understand *why* people think and act as they do? Explanations are simple and dismissive; they centre on religion and on language, on history and culture or on atavistic anthropologies or genes. But they do not answer the simple question. What is an individual's 'culture'? Why do religious beliefs sometimes lend themselves to kindness and virtue and sometimes to hatred and bigotry? What is there about other people's language and culture that makes people angry and threatened? These are the kinds of straightforward questions that tend not to be asked, let alone answered. The simplest, even the most naive questions are always the most difficult to answer.

The problem is that the more the excesses of human behaviour are reported the more the sense of the inevitable accumulates. The capacity to be shocked and horrified never leaves us, but it is confined to rare events when we should be disturbed every day. It is only the most extremes of behaviour that causes anguish in those distant from it, and, tellingly, the arbitrary murder of the innocent in places where it is unexpected, rather than the continual horrors of war. All these acts have explanations, and these are not the explanations of the abnormal or the exception. Explanations lie within the shared human experience. The problem then is that when things generally go wrong, when people misbehave, it is almost accepted as inevitable. It might seem inevitable but it is not necessary.

To assert the comparative lack of curiosity in exploring human nature does not mean the same thing as there being a dearth of explanations. There are many assumptions made about genetics or about the environment, that suggest that people know the answers even before they have looked for them. To take the pathology of crime as an example, there are many long-standing debates about whether the causes of criminality lie in the individual or in the environment. The difficulty in this debate is the fact that there is the assumption of inevitability, that things could not be otherwise, whatever the argument - "it's the way he is" or "it's the way he was brought up". And then one way of escaping rather than confronting this dualism is to redefine the problem in a constitutive criminology, seeing crime as a cultural artefact in the interpretation of the beholder. Such relativity can be the avoidance of seeking real understanding.

As the next chapter outlines, the studies of the human experience have rested heavily on what seems to be a given, that all rests on stages of development, that people move from innocence to experience, from childish limitations to the sophistication of adulthood. Furthermore there are assumptions made that there are regular patterns, through which stages follow one another. Thus the interest is partly directed towards the ways in which these stages of development are expressed, or on the influences that come to bear on them. The human experience is seen as a series of rational steps, in which it is normal to grow into some kind of wisdom, and abnormal to escape into the pathology of wrong doing.

Suppose we have got this wrong? Suppose these assumptions are misplaced? Suppose the experience people undergo in their early years is far more dramatic and complex? We like to comfort ourselves with notions of childhood innocence and infant incapacity despite the evidence to the contrary. That means we can create an atavistic dream world for ourselves and that we do not feel ourselves and at the same time avoid the feeling that we are being closely scrutinised or judged by those closest to us. Oscar Wilde sums up in his own way a widely held belief:

> We begin by loving our parents, after a while we judge them, rarely, if ever, do we forgive them..[1]

But even his is a developmental view. It does not consider the possibility that judgement and forgiveness might lie alongside rather than after the loving. Nostalgia or sentimentality about childhood is a form of self-protection. Pets are unthreatening. We would like to think that young children are equally unjudgemental.

One of the most important understandings that have been gained over the last few years is about young children's capacities. In study after study it is discovered that young children are able to discriminate, make judgements, analyse social situations and the complexity of human relationships by the time they are four. It is, of course, possible that they do so far earlier and it is only the difficulties of communication that keep this hidden. We are easily deceived into making judgements about ability according to the mastery over language. As children adapt themselves to the world in which they find themselves so they adapt their means of expression to the vocabulary of those around them. But long before they have linguistic mastery over self-expression, children are able to analyse and understand what they see and hear, as many of the following references will demonstrate.

Suppose we acknowledge the real ability of young children and see them not as unformed or half-formed creatures only gradually able to understand? Suppose we look at them more as alien beings suddenly plunged into a strange new world and looking at it askance.[2] If children have the ability to analyse what they see what do they make of it? If we realise that they come into the world with an intelligent critical gaze we might think differently about what they experience. We might also think differently about the circumstances we present to them.

The distinction between the capacity and potential of children and the actual realisation of this capacity is widely acknowledged. Whilst the 'exceptionally gifted' child is celebrated and a subject of some curiosity, it is acknowledged that such abilities should not be the exception but the norm. The capacity is there in every human being; it is the rule rather than the exception. But the capacity to think, feel and analyse remains for the most part unfulfilled. This book seeks to explain why.

An analysis of the literature of experiments that demonstrate children's capacities reveals three underlying characteristics. The first is the sheer complexity of any 'description' of human thinking, even abstract reasoning, let alone all the moral, emotional and social dimensions without which thinking cannot be understood.[3] The second is that to uncover and 'explain' the thinking process is a very difficult task, and time and again what is uncovered is limited by, and interpreted by, the methodology used. The third is the amount of interest shown in young children up to the age of five or six. Until that time the ability to respond, or categorise, to articulate or demonstrate examples of rational thinking gain all the undivided attention of researchers. But after the age of six, it seems, child development in the normal sense comes to an end, judging by the little attention paid to it. Thereafter, young people are no longer the subjects of curiosity but left happily or unhappily in the hands of their teachers. There are exceptions, especially studies of young people in adolescence. But these are virtually all about the 'abnormal', about aggression and broken relationships, about crime and failure. It is the shared experience of all young people with which we are concerned here. What is the consequence of such natural early ability. What has often been well researched in the cognitive functions of the brain. What does all this mean?

The process of reasoning is complex. To understand the essence of the physical world in the way children do is to understand an array of different phenomena all of which interact with each other. We might take this for granted but which we tend to assume these things are beyond the capacity of young children. And yet to survive, let alone understand, their environment, children must be aware of a variety of different concepts. These include the ability to classify and discriminate, to see each chair as individual but all chairs as one type of concept. Young children need to grasp, although not necessarily in formal terms hierarchies of classification: that a trout or a salmon are both fish, that a fish is a vertebrate and a vertebrate an animal. They need to understand scale as in maps or as in magnification. They need to know ratios of their own limbs are subject to the same laws as gears and pulleys. They need to understand the researcher's prime concern: the significance of variables in terms of the relationship between events, and to know how many variables can apply at the same time. They need to know about correlations between one thing or event and another; they need to know about probability and understand abstract models.

"Multiplicative compensation", "proportional thinking", "the exclusion of irrelevant variables", "probability" and "correlations" all sound like complex concepts. They are. They are certainly complicated to explain but not difficult to acquire in the normal process of growing up. They are all necessary towards the understanding of the immediate environment and are necessary long before they are defined or articulated. And these are just the physical aspects of the world. The experiments that demonstrate understanding sometimes discover the inarticulated necessity of such understanding. Thus in creating a sense of equilibrium it is necessary to demonstrate the fact that four variables are involved in a balance; two weights and two distances from the centre. Balance, aided by putting our arms out on a narrow plank, is itself a manifestation of this concept. Concepts can be understood long before they are demonstrated.[4]

The process of thinking, of analysing their surroundings both visual and aural is amply demonstrated by infants. But like parents we do not often realise that this close scrutiny of the world is a search for categorisation, for bringing reason to what in its infinite variety might seem like chaos. The ability to make general characteristics, to apply a theory of similarities and differences is part of the early response to the environment. What is usually studied are the observable manifestation of such categorisations rather than the intellectual capacity which drives them. What is less well understood are the emotional influences of what is observed, and the different means of organising the information. For no human being is ever passive. They might like to be, they might seem as if they are and it might suit others if they were. But at one level or another the individual is reacting, is drawing conclusions, is not merely gazing but being affected by what is observed. He and she are constructing their own world view, seeing themselves as individuals and realising that all other people they come onto contact with are doing the same thing. There is, them, their own gaze, that of millions of others, and the shared phenomenon that binds them all together.

What the researchers have done is to demonstrate at how early an age in their subjects they can *prove* these capacities for intelligent understanding. This does not mean that finding of the ability the means to demonstrate the proof is the same as the first existence of such understanding. But even assuming that the ability to understand is dependent on its demonstration we need to take in the fact that young children bring intelligence to bear on the world in ways that have been held as an adult preserve by the time they are three and four. It is a fact often resisted not in theory but in action.

There are two aspects of human life into which children explore very early. One is practical philosophy, the ability to reason. The other is the understanding of the complexity of human relationships, including the ability to deceive. The two are very closely connected as if the rational were always hand in hand with the manipulation of the irrational. Young children observe, with surprise and astonishment, not just the logic of human behaviour but the ways in which motivations are disguised. Young children see through appearances. They are able to generalise characteristics in common amongst different objects and concepts.[5] They go beyond superficial, surface features in making their discriminations. They are also able to make genuine causal inferences and demonstrate them around the age of three. For instance they infer the relationship between (say) a broken cup and a hammer or a wet cup and water.[6]

Long before they can be seen to make abstract causal inferences young children will have had to experience them: an adult leaving a room, a hand raised, or in the earliest months the way in which a mother will prepare her dress for feeding. Without causal inferences how could anyone survive? Such understandings, however, are not limited to the physical environment or to the direct intervention of others. They are also observed in the emotional logic of other people's behaviour. Before there is any ostensible interpretation of the words used a young child can see how her parents suggest actions before they take place: the expression, the hint of aggression, the slight exasperation. Causal inferences in terms of technological outcomes are merely the abstract end-product of everyday experiences. It is, in one sense, as simple as no food leading to crying.

Causal inference can be manifested in the most simple of ways, but it is also at the heart of complex human understanding. The capacity to see meaning, like the capacity to develop language relates the experience of young children to those of adults. So much can depend on adults realising this and action upon it; in fact in 'teaching' in the real sense, seeing teaching as interaction as opposed to a barrage of knowledge opened later. Even the youngest of children can be taught to turn their understanding into demonstrations of their understanding. There is, for instance, the famous case of 'conservation': is the amount of sand or water in different cylinders the same, whether it looks tall and thin or broad and wide. The ambiguity of the word 'same' does not need to be dwelt on here, but much has been made of the fact that children of five were not capable of explaining or acting on the demonstration of their understanding of this concept. The assumption followed that they were incapable of understanding the idea of compensation, even if they lived with the actualities of the concept from day to day. And yet it has been demonstrated that infants of 14 months can actually be taught the concept as expressed in experimental as well as experiential terms.[7]

The need to understand causality is to appreciate the connections between events. Some might seem simple and others complicated as in the recognition of the real variety ('chaos') that surrounds the consequences of every human action. The distinction between simplicity and complexity might lie in the fact that one action - breaking a cup - is not nearly as obscure as giving an order that someone else must carry out. But the distinction is also between the surface and the underlying causes and consequences. Enough repetitions of a raised voice, or an angry expression leading to violence and the causal inference will be as clear about human relationships as about a broken cup. Young children are able to see not only the connection between two actions but understand the distinction between them, each one with its own integrity.[8] They understand classifications which overlap, like shape and colour, by the age of three.

Concept formation, the classification of events so that they make generalisable intellectual sense, is a type of necessary problem solving.[9] Every new stimulus either reinforces or needs to be placed in correlation to those already understood. Whilst this can have negative consequence in the long term - the rejection of any new information which does not fit into the pre-existing pattern - it appears to be a necessity in early learning. The problem is that no one, including the intelligent recipient, can completely control what connections are made. As young children build up their structures of the world, their own classifications for making sense of the varieties of information, they can as easily see the connection between untoward actions, like brutality, in all in fearful consequence, as between the everyday more neutral logic that underlies the formation of physical constructs and natural law.

How can young children, seeing causality, make distinctions between those events that cohere, in terms of physical consequences, like balance, equilibrium and variety, and those that hang together in terms of human action? They appear to apply the same sense of logic to both. They scrutinise the patterns of behaviour as well as the patterns of furniture. They classify the way that people interact just as they categorise typologies of objects. Thus they are very quick to understand the logic of natural causes, like the origins of objects and causal understanding (how the sun began and why rabbits have long ears). By the age of four they are aware of the distinction between man-made change and natural causes to the extent of being able to be tested on it.[10] Far from assuming that natural things are created by people, they understand the integrity of the natural world, and the application of concepts to its functioning, for example that there are links between internal parts of the body and activity, that bones are important for the flight of a bird.[11]

The abilities of young children, rarely explored in normal circumstances, demonstrate the ability to be logical and to draw distinctions between the notions of hypothetical belief and evidence.[12] They realise very early that not all is as it seems, that people have their own motivations for what they say and do, clutching their own beliefs. They are able even to construct an empirical test to decide between two conflicting hypotheses. The notion, therefore, that the world as presented to them is one simple and homogenous whole, accepted as simple fact, is far from the reality of sophisticated scrutiny of the very young.

Testings - or demonstrations of ability - are not as valuable as findings, the realisation that the abilities are already there, indeed, a necessary part of the condition of living. When hierarchies of needs are mentioned there is a tendency to think of young infants as helpless in the hands of adults, or that their needs are primarily physical.[13] This might seem to make some kind of primitive sense - without the physicality of living nothing else exists - but it misses the point. Infants need the ability to think in order to make use of the opportunities of the physical. Being fed is not just a passive experience. As early as the pang of hunger comes the curiosity of interaction with the world. Certain needs cry out for attention, but the infant's attention is already engaged.

There are limitations to finding means of demonstrating the earliest abilities of children, but it has also been discovered that these can be taught and learned. Just as some tests seem to be designed to prove limitations so the same limitations are easily overcome if the tests are presented somewhat differently.[14] Children are aware of their own learning. When they are helped by being told about their own experiences, and when they have dialogues about the processes that they are undergoing they are not only learning as fast as ever but able to demonstrate it.[15] It is a question, it seems, of finding out how to prove such understandings. But logic suggests they exist long before the process of testing. The more sensitive the exploration of young children the earlier is the detection of their understanding of causality and random phenomena.[16]

These understandings are not confined to the logical acquisition of knowledge. They also take in the more complex causalities of emotion and the truth and falsehood of representations of things as well as the things themselves. By the age of four young children are able to consider alternative representations of the same object.[17] They are also able to understand the complex feelings of pride and embarrassment; the feelings that arise not just from observation of other people's behaviour, but examination of their own.[18] If young children led such uncomplicated naive lives, could they inhabit a world of such emotional complexity? Their feelings are by no means confined to the need for food and warmth, or even for attention and distraction. In addition they are analysing, whether they like to or not, the behaviour of themselves in relation to others and the differences between appearances and reality. Embarrassment often lies at the core of such complexity. It is the juxtaposition between the private and the public and the awareness of a distinction between the two.[19] It is the sense of being exposed, of being caught out. It is a highly sophisticated as well as social emotion, a charged sense of discontinuity between the self and the environment. It's a significant part of the world of 'childhood'.

If there is a clash between the private and the public there is also an overlap between experiences which are specific and experiences which, perhaps through repetition, become more generalised. Abstract thought arises from the sense made of any number of specific incidents.[20] It is not a pattern imposed upon the variables - at least not until the individual has decided in later years to control or ignore any actual details. It is, instead, a constant attempt to make sense of the phenomena they experience whilst they know that they are not to be taken face value. They do not exist, as it were, in themselves. They have a meaning. This meaning might lie behind a false appearance, an attempt to deceive. It is often difficult for young children to know the difference between appearance and reality but they know that the distinction exists - and that is the most significant fact. There is truth and falsehood and the stress on the individual to detect the difference. This is acknowledged or understood at an early age, and to understand the earlier years of human experience means having an insight into this fact.

One could say that this is not just a fact but a predicament. If all the information that is being presented is not only complex in itself, if all the information needs to be categorised and interpreted, what chance of making absolute sense of it when you are having at the same time to make distinctions between truths and falsehoods? The kinds of errors that could be made abound. How do young children distinguish between misleading appearances which are centred around an object's real and apparent *properties*, and an object's real and apparent identity?[21] And yet children see the distinction and make different kinds of errors according to the nature of the deception. Researchers might without reflection leap upon the fact that children, faced with such intellectual conundrums, make errors. More significant is their ability to make distinctions between different types of appearance and reality. By the age of three young children understand the division between appearance and reality. Already, they do not accept things as they seem to be. The issue for parents and other adults involved is what to make of this and how to give intellectual encouragement as well as emotional warmth. The tendency to concentrate first on the physical, and then on loving encouragement and only later in intelligent understanding has become stretched into a misconceived 'hierarchy' of stages. When all of these approaches depend so strongly on each other and belong together.

The human intelligence understands much more than it recognises it has understood. We are often unaware of our own understanding. Corrections are made, inferences are a source of knowledge, signals are given and received.[22] Study closely the behaviour and conversation of two members of the same organisation doing business just for two minutes and you realise that the levels of communication are many. All is not what it seems. There is far more going on than meets the ear. The inflexion, the innuendoes, the pauses all amount to a complex series of signals at a cognitive and emotional level. Some things are pure appearance, or pretence, a disguise or an attempt to hide. Other messages are clearly unintended, but understood. When young children observe the behaviour of others they do not know all the social and cultural artifice which surrounds all human action, but they do look closely. And they understand inference, even when they assume that others do not.[23] Their awareness of the world includes the realisation that they can see what is going on even when those they observe seem to believe all that they say.

Children have the delicacy to assume that other people's knowledge is based strictly on fact. But whilst they rest securely on this assumption young children also make inferences about the reason for and the limitations of other people's knowledge. There is a subtle and complex distinction, again, between the understanding of what is taking place, recognised intuitively, and the expression or demonstration of that understanding. Young children are able to acquire new conceptual categories with remarkable ease and with acute accuracy.[24] And yet, when they are formally tested in a laboratory they are so sensitive to the desire of the researcher and in a curious way so polite that they present ineffective strategies for their own learning. They are, in fact, presenting the first hint of the stranglehold of human adaptability, learning to please, to give the information that is so obviously, to them, required by the inferences of the other. Adaptability can be a sign of intellectual mastery, but it can also be turned into a limitation.

Understanding inferences means, in fact, recognising the requirements of dissimulation as well as actuality. is revealed in knowing how to adapt to circumstances. It is a 'pre-linguistic' form of dialogue. It derives from the fact that children are able to create a dialectic relationship with their surroundings already possess that most formidable component of categorisation, a language. They will introduce a concept which, once the label is well known, seems a simple category but, from the point of view of an intensely living individual, something complex. And yet, when the concept of death is explored we discover not only that young children have a sense of its overall meaning but of those sub-sets of attributes that contribute to real understanding.[25] They realise the inferences, of death's irreversibility, and universality.[26] They not only realise the ultimate distinction between the living and the inanimate, but also some of the meanings of dying that are left unexplored, or deliberately kept unexamined until the later reaches of old age.[27]

It is impossible to prevent young children contemplating all the big issues surrounding the meaning of life and impossible to ensure that they receive an ordered sequence of experiences that match a theoretical maturing. All parents will have noticed how direct their children's questions are - but will tend to dismiss them as touchingly naive, as if children did not really wish to know the answers. Besides we have observed the answers to simple questions are the most difficult to give. Thus there is a temptation to brush aside the children in their questioning. It is adults who created the myth of the naive simplicities of childhood. Many of the artificial explanations, like babies being delivered by storks, show a kind of well meant but misplaced mawkishness. It is as if adults cannot quite bear the thought that their children are having to face the deepest questions. This question about information is part of the adult way of coping, a way of coping with reality that children are being carefully initiated into accepting. It is telling that adults at the same time recognise that all the most penetrating and disturbing of facts actually present themselves into the consciousness of the child, through primary or secondary information, the dead bird on the path or the sensational horror presented on the news and yet pretend that they were either never seen or made no impression. The mythology of childhood 'innocence', interpreting a lack of ability to shoulder much responsibility as a pleasant and unknowing naiveté is contradicted by all the information they are observed to receive. This is a contradiction which is completely human; the facts at once recognised and dismissed.

The assumptions that adults make about children are, of course, part of the cultural process that teaches children how to adapt, how not to be too ambitious. It partly explains the distinction between their abilities and the way these are, in the majority of cases, under used. For children's ability to understand and their need to analyse are mitigated as well as enhanced by their social sophistication. Their very earliest judgements and insights are about human relationships. This includes the ability to guess what the other person wants. They can even make up for the social deficiencies of others.[28] This suggests a strong motivation to please as well as a clear insight into what people are thinking and feeling. Young children do not merely absorb what is presented to them, but return it. This is as true of emotions as of their analysis of the physical environment.

Together with the ability to handle complex information, children understand human relationships in a sophisticated way at a far earlier age than has generally been recognised. This is another significant finding which emerges from the extensive literature on young children's development. Indeed, one of the most significant factors in learning, which goes deeper than any 'pure' idea of cognitive capability, is the social aspect. Young children's motivations, their understanding of others and the sharing and description of knowledge are the basis on which academic learning rests. Long before they are able to express their understanding of social relationships they are able to demonstrate it.

Social relationships are not simple interactions. There is never a time when, as the popular mythology holds, a young child sees him or herself as merely dependent on others making demands that need to be fulfilled. The earliest signs of communication are attempts to please, to respond. Relationships are about social conventions as well as values, and concern moral tasks as well as the sense of ownership.[29] In fact children quickly learn that there is the potential for conflict as well as unity in relationships and in different points of view. They understand that if they have a point of view their parents might well disagree with it. This could be seen to be on good, logical grounds, but there will still be a conflict of interests. Every parent will have experienced the battle of wills with their young offspring. They might not have seen this as a demonstration of the child's ability both to detect and to reject a different point of view. Conflicts or outcries are early examples of the exploration of social conventions, and the tension between rules and emotions.

Learning always has a social context. It is impossible to separate some kind of logico-mathematical reasoning as if some kind of formality of thought could take place uninfluenced by all the observations that have been made of the variations in human behaviour and relationships.[30] The insights that we have now accumulated have demonstrated not just the paucity of information presented to children in experiments which are designed to limit themselves to the detection of hypothetical mental operations, but the fact that children necessarily bring with them a whole variety of complex social understandings. Their means of learning does not just take place in relation to their categorisation of inanimate objects, and their catalogue of linguistic groups, but in relation to others. The evidence is now abundant about young children's ability to understand other people's point of view.[31] This happens well before the age of four. They are anything but egocentric. They are able to detect the different processes of thought in other people and as soon describe another's point of view as anything else. Indeed, one can even see an ability to see what is really there, rather than what is in the strictest terms visible. For example they will draw the handle of a cup even if it is facing away from them as they are drawing. The adult has learned perspective: the strict rules of the visual. The child knows what is actually there. Similarly the child detects the hidden motivations and thought processes of others, and not just their face value.

Children have a theory of mind which is formulated the moment they can accept the difference between the I/me and you, which is by the age of two.[32] They are also aware of other people's emotions as well as their mental perspectives. One of the first things they learn about other people's emotions is the distinction between the fact that people feel things but also hide them. What a person displays can be a disguise, a pretence. After all, for the sake of the children, parents will almost inevitably hide some of their feelings.

Children also quickly develop moral insight. The moment there is a hint of falsehood there is a sense of right and wrong. The fact that children are also morally pragmatic, knowing what people can get away with, and are concerned with the outcome of actions as much as their motivation is an outcome of their experience.[33] It is the acute observation of other people's behaviour that leads to the sense of the everyday right and wrong. Whilst they acknowledge the difference between the happy wrongdoer and the sorry one, it is a relatively minor concern against the effects of the action itself. They do not expect people to feel good if they have harmed someone else, but they have also witnessed countless examples when this has happened. It is as if children are learning the sophistications of disguise, as if they learn bit by bit how to state a moral perspective according to what they *should* say rather than according to their experience.

Children's awareness of emotions, an awareness that is far earlier than their understanding of its terminology, is essentially an understanding of other people's as well as their own.[34] Emotions can be felt, but to be understood they need to be seen in the light of differences and similarities, in the overall human experience. Emotions are a central aspect to inter-personal relations, and personal feelings are understood in a social context. By the age of eighteen months children already possess an appreciable understanding not only of the way people feel emotions but, necessarily, the way in which emotions are communicated. Understanding is of the way that emotions are conveyed as well as experienced.[35]

The distinction which children make between the emotions which are clearly presented and those which are disguised or suppressed points towards their ability to see the underlying motivation and intentions of others. They understand the psychological experience of choice, not just in themselves but by the inferences of others.[36] They appreciate the subtleties of emotions and intentions before they learn how to create a dialogue about them, before they can share their analysis. The difficulties that researchers have faced are not just in learning about this but in demonstrating it. Nevertheless the evidence of early social understanding is weighty and consistent. Whilst the implications of this have not been fully understood the earlier notion that children only develop slowly in taking in the perspectives of others has been thoroughly overcome.

Young children are formidably social creatures. The world they eagerly analyse is the living and moving world of articulated as well as hidden thoughts and desires. By the time they are eight months old babies are clearly 'tuned in' to the different emotional expressions of adults.[37] By the time they are two they are interested in the implications of transgressing rules - as well as doing so. They can both argue with their parents and show sensitivity to the other person's point of view and the delicacy of their feelings. They have insight into the need in other people for being comforted; even young babies demonstrate this capacity. Young children understand other people's goals and intentions and they understand social rules.

This ability to understand others makes children capable of all the kindnesses and sympathies of human nature. But it also has potentially dangerous consequences. They are consistent observers, and they detect what adults in theory would wish to keep hidden. They are also inveterate overhearers. What they see and hear is then interpreted in the light of the knowledge they have already acquired. Long before social rules and conventions are formally explained to them they are amply demonstrated in the richness of everyday social life. But they also experience the failures of relationships as well as the comforts; they witness arguments as well as disagreement. Having the ability to know about points of view arises from the fact that they understand difference, that there is conflict. Seeing the difference between what is felt and what is said is the beginnings of being witnesses to the potential pathology of human relationships. What children require is the ability to have different points of view accepted and agreements negotiated. This is dependent on the sophistication of personal dialogues.

The fragility of the early years of the human experience lies not only on its dependence or circumstances, and relationships with others. It lies in the constant scrutiny of human behaviour. Young children and adults share a fundamentally similar construct of human action in terms of beliefs and desires; they understand the psychological reasons for actions.[38] The difference is that adults have found their own completed rationale, for good or ill, for their own and other people's actions which arise out of their beliefs. Children are constantly constructing their own theories. This is as fundamental a need as eating.

The understanding of other people's points of view and their beliefs also includes the recognition of false beliefs, of falsehood within the array of truths. This aspect of a theory of mind has proved to be of particular interest to those seeking to understand the experiences of young children. The reason for this is that the distinction between truth and falsehood, between the real and the fantastic, between fact and myth, is the most sophisticated demonstration of complex thought. But it not only gives a telling insight into the abilities of young children, but also a disturbing acknowledgement of the complexities of experience. There is no time of simple innocence, unaware and unknowing. The capacity for understanding, and, it follows logically, the experience of falsehood, of lying, of making a distinction between what ought to be and what is, comes early.

The tension between false beliefs and reality affects both the individual's understanding of him or herself and their interpretation of others.[39] The tension arises partly because young children have the capacity to make that essential distinction between theory and reality. Whilst they can accept that certain actions - like lying - are wrong, that does not mean that they will not make full use of falsehood. This discrimination is not just a matter of selfishness. It derives from the mixture of exploration and observation that marks out their entry into an existing and it seems complete world, with its rules to be obeyed or broken according to a whole and almost separate set of alternative rules. One guide to social behaviour is what ought to be. That is accepted as easily as the fact that the other guide to social behaviour is what an individual can use to his or her advantage. Naturally there is a constant tension between the two. At no point is there a complete and ultimate choice between one or the other. What children observe is that both sets of rules are treated with a similar respect, even when they are in contradiction to each other. They, like all others, can demonstrate awareness of morality without acting upon it.[40] After all, lies are mostly told about covering up misdeeds. Lies succeed. They retain harmony. They save time. They become, imperceptibly, a natural mode of conduct.

Children consistently demonstrate the moral sophistication of adults. They know right from wrong. They see the distinction between guilt and shame. They understand the distinction between moral imperatives and the role of external sanctions. They also realise their own capacity for bad behaviour and the psychological causes or excuses. All these insights can be demonstrated at length but here can only be summarised.

The distinction between moral rules and action is tellingly brought to light by young children's evaluation that lies are far worse than the misdeeds they seek to protect. They are aware of culpability; they are aware of the much more serious consequences of falsehood than carrying out inappropriate actions. The one becomes a consistent habit, a *modus vivendi*. It is only when the other is similarly habitual, when misdeeds become a way of life that there is a really dangerous social consequence. Thus they make a clear distinction between all those they observe being 'naughty', including themselves, and those whom they feel have an extra relish for doing so until a time might come where the distruction between good and bad no longer matters. The assumption that children have the limitation of simplifying their understanding of morality into the consequences of action, on external factors, on punishment rather than on internal factors like truth and intention, is not borne out. They see and acknowledge the complex fact that the lie itself, and the intention behind it, is as bad as an action which, whatever the outcome, was not actually motivated. Later on, as they grow older, so do children lean towards both the innate limitations of human nature and motivation, and the necessity of punishment as a regime of control.[41]

The question in many researchers' minds about young children's understanding of false beliefs and active deceptions has always centred on *when* they develop it rather than the fact that they do.[42] The argument is about whether the first signs are detectable at two or at four years of age. But the crux here lies in the word 'detectable'. The capacity to act in deceiving others is not the same as the ability to explain the deception.[43] It is interesting to note how quick children are to demonstrate the ability of deception. This can be observed in the way they employ a range of deceptive strategies in playing a game, acknowledging the possibility of false beliefs and trading upon them - at the age of two-and-a-half. Already they understand through the possibilities of truth and falsehood, of deceit and the covering of feelings, the sense of other people's points of view and how to manipulate them.[44] This is the kernel of a theory of mind; the recognition not just that people exist in relationship to each other but they have their own individual sense of the world, that each has a unique point of view.

Young children were once assumed to be in some way autistic. They were seen to be so limited in their understanding that simple egocentricity ruled their lives. Autistic people themselves feel emotion and express it strongly, but they find it difficult to make sense of other people's emotions. Young children are in no way autistic. They are almost as quick to detect other people's feelings as their own. They know about the limitations of the point of view, of subjectivity as well as the objective. They both understand false beliefs and can anticipate the likely impact of deceptive strategies on the behaviour of others.[45] They are in control, by the age of three, of information management. Given that people's mental lives are spent in manipulating experience to fit their own beliefs, in making sure that the edifice of the self is constructed in such a way that nothing should disturb it, this realisation of children's earlier experiences should come as no surprise. The fully human experience is a homogenous one. It is not saved up for some later time.

There is a distinction to be made between what children see and understand and what they would like to see. The contradiction between the desirability for truthful action and the temptation to lie is strong. But so is the contradiction between children's awareness of falsehood and their wishes that circumstances could be different. Three year olds, for example, do not *wish* to attribute deviant beliefs to others. Whilst they understand the relativity of beliefs, as between themselves and parents, they also find the contamination of fact with falsehood very complex.[46] There are, after all, physical facts, social conventions, values, ownership of property as well as morality. A fact in one case is not the same in another. There is, for instance, a genuine difficulty for three year olds in inferring that another person holds a false belief about a matter of verifiable fact.[47] That another person holds a different belief about a matter of taste or value is, of course, a far simpler matter.

But where does the distinction between reality and falsehood lie? Not only is verification a subtle, difficult matter but the representation of beliefs is a difficulty.[48] What appears to us to be a single state of the world - a matter of fact or reality - can be represented in different and apparently contradictory ways. But to suggest this is to assume that the 'world' or 'reality' is verifiable given the different points of view. No wonder young children find the concept of truth - physical or emotional, true and false - difficult. It is, in fact, almost impossible in the context of making a (post-modern, or post-postmodern?) distinction between ascertainable fact and point of view.[49] This is also, incidentally, the difficulty in summarising the case of what is true of all experience and making it distinct from sounding as if the case were no more than 'generalising' all 'children'.

Young children of three not only possess an understanding of the distinction between appearance and reality, but need to.[50] They have an insight into other people's minds before this is systematically demonstrable.[51] They can see the possibilities of false beliefs before they know how to act on this knowledge.[52] But the experience goes deep. Whatever their actions they know the morality of lying as being bad. Their moral discrimination and social understanding begin, therefore, at a very young age.

Into this ambiguous and complex world they come, seeing and adjusting. Children are close but not detached observers. Their sense of the behaviour of others and their engagement in the world is one which is self-aware and self-conscious. The responsiveness to relationships is as much dependent on their ability to adapt as the understanding of the motivations behind other people's behaviour. Their very physical experiments with their own limbs and with the constant mental exercise of play is the demonstration of their concept of themselves. Children are embedded in their own beliefs and attitudes. When they attempt to make sense of the world it is to make sense of *their* world.[53] Each has to mould the environment as it is unfolded and categorised to an individual, even idiosyncratic point of view. None of us thinks of our own mental state of interpretation or the meaning of life as anything other than absolutely normal and correct. It is only other people who hold mistaken beliefs. That is the one common attitude we all share.

If there is a sense of egocentricity it is held more firmly in adults than children. In the sense of conformity and inclusion, in the sense that a particular outlook is correct it is adults who accept their own understandings in an egocentric way. This is because it is assumed that there is no longer a disjunction between the points of view of the individual and the culture in which it is embedded. Young children, however, experience the tension between their own point of view and that of others. The pressure to conform and to accept clashes against the need to understand and analyse. This is a personal need and built on reflections that have to make sense of countless episodes and examples, before the mind has become accustomed to ignoring most of the messages - aural, physical and intellectual - that beset it. Children's early theory of mind derives not only from their growing realisation that other people have points of view, but that they themselves do.[54] It is the analysis of *otherness*, of the world that needs to be recreated into a coherent whole with a shared language and way of seeing, which comes first. Only then, as the experiences become a coherent whole and then fall back into their individual selves, do children realise that they themselves are merely one of the parts that make up the whole. A theory of the individual self is created not at the point at which children realise the otherness of other people but when they realise the otherness of themselves.

Children need to establish a concept of themselves, separate from the assumption that all fits into their, point of view. This is why relationships, and the insight into other people's outlooks is so important, why so much stress is laid on the ability to detect falsehoods as well as truths. The earliest experiences of behaviour are analytical. They reveal not only what should happen but the extent to which it is possible not to conform to it. Each person's behaviour gives coherent signs of moral or amoral codes; and these are taken to relate to the individual self. They are not slavishly followed. What is seen is seen as separate from the self, but it does relate to the individual child's sense of being. Children have a strong sense of self that becomes a global self-concept: the 'I am' and 'I do' untied from specific contexts. Even very young children, arising from their analysis of the relationship between themselves and other stable and unstable experiences, create and maintain a continuous sense of who they are.

The concept of self does not, however, lead automatically to a sense of self-belief. It is too dependent on experience, on what is believed. And yet the assumption has often been made that young children have an automatic and optimistic self-confidence. There is no doubting the importance of encouraging a healthy and robust self-confidence whatever the abilities and aptitudes, but this is not something that happens in all circumstances or all the time. It is an outlook that needs to be developed. When young children explore their circumstances they have to acknowledge the pain as well as the pleasure, the fragility as well as the sense of safety. There is, after all, no relationship without the potential of conflict whether it is between the child and an adult or the observed behaviour of others.[55] A separate sense of self includes the understanding of difference. At some time or another, whether acted out or imagined, the potential of conflict will be actualised. Children's very sense of fairness arises out of an almost philosophic stance at the pluralistic conceptions of behaviour that they observe.[56]

Children observe varieties of behaviour. In a physically stable world that needs to be made into a coherently understood whole there is always one element of intense instability. This is the behaviour of other people in relation to each other and to the child observer. Behaviour is never constant, but changes its mood and tone, as in the variety and individuality of tone of voice that is learned long before other manifestations of language.

In recent years there have been numerous studies of children's early thinking in terms of a theory of mind. There might be differences of opinion about the exact point at which a child manifests this ability, or how it can be detected, or whether such theories depend on language, or an understanding of language. What is well established, however, is the existence of children's sophisticated thought, indeed the necessity for them to have a 'philosophy' of their own. This is a capacity that adults either lose or associate simply with language or simply absorb so deeply that they no longer think about thinking. Whilst there is a tendency for adults to develop a 'folk psychology' of their own, and whilst they would eschew anything that sounds as fanciful as a 'theory of mind', it is an absolute for children.[57] I would argue that it exists long before it can be demonstrated.

The existence of a theory of mind, including a systematic ability to analyse and detect the distinction between our own thoughts and beliefs and those of others is well established by the age of four, by which time, children can use language well enough to explain abstract thought. They are able to explain the point of view, or the amount of knowledge, say, that the hero of a story - as opposed to themselves - possesses.[58] Whilst there are doubts about whether younger children possess a concept of mind which is representational and which includes sustainable belief systems, these doubts arise because of the difficulty of devising tests that would elicit such ability.[59] Children's competence is formed long before it is expressed. Young children have a genuine understanding of mental representation. They know that beliefs refer to and represent external realities, and that people act on the basis of them.[60] They also possess the notion, that beliefs can misrepresent reality as well as express it.

Young children therefore detect the distinction between reality and belief systems, and the fact that each person's belief system is real to him or herself, even if it is manifestly false to others. The very need for stability, for the understanding of a consistent world is undermined by this notion of an insecure and complex, changing reality. Just as children decode what they see as reality, so they understand that the ability to make sense of the world is itself an individual system of beliefs. The very need to create a personal interpretation, without which the mind could not function, and the very ownership over this systematic categorisation, draws attention to the individuality of personal interpretation.

There are various levels of thinking which, taken together, make for a far more sophisticated analysis of experience. Some of the necessary understandings might seem simple taken separately. Put into a whole, however, and a different picture of intelligence emerges. That some things are alive and others not, that some things are formed through outside agents and others grow naturally, that there are continuing connections between things and people and the balance of syncretism and juxtaposition all amount to a necessarily complex understanding, where the separable parts can make a whole (like the parts of a bicycle) and when meaning depends on the connections between ideas, as in a story.

Young children have a intuitive sense of concept formation. They are practical in their ability to associate specific features and individual concepts with a linking theory that makes sense of them.[61] They are like scientists as well as philosophers constantly seeking out evidence that adds to their understanding. They have a theory of mind that includes the analysis of intention and deception as well as the immutability of fact.[62] Not only are they never mere passive receivers of information, but they also conceive the mind as being an active interpreter of information.

We are aware that children make a systematic distinction between the world and mental representations of the world: hence truth and falsehood.[63] It is impossible to explain or account for points of view, including deception, without admitting psychological explanations of beliefs, desires and intentions.[64] It is impossible to make sense of events that can be explained and predicted and which all interrelate in the past, present and future, without the set of rules, without a series of references from one event to another. Out of this arises the necessary 'theory'. It is not just a matter of dealing with everyday and immediate entities but of exploring the unknown.[65] We know, for example about planetary motion. It is real, and a theory. It is true, but not experienced.

Children's sense of experience is both immediate and abstract. To talk of 'theory' is not, however, to distance thought from reality but to draw attention to the reality of thought. Bishop Berkeley in the 18th century might have been seen to be taking things too far when he argued that the only reality was what is experienced through the senses but he did draw attention to the supremacy of the inner realities of thought and response. What is remarkable about young children, if not Berkeley, is the realisation of the reality of other people's point of view. And what, in one sense, could be more theoretical than that?

Other people are, however, also all too real. No understanding is complete without an acknowledgement of their reality and their separateness. What young children need to understand includes the possibility of pretence as well as the connections between particular objects and what they might be symbolic of; like pretending that a banana is a telephone.[66] This is just one example of children's ability to have an introspective insight into the display of mental states. Play is the outer manifestation of points of view, of the enacting of different styles of being and interpretation. Three year olds have an explicit understanding of the distinction between real objects and representations, between events and thoughts and images. Long before then they are aware of the conditions affecting perceptibility, and the connections between hearing, seeing, smelling and touching and their relationship to mental processes.[67]

The only factor that prevents the exploration of young children's practical and applied theories of thinking is the limitations in the approach of scientific evidence to have the actuality deductively realised. By the time abilities are manifest in explicitly theoretical terms they are demonstrated in action. The concept of intentionality, including the ability to command as well as to attribute intentionality in others - 'Daddy read' is such a demonstration.[68] The insight into other people's behaviour, that they act in accordance with the beliefs they hold, even if they are false, is another.[69]

The difficulty for young children in their sophisticated reading of the world is that the world as presented to them is an ambiguous place. If some of their earliest insights include deception and false beliefs, what kind of straightforward reality can they take hold of? They need to understand the distinction between intention, as in a point of view, and the effect on the listener. It is the latter, as in the case of overheard remarks, that counts. There are faulty intentions and faulty utterances.[70] There are also the very personal interpretations of what is said, whatever the speaker intended. And this is as true of other people as of themselves.

We can establish the essential facts about the early experience of human beings, and re-think some of the mythologies. We know, for example, that very young children have the mental capacity to analyse what they see and experience: indeed it is a human necessity to do so. What we have not recognised in the past is the severity of the scrutiny that lies behind the seemingly innocent gaze. Children are witnesses who could be likened to strangers coming from an alien planet. They see the world in a fresh way, surprised but accepting, taken aback but adapting. The reason that this capacity has not been recognised in all its power and its fragility lies partly in the refusal to see it, partly because it is hard to prove experimentally facts which concern language before language has been developed and partly because their very adaptability has all the appearance of innocent acceptance.

The powers of the mind are therefore much more than an untapped resource or an unused ability. The interpretation of the world is a constant necessity, from the relationship between the movement of limbs and the effects of movement to the categorical interpretation of segments of visual and acoustic phenomena. If such concentration were kept up rather than smothered then we would accept as normal what we now think of as the unusually gifted. Most of the studies of young children have concentrated on the way in which understanding is ordered and classified. Categorisations underlie the means by which the world is reconstructed in the mind. This is, however, not only a process of thought, of analysis, but is the first sign of the way in which the mind has the capacity to limit itself as well as to explore, to learn how to ignore or leave out details as a way of fitting new information into what already exists.

This process of adapting sensory experience into existing mental patterns underlies mental capacity. But such powers of thought are not abstract. Research projects keep discovering the early ability to understand others, and the fact that each individual has his or her own mental framework.[71] Without such a realisation there could not be proper relationships, and relationships are the essential life line for young children. The understanding of a 'point of view' is crucial.

Understanding other people is made the more complicated by the fact that there can be mismatches between beliefs and action. The other person can have a different point of view. This can be correct, or not. The exploration of notions of truth and falsehood, appearance and reality reveal understanding of an environment complex enough for adults to find difficult. When young children analyse what they experience they are not merely accepting all as given.

The ability to understand false beliefs means that children's understanding of themselves as individuals in a crowded world goes far beyond egotism. The fragility of young children's upbringing and the uncertainties that surround it derives from this less than peaceful and optimistic sense of self. Their sense of self is not just a series of demands and fulfilments, desires and disappointments, but a realisation that there are bound to be disappointments, and that one is linked to another. Gratifications will come, but they are not automatic.

Young children possess as the most fundamental of their needs something which we tend later to forget or overlook - a theory of mind, and a sense of self in relation to others. What they observe and experience builds up into a consistent interpretation; intelligent and emotional. They do not only think but are aware that they do so. They not only act on beliefs but define such actions for themselves. They understand the concept of thought.

This capacity placed in what to them is like an alien world is not just powerful but fragile. As young children get older they quickly learn to adapt, and learn what to ignore, how far to explore inner issues and to what extent to suppress them. But during the crucial early years all kinds of information, not just about the physical world but about society, is presented to them unabated and unmitigated by explanation. Human behaviour in terms of their immediate family, their parents and siblings is displayed before them, supported by the cast of millions, glimpses of television and insights into human behaviour in all its difficulties. Looked at in this way the modern world, like those ages that preceded it, does not present itself as one of sweetness and light, of stability and order. Those who read and hear the news everyday are aware of all the conflicts on various scales, and like the ploughman in Breughel's famous picture, carry on, disregarding the great events.[72] But for young children such facts cannot be ignored. Learning how to disregard them is part of the process of growing up. At the beginning facts are received in all their vivid immediacies.

Each individual has his or her unique set of interpretations. But there is a common core of experiences, and a style of adaptation that belongs to each of them. It is this that we need to understand in order to help, it is this central and generalisable fact of experience that we need to be sensitive to, if we are to bring out the uniqueness and develop the capacity of each child.

The highest level of social and intellectual competence in the adult world has its basis in the minds and experiences of all children.

Recognising this can be difficult given the ideologically constructed 'gaze' of the adults.

Notes

1. Wilde, O. *Lady Windermere's Fan*, Act III.

2. There is a school of poetry, however short-lived, called the 'Martians' for their attempt to scrutinise the world as if they could bring a fresh and unsullied gaze to everything. For them it meant some spare and original reinterpretations. For children this is no self-conscious attitude.

3. The many papers in a journal such as *Child Development* demonstrates an accumulated insight into the early development of human reasoning, although it is the time and fact of the case that is often reiterated rather than the consequences.
    Cullingford, C. *The Nature of Learning*. London, Cassell, 1990.

4. The distinction between the two will be taken further in the short discussion of Piagetian research.

5. Gelman, S and Markman, E. Young Children's Inductions from Natural Kinds: The role of categories and appearances. *Child Development*, Vol.58, No.6, pp.1532-1541, 1987.

6. Das Gupta, P and Bryant, P. Young Children's Causal Inferences. *Child Development*, Vol.60, No.5, pp.1138-1146, 1989.

7. MacLean, D and Schuler, M. Conceptual Development in Infancy: The Understanding of Containment. *Child Development*, Vol.60, No.5, pp.1126-1137, 1989.

8. Sugerman, S. *Children's Early Thought: Developments in Classification*. Cambridge University Press, 1983.

9. Kintsch, W. *Memory and Cognition*. New York, John Wiley, 1977.

10. Gelman, S and Kremer, K. Understanding Natural Cause: Children's Explanation of how Objects and their Properties Originate. *Child Development*, Vol.62, No.2, pp.396-414, 1991.

11. Again, to anticipate, this disproves the suggestion of Piaget.

12. Sodian, B; Taylor, C; Harris, P and Perner, T. Early Deception and the Child's Theory of Mind: False Trails and Genuine Markers. *Child Development*, Vol.62, No.3, pp.468-483, 1991.

13. Maslow, A. *Motivation and Personality*. New York, Harper & Row, 1954.

14. See Donaldson, M et al., next chapter.

15. Pramling, I. Developing Children's Thinking about their own Learning. *British Journal of Educational Psychology*, Vol.48, No.3, pp.266-278, 1988.

16. Kuzmak, S and Gelman, R. Young Children's Understanding of Random Phenomena. *Child Development*, Vol.57, No.2, pp.559-566.

17. Astington, J; Harris, P and Olson, D (eds.) *Developing Theories of Mind*. Cambridge University Press, 1988.

18. Seidner, L; Stipek, D and Fesback, N. A Developmental Analysis of Elementary School-aged Children's Concepts of Pride and Embarrassment. *Child Development*, Vol.59, No.2, pp.367-377, 1988.

19. cf. Ricks, C. *Keats and Embarrassment*. Oxford, Clarendon Press, 1974.

20. Marini, Z and Case, R. The Development of Abstract Reasoning about the Physical and Social world. *Child Development*, Vol.65, No.1, pp.147-159, 1994.

21. Taylor, M and Flavell, T. Seeing and Believing: Children's Understanding of the Distinction between Appearance and Reality. *Child Development*, Vol.55, No.5, pp.1710-1720, 1984.

22. cf. the work of M Argyle.

23. Sodian, B and Wimmer, H. Children's Understanding of Inference as a Source of Knowledge. *Child Development*, Vol.58, No.2, pp.424-433, 1987.

24. Kemler Nelson, D. When Experimental Findings Conflict with Everyday Observations: Reflections on Children's Category Learning. *Child Development*, Vol.61, No.3, pp.606-610, 1990.

25. Speece, M and Brent, S. Children's Understanding of Death: A Review of three components of the death concept. *Child Development*, Vol.55, No.5, pp.1671-1686, 1984.

26. Richards, D and Siegler, R. The Effects of Task Requirements on Children's Life Judgements. *Child Development*, Vol.55, No.5, pp.1687-1696, 1984.

27. Lazar, A and Torney-Purta, J. The Development of Subconcepts of Death in Young Children: A short term longitudinal study. *Child Development*, Vol.62, No.6, pp.1321-1333, 1991.

28. Richman, N; Stevenson, J and Graham, P. *Pre-School to School: a behavioural study*. London, Academic Press, 1982.

29. Flavell, J; Mumme, D; Green, F and Flavell, F. Young Children's Understanding of Different types of Belief. *Child Development*, Vol.63, No.4, pp.960-977, 1992.

30. Marini, Z and Case, R, op cit.

31. Cox, M. *The Child's Point of View*. Hemel Hempstead, Harvester Wheatsheaf, 1991.

32. ibid.

33. Nunner-Winkler, G and Sodian, B. Children's Understanding of Moral Emotions. *Child Development*, Vol.59, No.5, pp.1323-1338, 1988.

34. Kokob, S. The Primary School Child's Language of Emotions. *Educational Psychology*, Vol.9, No.4, pp.273-285, 1989.

35. Bretherton, I; Fritz, J; Zahn-Waxler, C and Ridgeway, D. Learning to talk about emotions: a functionalist perspective. *Child Development*, Vol.57, No.3, pp.529-548, 1986.

36. Donaldson, M. *Human Minds: an Exploration*. Harmondsworth, Penguin, 1993.

37. Dunn, T. *The Beginnings of Social Understanding*. Oxford, Basil Blackwell, 1988.

38. Bartsch, K and Wellman, H. Young Children's Attribution of Action to Beliefs and Desires. *Child Development*, Vol.60, No.4, pp.946-964, 1989.

39. Flavell, T et al., op cit.

40. Bussey, K. Lying and Truthfulness: Children's Definitions, Standards and Evaluative Reactions. *Child Development*, Vol.63, No.1, pp.129-137, 1992.

41. Cullingford, C. *Children and Society*. London, Cassell, 1992.

42. Sodian, B; Zaitchik, D and Carey, S. Young Children's Differentiation of Hypothetical Beliefs from Evidence. *Child Development*, Vol.62, No.4, pp.753-766, 1991.

43. Chandler, M; Fritz, A and Hala, S. Small-scale deceit: Deception as a marker on Two, Three and Four-year olds' Theories of Mind. *Child Development*, Vol.60, No.6, pp.1263-1277, 1989.

44. Harris, P. *Children and Emotion: The Development of Psychological Understanding.* Oxford, Basil Blackwell, 1989.

45. Hala, S; Chandler, M and Fritz, A. Fledgling Theories of Mind: Deception as a Marker of Three-year old's Understanding of False Belief. *Child Development*, Vol.62, No.1, pp.83-97, 1991.

46. Flavell, T et al., 1992, op cit.

47. Flavell, T; Flavell, E; Green, F and Moses, L. Young Children's Understanding of Fact Beliefs versus Value Beliefs. *Child Development*, Vol.61, No.4, pp.915-928, 1990.

48. Moses, L and Flavell, T. Inferring False Beliefs from Actions and Reactions. *Child Development*, Vol.61, No.4, pp.929-945, 1990.

49. Astington, et al., op cit.

50. Perner, T; Ruffman, T and Leakman, S. Theory of Mind is Contagious: You catch it from your sibs. *Child Development*, Vol.65, No.4, pp.1228-1238, 1994.

51. Woolley, T and Wellman, H. Young Children's Understanding of Realities, Non Realities and Appearances. *Child Development*, Vol.61, No.4, pp. 946-961, 1990.

52. Lewis, C and Osborne, A. Three Year Old's Problem with False Belief. Conceptual Deficit or Linguistic Artefact? *Child Development*, Vol.61, No.5, pp.1514-1519, 1990.

53. Flavell, T; Green, F and Flavell, E. Children's Understanding of the Steam of Consciousness. *Child Development*, Vol.64, No.2, pp.387-398, 1994.

54. Eder, R; Gerlach, S and Perlmutter, M. In search of children's selves: Development of the specific and general components of the self-concept. *Child Development*, Vol.58, No.4, pp.1044-1050, 1987.

55. Howes, P and Markham, H. Marital Quality and Child Functioning: a Longitudinal Investigation. *Child Development*, Vol.60, No.5, pp.1044-1051, 1989.

56. Thorkildsen, T. Pluralism in Children's Reasoning about Social Justice. *Child Development*, Vol.60, No.4, pp.965-972, 1989.

57. Wellman, H. *The Child's Theory of Mind*. Boston, MIT Press, 1990.

58. Perner, T, et al., 1994, op cit.

59. Hala, S, et al., 1991, op cit.

60. Wellman, H, 1990, op cit.

61. Barrett, S; Abdi, H; Murphy, G and Gallagher, T. Theory-based Correlations and their Role in Children's Concepts. *Child Development*, Vol.64, No.6, pp.1595-1616, 1993.

62. Wellman, H, 1990, op cit.

63. Astington, J, et al., 1988, op cit.

64. Fodor, T. *The Language of Thought*. London, Harvester Press, 1976.

65. Wellman, H. First Steps in the Child's Theorising about the Mind. In Ashington, J, et al., op cit., pp.64-92, 1988.

66. Leslie, A. Some Implications of pretence for mechanisms underlying the child's theory of mind. In Ashington, J, op cit., pp.19-46, 1988.

67. Taniv and Shata.

68. Poulin-Dubois, D and Shulta, T. The Development of the Understanding of Human Behaviour: from Agency to Intentionality. In Ashington, J, et al., op cit., pp.109-125.

69. Wimmer, H and Perner, T. Beliefs about Beliefs. Representation and Constraining function of Wrong Beliefs in Young Children's Understanding of Deception. *Cognition*, Vol 13, pp.103-128, 1983.

70. Beal, C. Children's knowledge about representations of intended meaning. In Ashington, J, et al., op cit., pp.315-325.

71. Cullingford, C. *The Nature of Learning*. London, Cassell, 1990.

72. "In Breughel's *Icarus*, for instance: how everything turns away.
Quite leisurely from the disaster; the ploughman may
Have heard the splash, the forsaken cry,
But for him it was not an important failure; the sun shone
As it had to on the white legs disappearing into the green
Water; and the expensive delicate ship that must have seen
Something amazing, a boy falling out of the sky,
Had somewhere to get to, and sailed calmly on."
W H Auden, *Museé des Beaux Arts*

2 Instant epistemologies: the myths of child development

The delight taken in recording the charming misunderstandings of children always has an uncomfortable edge. How sweet, we think, that children can so misinterpret as we, as adults, understand so well. "I want a drink" she says. "And what else do you say?" I respond in the cajoling way of adults to encourage at least verbal politeness. "And a biscuit". Or "We are breaking up next week". "Breaking up? Who is?" One reason for the discomfort is the underlying realisation that we are indulging our sense of superiority. It makes people feel slightly special when they can be supercilious to others. There is no easier group over whom to rejoice in superiority than those who are younger. An imbalance of politeness is taken for granted. The old can say what they like to the young. "What's your name, boy, and how old are you? Well done! Carry on".

The word 'childish' is a curious put down. It encapsulates that sense of human helplessness and stupidity from which we seem to have recovered. As least there are some to whom we can all feel superior. 'When I was a child I spoke as a child. I understood as a child ... but when I became a man I put away childish things'. Such a sense of maturity seems natural given all the immediate evidence of the helplessness and inarticulacy of babies. The whole edifice of the authority of parents and the system of education depends upon the superiority of one over another. The cultural roots that suggest firm authority and then control also turn them into warm sentimentality. Being superior to children seems to make us feel better.

The other discomforting aspect of the innocence of misunderstandings comes when we realise that some of what we find funny is painful to the child. "Go and see the head" (which head?) "We are breaking up next week" (that sounds terminal). For the interpretative gaze of young children the unexplained and customary remark has an immediate meaning to their own interpretation. A young child watches an old slapstick movie on the television. People are throwing custard pies at each other. Very jolly. But the image of a smiling face suddenly transformed into a blank white dribbling mess is also frightening. Or the vicar in his sermon mentions in passing that people were 'party' to an action. "Where's the party?" asks the hopeful child. There is the Laurie Lee anecdote about being told to sit "quietly at the table for the present". To his intense disappointment the present never turns up.

Seen in all its mistakes childhood might seem to carry the charm of the absurd. The struggle to make sense of what is either inexplicable or unexplained appears as a series of misapprehensions but it does not feel like that to the individual. In our amusement at the seemingly carefree talk of young children we see those aspects that lend themselves to chat-shows and forget the evidence that they give of minds wandering over uncharted experience. In exploring the territories of the mind it is the young children themselves who are their own guides and adults look on not only thinking that they cannot be helped, through incapacity of some kind, but relishing the fact.

The mythology of young children's incapacity which is unfolded in the concept of "developmental stages" has a psychology of its own. There is a natural superciliousness in being adult that finds its easiest target in the seemingly unseeing, and therefore forgiving, eye of the infant. But the notion of childhood as carefree and children as gentle, optimistic and untroubled souls reveals another psychological trait. As Bettelheim puts it

> The ... myth of childhood innocence dies very slowly. It is because of our own hostility in infancy which we are trying to deny. It really has to do with being unable to accept all the hostile, aggressive thought we had in infancy ... Because our adult status is so recently acquired we have to protect it at all costs.[1]

There is a kind of amnesia that surrounds the memories of childhood. Having acquired the protection of self-centredness it is both easy and profitable to forget what we have all experienced in childhood, those traumatic events, big and small, that had us not as onlookers but as direct participants in them. For example, in cases of divorce, the children will usually believe that it must be their fault. They have not learned to distance events but are deeply and emotionally engaged.

Everyday events are full of potential trauma. There might be some moments of bliss, of absorption in an activity, for the intensity of response is directed at pleasure as well as pain. But there are also those moments of intense fear or anxiety, waking up in the night, feeling abandoned, feeling betrayed. Fear is always part of the human experience, but for young children it is hand in hand with a sense of guilt, a real sense of inner disturbance. As we grow older we learn how to distinguish and how to externalise, how to put realities to one side. Part of this process is the mythologising of childhood.

There is an irony that the growth of the mythology of the innocence and bliss of childhood has coincided with a growth in the communication of the opposite. Children have always suffered. But whilst they were caught up in the terrible catastrophes of human history and witnessed them face to face, it is only more recently that the universality of such experience is communicated to them directly if second hand. Their developing sense of the relative partly derives from a growing realisation of the chance of where they live, and the understanding that if they had been in a certain school at a certain time they would have suffered likewise. Their own circumstances slightly but palpably does not feel as safe again. The very assertion of childhood optimism coincides with some of the most terrifying events.[2]

Childhood is not just a condition but a social construct. Whilst it has many contradictions and multiple realities, it is still assumed to be a consciousness seemingly separate from adulthood.[3] Childhood is a fairly recently invented construct.[4] There was a time when childhood was not seen as something to be kept separate, to be preserved as a kind of innocence. In the middle ages, in a time of great piety and violence, of great and unbridled passions, the children were a natural part of adult life.[5] There was no explicit separation between the private and the public. The Lord of the Manor in the Great Hall had his place, but all his people were visibly close around him. Only later would there be separate staircases for servants, and a greater stress not only on privacy but one almost expunging certain everyday realities.

We live in a time when everything is ostensibly moderated and controlled, when the subduing of passion, at least on the surface, is considered necessary. Of course there are the vicarious passions, the anger of sport and the bloodthirstiness of videos, but these are kept in their place. We also have all the civil authorities, like the police, to control what was earlier left to self-control. But before the 1500s there was not the same distinction between the public and the private and no such developed sense of shame. All acts were carried out in a far more open way and little was hidden from the children, so as to preserve their innocence. In a sense it is adults who in becoming less 'child-like' have reconstructed a new concept of themselves, learning to repress feelings rather than express them.

Against such a subdued and controlled concept of the world the notion of childhood as a time when all is seen vividly and unsupressed seems too difficult to accept. And so it is turned into a myth, a nostalgia for the good times when it seemed that there were few responsibilities - few engagements with preserving the social order. What adults seem to be unwilling to accept is that there was a time when the world was dramatically present rather than mentally controlled. Young children's understandings arise partly out of the negotiated interpretations, to some extent in conversation with others, and partly out of a study of the social and historical symbols that we call 'culture', an understanding of something beyond the personal.[6] It is this steady gaze at the shared inheritance which includes grief as well as joy that, it seems, adults wish to deny.

This view of childhood limitation and the intellectual superiority of the adult is upheld, even developed, by researchers into childhood. Nowhere is this clearer than in the Piagetian-style experiments setting out to prove how deficient children are in mental abilities. Reviewing these tests makes one wonder how much energy was placed into trying to prove a deficit model - to demonstrate how slowly and in how abstract a way that children grow into an adult relationship with their physical and social surroundings. Piagetian tests seem designed to prove the egocentricity of the child; and instead reveal the tests' insensitivity to the point of view of the child. Ever since Plato posited different stages of maturity the idea of intellectual development seemed attractive, although it was only attempts to prove such notions empirically that these stages were tied to certain ages. Plato's view remains attractive in that they allow a moral dimension, with people tied to a particular phase.

The deficiency of the experiments has been demonstrated time and again, but the main reason for citing them here is not just to criticise Piaget but show what these tests, and their alternatives, reveal about the thinking of young children. In almost every case a famous original - about points of view, or the law of conservation - has been amended by an alternative test to include the way that the mind usually operates, and then it has been discovered that children can, after all, do what the original tests were designed to deny. What is so clever about the tests is the way they leave out the actual experience of children and the way they understand this experience, and instead concentrate on abstract reasoning. Children's thinking is complex and deep but it is not abstract in this way. They are dealing with the real world, of actual people and points of view, of ambiguities and emotions. Piaget's tests manage to leave out all that is not purely 'scientific'. This is why they need to be carefully controlled to be repeatable. They have a deductive logic of their own.

Piaget actually suggests that children do not see the world 'as it really is', as if they somehow ignore all the evidence that confronts them.[7] The problem for children is that they see the world all too clearly but they cannot understand Piaget's task since it is psychologically abstract.[8] Replace algebra with real people, and explain, and children understand. What children need is exactly what Piaget assumed they lack - the exact nature of the psychological problem and the human motivation behind the problem.[9]

The famous test that sought to demonstrate children's egocentricity by presenting them with a model of three mountains was similarly overturned when instead of giving children photographs of different perspectives, they were presented with the possibility of demonstrating their understanding by manipulating the actual model. When this rather abstract model of mountains was replaced by a model of something more familiar - people and animals - young children did even better. It is the real world they are dealing with, rather than trying to guess what answer it is that the researcher wishes to hear. What is often clear is that when young children are confronted by Piagetian tests they refuse to be manipulated and refuse to answer over-simple questions which seem to have little point.[10] This does not show limitation but a 'social' reaction to the circumstances.

The test that presented children with two different jars full of water, one tall and thin and the other squat, also proved the difficulty not of understanding conservation but what the nature of the task was, and what was being demanded. It is the linguistic problem of having to choose between two different definitions and the abstract task of saying what something would look like from a different point of view - why? - that is difficult. The problem, as Margaret Donaldson has suggested, is that Piaget never really understood the minds of children.[11] His very rationality excludes the complex richness of children's experiences. He failed to take into account their uses of language. What children do *not* do is to divorce abstract problems from the reality of everyday life. If a 'test' is made to appear a real task, for example when water is replaced by pasta shells and the task is made into a competition, then children see the point and do what the experimenter is trying to ascertain.[12] Tests need to be real or they are of no interest. After all children are attempting to understand physical and social phenomena all the time. They do not need distractions.

Children like to solve puzzles. They apply their sense of logic to puzzles in everyday life. They are not good at logic abstracted from the domains of meaningfulness.

> If p then q
> Not q
> Therefore not p

is not as easy to follow, for anyone, as

> If there is a wedding there is a man involved
> There is no man
> Therefore no wedding

If there are four cards

and a rule which states "if a card has a vowel on one side then it has an even number on the other side", the test is "Name only those cards which need to be turned over in order to determine whether the rule is true or false".

and give the rule: "if a letter is sealed it has a 2nd class stamp on it" and the same question is asked, then everyone finds it far easier to do.[13] Why?

The answer to the question is that the brain does not lend itself easily to the tasks of logic abstracted from meaningfulness, without some connection to the social context. Numeracy and scientific reasoning can be acquired and can become a lucid and bracing language but they develop out of the study of actual circumstances. It is sometimes thought that the most gifted of young children are those who are very musical or very mathematical. A few sometimes pass examinations years before their peers. But these are exceptional only in so far as they are allowed to be and only in so far as they place their powers of mind in these directions. The same rapidity of understanding and clarity of thought is actually carried out by most other children but they are given no credit for it. It is as if there were a conspiracy of silence, as if acknowledging this would cause too many difficulties.

If young children are so clever, how do we explain what happens subsequently to all this ability? What we are doing to ourselves is a question we do not wish to face. One of the reasons for the popularity of the Piagetian theories is their combination of what appears to be scientific intelligence and emotional comfort. The tests on which the theory is based also have the advantage - if that is the right word - of demonstrating the cleverness of the researcher rather than exploring the truth of the subject. Habit is a powerful mental force even if an undeliberate one. It is the seeking out of the familiar or comfortable understandings and reference points. It is a powerful need and an influence which affects researchers as much as anyone else. The need to be in a 'network' of mutual understandings and references implies the creation of agreed positions with support from agreed authorities.

One of the reasons that Piaget ceased to look at the reality of children's inner lives was the sheer force of habit, or the familiar. Once the stage theory was established, from primitive sensorimotor intelligence through concrete operations to the sophistication of abstract thought, everything could be fitted into it - language or play, morals or physical education. There is nothing more attractive than the familiarity of a fixed point of view. The thought that it might not be true is simply not considered because life is simpler if it is not considered. What a scientist finds attractive - before chaos theory at any rate - is the neatness of the complete, the model that describes all, even if it does not explain it. The kind of model that Piaget worked to was necessarily abstract, without the contamination of social reality. Allied to the subtle attractions of the supercilious is the warmth of the familiar. The seemingly obvious idea that children grow mentally as they grow physically, that there is a logic in the development of the brain as there is an order in the sequencing of cellular growth easily subsumed all other considerations.

All this not only explains what underlay Piaget's approach, but the attractions it held for others. Indeed, Piaget has become a symbol for a style of thinking that is more extreme in some of the followers than his own. His own writing is still interesting and contains many subtle insights. But the way it has been used is quite another matter. There is no need to 'deconstruct' Piaget's own works - that has been done often enough - when the real damage that has been done is the universal application of it to so many other, often inappropriate research designs. The complex and messy variety of abilities and experiences that come together in the progress of the young child in the world have been ignored, and people have suffered as a result. The problem is that what on one level has become academic folklore is on another level a reference point against which to make judgements. Out of the principles of 'science' can evolve a doctrinal canon.

There is a body of still accumulating evidence that demonstrates the limitations of the Piagetian approach. There is so much of this we should have little difficulty in accepting consistency and power of the arguments. But the consequences of this knowledge have rarely been explored. The hints of what it might mean - to parents, and to the education of a young child - are, however, clearly stated. There is a general shift in emphasis from the concept of the child as lonely scientist, constructing hypotheses in abstract isolation to the concept of the child as a social being, learning in reaction to a context.[14] The importance of role-play and seeing the point of view of others is acknowledged and language given a greater prominence.[15] The ability to learn by observation and the translation of these into understanding without limitation is accepted.[16]

What is clear is that the idea of the child as a limited, or autistic, egocentric is not supported by the accumulating evidence in, say, the annals of *Child Development*. Even young babies adjust their gaze in a way that demonstrates their interpretation of the other person's perspective.[17] Cognitive acts cannot be separated from the subjects on which they depend, for thought does not consist only of the epistemic - the operation of mental acts on the world. It includes the 'ontic' - the means by which the circumstances are construed and represented, made into 'reality'.[18]

Stage theories are one of the shadows caused by the concept of the child as not only weak and helpless but dependent, and learning by imitation. Because the infant can respond to a gesture does not mean that he or she is merely copying it. But just as the tests were designed in such a way as to cause as well as seek out deficiencies, so the interpretation of all the observed data allowed no recognition that there would be thought behind the gestures.[19] Even in moral reasoning the power of imitation was held to be supreme, as if the acceptance of adult constraints only later develops into respect and co-operation.[20] Piaget often asserted that young children could not 'decentre', that they were so bound up in egotism and therefore in the simple acceptance of what would happen to them - the adult authority - that they could not see a different point of view, with contrary motivations.[21] The assumption that the child does not see the world 'as it really is', is like an accusation of stupidity, of fatal limitation. If all that is seen of the world is a series of unconnected segments, without cause and effect, without their own meanings, how could young children cope? The Piagetian answer is that they do so only in a limited way, that the 'real world' would be too much to cope with.

The problem is that children have no choice but to cope with the real world in all its ambiguities, personal and social motivations and intellectual richness. It is the very complexity of the world that they need to understand. They do not grasp the disembodied, psychologically abstract tasks given to them. Not because they are abstracted but because they are meaningless. Contrary to what Piaget says, the child is aware of him or herself, which is not the same as being egotistic. This awareness is a sense of relationship to others; close or distant, understandable or inarticulate. Not only are there different levels of thought engaged in the child but different levels of thought recognised in others. The objective and the subjective, the emotional and the rational are all there. When Piaget tries to make the crucial distinction between [directed] thought and the 'autistic' he cuts living reality into segments.

> Directed thought is conscious, ie. it pursues aims that are present in the mind of the thinker ... Autistic thought is subconscious, ie. the goals it pursues and the problem it sets itself are not present in the consciousness.[22]

For Piaget the crucial distinction is between the egocentric, the helpless purely imitative autism of the very young and the gradual unfolding of directed, rational thinking.

But is 'gradual unfolding' really the correct description? One crucial aspect of stage theories is the sanctity of the order, the idea that everything has a logic, that certain events can only take place if previous events have taken place. The rigidity of the separate stages suggest that there is a pure and simple logic to development, that learning can be understood as a series of small steps, in a behaviourist sense. Instead of a profusion of events and an attempt to create order out of the chaos of experience where there are no psychological filters against certain sights and sounds, the notion of the stage is that the understanding unfolds slowly and with precision. It is as if it were possible to be so out of tune or unaware of experience that only those aspects that would fit into the limited understanding would seem to exist. Such control would, indeed, be some kind of mastery on an adult scale; the ability to choose what to accept, according to established principles.

Stage theories were developed through particular types of experiment. These supposed that children have to interact with the environment in order to develop an understanding of it.[23] For the sake of measured observation this interacting would be physical; as if nothing that was not seen or handled really counted. 'Out of sight, out of mind'. We now know that young children are aware of hidden objects; and the absence as well as presence of other people. But stage theories are like theories of biological growth. They suppose that what happens is what is observable and physically demonstrated. Many writers have criticised Piaget for only observing (very few) children of the same background as himself.[24] But the background of the children is neither here nor there. Piaget would always see the same things, being rooted in a cultural gaze of social control.

Observations of young children have sought out a pattern of growth, whether of norms or stages, that presupposes limitations, and that suggest that what is hidden from view does not exist.[25] These developments in deductive reasoning are seen to demonstrate the rudimentary nature of abstract thought, and young children are held to be perfect material for the study of thought broken into distinct parts. Always, as in the many Soviet experiments, there are the patterns of age placed against deficiencies sometimes even if less rigidly than Piaget: 'At the age of four children do not employ general propositions', or 'at the age of five children employ general prepositions but these don't reflect reality'.[26] Attention paid to real children would bring these statements immediately into question.

The desire to create a pattern of mental growth derives partly from a particular experimental method, and also derives from the notion that development occurs through an invariant hierarchy of stages, and that each stage has to be successfully negotiated before the next one is reached. The problem with this is what it leaves out. The experiments have been shown to be wanting. The theory is also damaging to our understanding of childhood. There are alternative models but they tend to be based on exposing the limitations of Piaget's views rather than replacing them.[27] They seem still to adhere to the Piagetian notion of the separation of development and learning into two separate processes.

The understandable problem for stage theories is that they wish to separate different concepts from the confusion of elements. It is a natural scientific approach, to try to study a problem by breaking it into manageable pieces. With mechanical things, as with the body, this is possible. But to conclude that language can be separated from thought, intrinsic from extrinsic motivation, the activities of the mind and the body, is to presuppose that what can be observed is all that takes place, and to impose a biological pattern of unfolding stages, whether distinct or not, on the hidden activities of the brain. Piaget asserted that man cannot understand the universe except through logic and mathematics, and that he can only understand how he has constructed logic through studying himself biologically.[28] What stage theories lack is the acceptance of a social and cultural reality in which children are embedded.[29] Suppose children have no such limitations?

Piaget was by no means the only influential figure developing stage theories. Even since Plato they have had their attractions. This is at least partly because they promote an end point of ultimate reason and wisdom - just you and me. In Plato's case the stages include the instinct for collecting information followed by the fiercely moral phase before turning at last into the sense of irony.[30] But at least this theory allowed for the possibility of people *not* developing or being caught up in such unambiguous passion for a cause that they are unable to see other people's points of view. And such a broad sweep in understanding is more about the uses of thought and emotion than about the abstract abilities. Erikson also suggests stages of growth and understanding from infancy to old age, with the last element in social order being wisdom.[31] If that is the ultimate then everything before it is bound to have its limitations, all being placed in hierarchical order.

What Erikson does is to give his eight stages different dimensions, including emotions and attitudes, understandings as well as demonstrations of ability. He also suggests a series of tensions between, for example, basic trust and basic mistrust, between autonomy and shame and doubt, between initiative and guilt, between intimacy and isolation.[32] All of these, like tensions between happiness and despair, we will all recognise. As in Gesell's notion of different types of experience like some kind of spiral or gyre we feel as if we have been going through phases of experience. All the dichotomies of life, the psychological sense of self, personal relationships, and understanding our place in society, are felt, even if suppressed, all the time. What Erikson does is to explore the relationship between the personal and the social. The sense of the tension between the sense of identity or diffusion of identity is linked to an understanding of peer groups, to ideologies and to the sense of 'being oneself'. The idea of intimacy versus isolation, partnerships and friendships, finding oneself in others and social co-operation, are all linked.

But they are all placed into a pattern of eight stages, divided into infancy (trust versus mistrust), early childhood (autonomy versus shame and doubt), childhood (initiative versus guilt), pre-adolescence (accomplishment versus inferiority), adolescence (identity versus role confusion), young adulthood (intimacy versus isolation), adulthood (generality versus stagnation) and old age (integrity versus despair). Even the briefest outline of the concepts suggests something familiar about the tensions inherent in life. But are we to assume that the child does not feel any role confusion, or that the sense of isolation never affects him or her? Does shame or doubt simply fade away? Would that it were so! That the human experience changes and develops over time is accepted. But at all times the mixture of emotion and understanding are similar. We might deal with them differently but no-one feels a separate person, a separate integrity, from the time they were ten or fifteen years younger. Erikson also links different stages with different types of significant relationships, starting with the maternal relationship, through parents, the basic family, to neighbourhoods and schools, through peer-groups and models, partners and friendships, to divided labour and a shared household and ultimately all mankind. Understanding, or a sense of relationship is extended over an ever increasing circle. But take the experience of an eight year old. As later chapters will demonstrate, they are as acutely aware of a shared household, of peer groups, of neighbourhoods and the world outside as they are of their basic family.

The idea of different stages of understanding and development must be attractive to have such a hold on the literature of childhood. It extends into an adult's sense of self. It is parodied by the lachrymose Jacques in his set speech about the seven ages of man.[33] After all, the sense of time passing, and the inevitability of old age and death - 'sans everything' - is a central part of the human condition. But it is not one limited to maturity. It is shared, as are all the other emotions, if not some of the physical symptoms - by young children. The idea of stages is, Shakespeare apart, dominated not so much by ending in death as by ending in maturity. It is as if the writer or researcher were looking back from a position of lofty wisdom, on the limitations of those periods through which he has travelled.

Nowhere is this sense of the goal of wisdom more apparent than in the moral stages as outlined by Kohlberg.[34] His was a model based essentially on the notions of Piaget - who also included moral reasoning amongst his subjects. It is one which has six stages that suggest that only at the end, with maturity, are we capable of individual principles or fully developed conscience. The ultimate goal is the universal value of the individual. This sounds admirable. It is something valuable for which to aim. It clarifies and describes the complexity of moral behaviour, the subtle distinction between right and wrong, the tension between personal and cultural morality and convention. The problem with this theory is, however, the assumption that moral questions, which are always complex, are not understood at an early age. It is as if young children are 'amoral' beings, at first slowly learning that good behaviour is only a matter of obeying rules, or that the only merit is avoiding punishment. The problem with the theory is that it looks at all the different aspects of behaviour, conformity and understanding, truth and falsehood, intention and accident, and stretches them out in a continuum. It seems neat to suggest that a true understanding of moral behaviour is only learned through a series of stages, but this does not mean it is true.

Kohlberg suggests that in young children human life is confused with objects; and yet we know that at the same time children understand mortality.[35] He posits the idea that children conform to obtain rewards and have favours returned, that they are, in fact, unaware of any deep sense of right and wrong. And yet we know that children are aware, before they can really express it, of the distinction between right and wrong. Kohlberg based his theoretical position on looking at older children, mostly adolescents. He did not show great interest in young children. Had he done so he would have found something quite different and far more complicated. By the age of six young children are quite clear about the distinctions of justified or unjustified behaviour, that fine line when fighting is play and fighting is dangerous.[36] They are also aware of the differences in the status of authority, between that of the peer-group and that of the teacher, and the difference between accepting authority because there are imposed rules that those in authority wish to have obeyed, and the fact that these rules are necessary, and a kind of social etiquette as a way of learning good behaviour.[37] Children realise that rules are outcomes of behaviour, a result of need not just to avoid danger, but to establish right from wrong.

Childhood is a testing time for the discovery of relationships, in which morality plays a central part. The choosing or rejection of friends is not just an arbitrary personal matter. It causes pain as well as pleasure. Because of this young children are aware of the importance of 'good' behaviour as well as the consequences of 'bad' behaviour.[38] They admire and wish to emulate those who have a moral code that leads to gentle treatment of others. They are witnesses, after all, to teasing and bullying. They see the distinction between the intention behind the act and the act itself. Contrary to Piaget's ideas, they see that the deliberate destruction of a small cup is worse than the accidental breaking of an antique. But they also realise that to the owner of something valuable its loss can far outweigh the reason for it. The small cup might quickly be forgotten, whatever the moral shock; the loss antique will long be resented.

The world of young children with its intense and inhibited social relations is one of constant and complex moral decision making. These are all centred firmly on a pragmatic understanding that whilst all are agreed on what ought to take place, a lot that is wrong is also part of daily experience. Adult moralists might look at their own behaviour as constantly fastidious and exemplary. They are also unembarrassed to accept that other people's behaviour clearly does not obtain the heights of their own standards. Young children are more pragmatic. They accept that they themselves have not always behaved as they ought to; they have lied and they have teased. Perhaps Kohlberg would suggest that this is undeveloped morality, that children do not know what they are doing deeply enough to avoid doing so. Young children, in fact, are perfectly aware of what they are doing, but they also know that immorality has its rewards.

The most obvious example of the way in which bad behaviour can be rewarding is lying. This can mean that something that they do not want to do can be avoided; it is more convenient to say 'yes' to "Have you washed your face and brushed your teeth?" when the answer should be 'no'. It is the most obvious way of avoiding punishment. But children also know and say that lying is worse than hitting. It might be the everyday art of getting away with things but this does not mean it is right. They are also aware that lying can, on certain occasions, be good, like the white lie that keeps a sibling out of a room whilst it is decorated for her party which is to be a surprise. Young children demonstrate an awareness of small distinctions in moral behaviour, like teasing being worse than fighting - unless, of course, the fighting becomes brutal. In questions of morality it is easy to generalise but not so easy when faced with an actual case. Then it all depends on the circumstances in which it takes place.[39] Is it a game that two boys are playing or is one harassing the other? This awareness of the importance on the environment and the subtlety of the questions involved is why children are so obsessed by the concept of fairness. Of all moral undermining nothing is worse than the failure of a collective social etiquette. Authority is placed into the hands of the teacher because he or she is a necessary and agreed agent, not because power is seized by them. Once there is a sense of the breakdown of this trust, once the cry of the individual about being singled out becomes too strong, then there emerge all the demonstrations of 'alienation'; truancy and a psychological refusal to accept the system in which justice is supposed to prevail.[40]

The moral problems with which young children are confronted are subtle and complicated. They understand the tensions between rule and ritual and between rule and principle. What does seem to be apparent in young children in their understanding of the world is their sense that they have done wrong. This gives an edge to their sense of the importance of morality. They also accept that there are some people who will always be bad; how else are there so many criminals, from those who carry out abhorrent deeds like murder to those who break more conventional rules like the speed limit.[41] In this understanding the attitude of children is a conservative one, that rules and punishments are necessary because otherwise society would collapse into anarchy. They do not suppose that their world is full of innocent optimism, where gentleness and understanding prevail.

On the one hand, then, we have empirical evidence of young children grappling with moral problems from the moment in which they engage with others. On the other we have the theory of stages through which children only slowly come to understand complex questions of morality, only slowly realising that behind the rules lie reasons. The latter seems on the face of it more attractive, and far easier to deal with. But the evidence, as we will see, suggests otherwise. Because the first institutions which children experience are so dependent on rules, and on sanctions, this does not mean that children are unaware of anything more personal in the reasons for moral behaviour. Indeed it is children themselves who stress the need for clear rules, for fairness and for social justice.[42] It is their acceptance of the necessity for authority, and their acceptance of the prevalence of bad behaviour that gives legitimacy to the rules. Once they no longer sanction them, once the agreement breaks down, then we have the problems of truancy and bullying. It was once thought that these signs of social problems were exceptional and rare. This prevailing attitude was one result of the picture of childhood based on stages of innocence; including children's inability to see the reasons behind rules. The irony is that Kohlberg's theory is attractive because it joins action with understanding; if children behave badly or lie it is because they do not know what they are doing. Once they know it is presumed then they will be as good as you and me.

The theories of stages outline a series of developments that depend on a gradual unfolding of abilities, cognitive, social or moral. But what makes them attractive is not only the sense of superiority in achieving wisdom but the way in which they also suggest a potential solution to the fundamental question of human nature: why and how do things go wrong? Whilst Piaget is essentially descriptive, and assumes that people will inevitably progress through every stage, both Kohlberg and Erikson delve into the emotional and moral aspects of experience. Erikson in particular raises the question of conflicts that we all recognise; trust and suspicion, guilt and shame, autonomy and identity. Whilst the confusions are described differently according to the stage, the conflict is one we all understand, between opposing forces that lie deep in the psyche. This attempt to explain the inner development of the individual through a series of stages is also exemplified by Freud.

This is no place to open up the continuing debate about Freudian theories or their alternatives, or even to point out the often damaging criticisms of the theory and its consequences. It is enough here to remind ourselves of the hold such a theory has on the imagination. Beyond reason and outside morality human behaviour is explained as a series of stages which have been related to those of Piaget and Erikson. That they have little in common and deal with different aspects of human nature does not prevent the temptation of placing development into a pattern. In Freud's terms the Oral and Anal stages, the second of which is from 18 months to 3 years, are followed by stages that follow each other in regular pattern, from 3-5 and from 6-11. Thus the psychoanalytical stage of 'latency' is placed besides Piaget's 'concrete operations' and Erikson's 'Industry versus Inferiority', with 'technology' as the element of social order. Psychoanalysis and the treatment of psychotic disorders might seem far removed from cognition, but all stage theories give more than a hint of the human condition being immutable, as if people were not completely in control over what was taking place. It suggests how fragile young children are; but here it is suggested this is not because of their sensitivity but their helpless limitations. And it suggests a sense of the inevitable.

Freud's theory of stages also includes the notions of regression and fixations; the premise that the stages need to be got through, but that there is no inevitability about this. It suggests that in the progress towards being a normal adult, wise and well-meaning, it is possible to remain locked in an earlier stage, never to grow up. Thus the dismissive phrase 'how childish' carries an even greater weight of meaning. Just as in Plato's stages, and in Erikson's and in Kohlberg's, the incomplete person, the one who does not fulfil his or her moral potential, or the one who is seriously disturbed is the one who has not 'grown out' of a particular stage. Piaget's stages might seem more inevitable - as they are more biological - but even here the notion of 'autism' or childish 'egocentricity' is one that smacks of the sense of regression. Childhood is seen as a series of stages through which one must pass to become an adult in the full meaning of the word. In terms of the observable physical changes this might seem proven. But these theories in their very use of concepts like 'regression' and 'fixation' point to the limitations of childhood. It might seem like innocence or it might appear like stupidity, but the sense is that a child is incomplete, not having to deal with and not being capable of dealing with the real world full of moral conflicts and ambiguities, of complex questions and incomplete answers.

There has been a recent shift in emphasis for the firmly fixed theories of stages of development, or if not more than a shift, then at least an understanding of what the theories have left out. The Piagetian concept of the 'active scientist' working out solutions to problems in isolation has been to an extent replaced by Vygotsky's notion of the child as a social being, learning in a context of shared language.[43] Vygotsky, Bruner and their followers find the importance placed on the influence of peers and teachers as educationally refreshing. They do not isolate the inner workings of the mind from the social environment. They stress how much learning takes place through dialogue and through working with other people. This is not to say that Vygotsky suggests that everything rests on the influence of the environment, as some Soviet theorist have tended to do. His concept of the 'Zone of Proximal Development' describes the gap between what a child can achieve alone, which is their potential development as determined by independent problem solving and what a child can achieve through problem solving under the guidance of, or collaboration with, adults and more capable peers. It is as if a child can achieve so much developmentally; but that he or she can be helped by others by the offering of what teachers refer to the 'scaffolding' of support.

Vygotsky's emphasis on the importance of the social circumstances both reflects changes in attitudes to language, and is a deliberate reminder of the importance of others, like teachers, in the development of learning. There are many examples of psycho- and socio-linguists discovering, again, the significance of language in the development of thought (can they even be theoretically separated if language is conceptual?) and language as in the term 'speech act' as something which affects as well as affected by the environment.[44] The studies of language as it is 'used' underlies the importance of the social circumstances.[45] At one level this might seem obvious since we all speak of 'native' language or languages. At another it suggests that for all the importance of minute rules of transformational grammar, language is a social as well as intellectual phenomenon or is nothing.[46] If language is so important in the mind and development of the child then so is the social environment.

The influence of Vygotsky suggests a reaction to the Piagetian notion of fixed stages and the sense that little can be done to aid the mental abilities of children. Those who have found the notions most useful are those who, like Bruner, seek to find a developmental theory that supports teachers and enhances learning.[47] The stress is upon language in mental development and on a culture that cannot be invented by a child. They emphasise the importance of role play, of being able to see others' points of view. The concern is with a social construction of reality. But they still accept the notion of stages of development. The emphasis has shifted to what can be done to aid progression.[48] They have not turned their back on the significance of those stages. They have not faced the possibility of a more dramatic and sudden confrontation with the world.

Vygotsky's emphasis is primarily on language, the means of communication and the means of learning. The use of language, as in the undermining of the theoretical Piagetian experiments, suggests a different and more subtle array of understandings which, as Bruner famously suggests, means that anything can be taught to children at any time provided it is presented in the appropriate language. But how far back does one go? Before there is an obvious language through which to express ideas or confirm them? For Vygotsky speech is activity, which is part of the productive and cognitive activity of man that allows for motivation, purpose and structure. Speech is a means of solving a communication problem. The emphasis is still upon cognition. Speech makes the process more social. Cultural influences - the circumstances of the environment - are clearly important. But there is still little explanation or no explanation of the emotional and moral impact of the real world on the young child. The emphasis is, reasonably enough, on the means by which children can be helped. This suggests accepting the social world as well as cerebral abilities.[49]

There is a parallel between the shift of emphasis from cognitive stages to social development and the changing attitudes to schooling. The debate about the latter is simply about the difference that education makes, or does not make.[50] Sometimes the emphasis seems to be almost wholly on the little that schooling does to change the social and economic factors that surround children. Sometimes the emphasis is on the ways in which schools can make a difference, given very similar profiles of children's backgrounds. As is the case with the surveys of the importance of the early years, the effort is towards countering a sense of the inevitable, a sense of helplessness. The concern is with schooling, with the relationship of the individual and the teachers, between what the child brings into the formal system and what the teachers can do. What remains relatively unexplored is what the child makes of the world, and what can be done about it long before formal education takes place.[51] There are many who would suggest that even at the time of entry into the pre-school 'stage', the child has been marked for life.[52]

Neither Piagetian theory nor the countering emphasis on social factors really explores that hidden territory of the inner mind. Invoking names like Freud merely emphasises the difficulties in giving satisfactory explanations. But this difficulty partly arises because there have been few attempts to try to understand through the individual's point of view. Of theories there are a number. But most interest in the subject is naturally untheoretical. There are many arcane accounts of personal meaning but how these are formed is a relatively unexplored subject. This is because instead of fresh attempts to understand, based on empirical evidence, we are offered hypotheses, the placing of a theory around only evidence as appears neat in shape, logical and inevitable. Stage theories are patterns woven around the core of reality. They disguise as well as they explain.

There is, however, another reason why the subject of human nature, looked at openly and freshly, is not often explored. This is because of the domination of contraries: the binary divides between one force and another. Within stage theories like Erickson's, or Freud's, are inbuilt bipolar conflicts. The most significant of all is that of Nature or Nurture: the individual *or* the environment.[53] That there are factors of innate personality that mark out each human being as individually distinguishable is clear as genetic coding or DNA. That environmental factors are part of the creation of the individual is as obvious as language. The question is how the two factors work in relation to each other.

The debate about the individual and the environment has been marked by taking up extreme positions either side. It tends to be political. Thus the geneticist will find reasons for the success or failure of social groups in factors to do with genetic inheritance even if these are, to all intents and purposes, meaningless.[54] Debates about the concept of 'race' encapsulate this stance. Those who wish to create a new social order will have a natural tendency to assume that the environment can be so manipulated that people can be created in the manipulator's image. What is disturbing about the level of this debate is not the political or racist manipulation of the evidence, but that the very argument is meaningless. At one level one can see why there should be an argument; where exactly is the 'zone of proximal development'? At another, however, it obscures the reality of the way in which the mind operates, and the way in which it absorbs and re-orders the experience of the world.

Shakespeare had no difficulty in accepting the tension of the two factors of personality and the environment in the forming of a creature such as Caliban

> You taught me language; and my profit on't
> Is, I know how to curse.[55]

It appears that such understanding of both factors has been replaced by a kind of dialectic between them both. There is a constant either/or in the argument, trying to disprove one or other position rather than accepting that any dichotomy between the two is meaningless. These are often naive dichotomies, very eruditely developed. It is, after all, easier to argue *against* a set position. It is also intellectually satisfying. To do so you need a contrary position of your own. But argument of this kind is also part of our cultural inheritance. The self confidence of politicians and the need to damage the opposite party overcomes reason, the point and counterpoint of barristers overcomes justice, and the seeking out of a contrary point of view to balance or undermine that of the person just interviewed overcomes truth.

The fascination with argument can involve people so much that they forget to ask, let alone answer, simple questions. This can be demonstrated, as an example, in the debate about reading standards and how people learn to read. The process of learning to read an alphabetic language is a fascinating one and demonstrates a great deal about the human mind. But the debate is carried out in terms of either/or when one or the other dominates in turn. At one point the emphasis is all on technique and methods, *how* can children best be taught. At another point learning to read is assumed to be nothing more than a psycholinguistic guessing game that can be learned, but not taught. Instead of the full exploration of the process of learning, and what can be done to help it, we are offered either a series of new methods - often very expensive - or the advice that the least effective means of helping is even trying to do so.[56] It is an example of the everlasting false dichotomy.

This fascination with a binary divide is motivated by a desire to find what can be measured. The rule of tests, of experiments, either to prove cognition or its absence, to isolate an environmental factor so that there is no longer evidence too complex to describe suggests the triumph of the academic over the intellectual, the dominance of measurable knowledge over immeasurable understanding. We might not understand the whole but we can demonstrate our understanding of the parts which make the whole. We are quicker to spot the opposites than the composite.

This is a natural outcome of the way in which people think in terms of categories and groups, and the way in which they are aware of tension. Erikson's descriptions of psychosocial crises, whilst hanging on a string of stages, are recognisable as potentially diurnal conflicts. The sense of isolation is clearly the opposite to feelings of intimacy, a sense of industry in making things opposite to a sense of inferiority, a sense of being part of a general movement opposite to self-absorption. We have already questioned why these should not be part of anyone's experience at any time; but the more important notion is the way in which diverse experiences hang together. Whilst we are given a range of opposites which we recognise, our actual experience is more complex. The range of extremes felt by manic-depressives is not the normal experience of the majority for whom conflicting emotions, are part of the everyday, in which even contradictory forces are at play.

Nevertheless, binary opposites continue to fascinate because they are a simpler measure, a simpler tool of understanding than seeing the whole. And there is an excitement in extremes, in conflict and in dividing people, like experience, into categories. Whilst Shakespeare pays due respect to the way that people believe that things happen according to their stars these are seen to be an ironic undertone to real events.[57] The respect is not for the concept but for the fact that people find it easier to come to terms with the world if experience and personality can somehow be labelled. It is such relief to nurture simple explanations; take away some of the ache of responsibility. It should be noted that these beliefs are limited to adults and not part of the experience, or reality, of young children.

The idea of divisions, of categories and of opposites has been with us since the I Ching. They have been given physiological support from the study of the hemispheres of the brain. "The left hemisphere ... is predominantly involved in analytic, logical thinking, especially in verbal and mathematical functions. Its mode of operation is predominantly linear ... sequential ... logical...",[58] "The right hemisphere ... seems specialised for synthesis. Its language ability is quite limited ... orientation of space, artistic endeavour, crafts, body image, recognition of faces...".[59] We therefore derive from these not one mode of awareness, but two modes of consciousness as distinct as night and day; the intellectual and the sensuous, the explicit and the tacit, the sequential and the simultaneous, the creative and the receptive [Yin and Yang/male heaven and female earth, from the I Ching], the casual and synchronous, the verbal and the spatial and the intellectual versus the intuitive. These are all recognisable as alternatives. What is less clear is how they intertwine in our lives.

That some kind of categorisation takes place is clear. Each concept like a word puts order on to what is perceived. There has to be a measure of generality that encompasses a class of objects, like 'chair' or 'cat'. It does not follow that the way in which people construct their own sense of reality either places people into such categories beyond male and female, or that there should be a set of bipolar constructs, of either/or.[60] As we grow older and at the same time simplify our perceptions and learn how to account for them so the binary opposites seem both more plausible and more explicable. It does not follow that what young children see and hear is so easily and simply measured. The sense that there is a schematic order in categorisation is strong. But a theoretical movement from the inactive, through the iconic to the symbolic is still based heavily on stages, on limited understanding becoming more formalised.[61] The irony is that the ability to simplify, to reduce experience into a set of limited explanations is something learned by adults but assumed to be true for children.

The fascination with opposites is a natural part of the human beings attempt to make sense of the world, it is the simplest of all categorisations, the crudest of all judgements, like 'men come from Mars, women from Venus'. But it is a simplistic adult game.[62] As a way of explaining the chaos of early experience they cannot take us far. They might be ancient pointers to the variety of human experience but they emerge from the logic of the afterthought. Binary opposites are experience in hindsight. Dialectic, like binary divides, might seem a convenient way of accounting for things but it can also obscure the contradictory nature of truth. It is like the extreme love of argument for and against, carried out in all the vulgar splendour of the law, immutable to the extent that the still small voice of truth or justice is lost. The actuality, the discovery of what is at the core, what is at the ontological centre of the soul is not a balancing act, some kind on trick of the tightrope with balances. Nor is it a choice. There are many decisions for young children but few simple choices.

Weighing evidence is a metaphor that invokes scales, like the symbolism of blind justice, blindfold lest she see the truth. It implies that there will always be a counter argument as well as an argument, that whatever is weightily argued will attract a counter argument. It means that to every argument there can be an alternative point of view; indeed, that it is only the point of view that counts. This is a monument not just for cultural relativity but for a sense of the importance of personal egotism. It all depends on what you mean. Young children's experience of the world is more complex than that. They see the distinction between the iconic and the symbolic, not one after the other. They acknowledge the very bulk and complexity of information presented to them before they learn to categorise and dismiss it. Such things are not easily measured in any scale.

The weight of evidence that emerges from the study of young children all demonstrates their abilities and their analysis of their social as well as physical environment. But there is an irony of misinterpretation even in this. What is being sought in young children's abilities is cognition, the adult refinement of thought as demonstrable and abstract. There are problems with this. One is the supposition that adults think in a purely rational way, that thought patterns are not arbitrary and accidental, contradictory and many layered. The ability to apply abstract reasoning, to think in terms of mathematical logic, or to remember great heaps of information is undoubtedly there. But how often is it used and by how many? The normal patterns of 'cognition' of thinking are far more dependent on context, on what is being reflected upon and the 'story' or the 'history' that the mind carries to the experience. In Piaget's experiments the motivation was to isolate the purest forms of cognition, to abstract them from language and from social understanding. Even now the experimental work on cognition is attempting to isolate just one process in the more complex, more messy process which is thinking. The mind is a powerful instrument but it is not a machine. It is in the very complexity of association and imaging, as well as in its critical scrutiny that makes the mind so powerful.

The difficulty for young children is that they are forced to gaze on a messy world, and not on some inward representation or invention of it. They do so without having the learning skills of filtering it, organising it, or making it fit into some neat shape. They have not learned the perhaps necessary limitations of logical thought. Instead they react to the reality of complexity before learning to simplify it into manageable portions. The hypothesis that supports research into cognition is that young children as well as adults respond primarily to cognitive representations of their environment and experiences rather than to those experiences themselves.[63] The alternative insight is to accept that each experience is not just a representation of a cognitive interpretation but dependent on emotional as well as mental reactions. All interpretations of events, in adults as in children, is necessarily subjective, and this implies a form of idiosyncratic inaccuracy. Each similar experience will be different for each person. They cannot be exactly the same in the scientific sense. And even in the processing of information there are elements which are deeply affected by emotions. Impulsive children, for example, show different and less developed cognitive abilities, and, on the other hand, depressive children show a lack of self evaluation. These are not just the either/or of the extremes, or the pathological edge of the human mind, but both parts of normal thinking.

The habit of logical explanation has led research to pursue a series of stages; it has also attempted to isolate the different variables that make up what we think of as thinking. There are 'models' of social information processing that attempt to rationalise a response to the environment by dividing it into encoding cues, forming a mental representation, searching for a response and enacting it as if each part could be directed.[64] Models of cognition, like models of memory concentrate on a pure form of encoding, storage and retrieval of information, seeing the mind as an instrument not unlike a computer, ostensibly untempramental and capable of many different connections in the overall circuit.[65] But the moment that emotions are brought in, even the simplest skills of memory are affected.[66]

In order to understand the young mind we need to accept what we know about adult ways of thought. The mind has the ability to accept that things can be true and untrue at the same time; it can accept contradictions and illogicalities. It responds as children do according to the way that it is asked; it is affected by all the power of language as much as by the clarity of the task. It muddles recall and recognition; a distinction between being able to store things in the memory and realising that it has been through the same visual or aural experience before. Thus associations deeply and subconsciously affect cognition. The very ability to ignore information is an important factor. The 'don't know' syndrome hides a great deal of knowledge. But then knowledge is affected by beliefs. And false beliefs are powerful as true ones.[67]

The juxtaposition between the idea that young children develop a theory of mind, and the sociocognitive tradition which emphasises intellectual progress as a function of social interaction should not be an opposition.[68] One depends on the other. The internalising of knowledge is a function of critical interpretation as well as a kind of incorporation into social interaction. The very division of psychology into clinical, developmental and environmental approaches has led us into some false dichotomies.[69] Of course the subject of the human mind is too vast to be wholly understood by itself, but its experience can be interpreted differently from the divisions that say less about exploration than about the demarcation lines of academic tradition.

There are always many levels of experience, the human which affects all people equally, the cultural and the individual. By accepting this bald fact, we already accept that the Nature and Nurture debate should not be an either/or.[70] The individual and the environment are in a state of constant tension, and the environment is the shared opportunity for experiences that remain individual.[71] All the recent research demonstrates the importance of socialisation in the forming of the mind, but it has not yet led to the explanation of the difficulties people have, nor the development of pathologies, as well as false beliefs and the constant discrimination between truth and falsehood. One of the difficulties we face in gathering evidence is the fact that so much attention is paid to the unusual - the 'failures', the disadvantaged, the afflicted and the disaffected, as if they were disconnected, from, and as if there were an unproblematic area of the 'normal'. Perhaps it is because we like to think of ourselves as not only perfect but self made, that we do not recognise the arbitrary and accidental nature of each person's experiences. Just as we are affected in the way we think by our idiosyncratic experience, so research into young children is subtly and inevitably affected by the beliefs of the researchers. We need to recognise that the purest of reasons is formed out of a kind of prejudice.

The debate about nature and nurture, like so many academic and research questions, is in the general sense political. They are driven to prove a hypothesis. But if we draw back and contemplate the way which children analyse and explain their own experience we learn more about that than their innate abilities. Whilst young children have a theory of mind, this does not mean that these theories are any more refined than the theoretical position of adults. They are more necessary and therefore more conscious. But they are also rich and complex. Young children possess intuitive beliefs and their own theories.[72] The question is how this influences how they form their ideas. Is it possible that young children take in every piece of information, every distraction before they are able to label and to distance them? Far from only perceiving the most general and simplified chunks of information, they are surrounded by surface information which they then have to reconstruct into meaning. Whilst social conventions affect them there are many different patterns of connection in the young person's mind.

We will never know what goes on in the young person's mind by observation or experimentation alone. This is partly because of the difficulty in seeking out the inexpressible, and partly because by the time language makes its necessary impact it will have imposed its own cultural constraints on the mind. What we can do is to see some of the consequences of early experiences in young children's subsequent reasoning - an area surprisingly unexplored. We do know about the powerful ability to interpret, but less about the long term influence. There has been extensive research on the discriminatory abilities of young children, on their social understanding and the potential of theoretical reasoning.[73] There is a filter to early experiences which leads to the subsequent development of different formulations of interpretation, but even through this we can gain at least a glimpse into the way in which the world is viewed.

The middle point between the idiosyncratic experience of the individual and the general human experience we all have in common is 'culture'; the particular events that are shared by particular people at a particular time. Whilst this does not mean that certain events will necessarily lead to certain outcomes, it suggests that we should be aware of the consequences of cultural experience, and that something could be done about it, if we cared enough. Vygotsky asserts that every function of children's cultural development appears twice, first on a social level and later on an individual level. What the extensive research since has shown is that the social and individual happen at the same time and are inextricably linked. Vygotsky also asserts that higher functions originate as actual relations between human individuals. But think again of the young person's gaze. This is indeed directed towards relationships but relationships with a whole mass of information. The firm 'theory' of mind is seeking out the distinction between what is responsive and what is not.

The notion of 'culture' is a constraining as well as enriching one, as Bourdieu reminds us.[74] Culture is formed by making distinct connections between groups of ideas or objects or tastes that automatically forms into those which are included and those which are excluded. There will always be more of the latter, just as there will always be more languages not understood than understood. Young children are continually being presented with information at two levels. One is the raw perceptual data that all people experience, of warmth and cold, light and darkness, sounds and silence. The other is the shape of the environment in its surface patterns, the artefacts, the voices and movement. When children gaze at the world they see the two intertwined and as inseparable as they later become. We should therefore not assume either that children are unaffected by cultural archetypes nor that they are wholly dependent upon them.

Again we need to remind ourselves of the limitations and idiosyncrasies of the adult mind. The mind does not follow logic. Its interpretations of probability are often biased.[75] Cognitive illusions, like perceptual ones, do not disappear when they are recognised as such. The stick in the water is seen as bent even when we know it is a result of the refraction of light. There are as many 'statistical illusions' as statistics. People systematically give illogical answers to questions of probability. For intuitive judgements are not dependent on logical probability but on some kind of rule of thumb. Human rationality quickly becomes biased when faced with uncertainty.[76]

One of the biases exhibited by people is towards the development of young children. Even when they are giving demonstrations of their abilities these can be interpreted as being unsophisticated. For example, there is a distinction to be made between the concept of mind as a separate entity and the mind as integral to the personality. Young children understand that people possess thoughts and beliefs; adults tend to personify the mind as a separable and independent processor.[77] Which is in fact more sophisticated? As people get older they rely more and more on memory when faced with tasks; does that mean that their approach is necessarily more reliable?[78] Young children look afresh at every new experience. They do not make the same distinctions between recognition and recall. They do not make the same distinction between internal and external cues. This makes them both more capable and more vulnerable.

Attempts to impose an order on the experience of the child for the sake of coming up with a logical, and ideally, testable model have tended to depend on theories of developmental stages and on binary opposites. Suppose the experience of childhood consists not only of a fully working mind but the experience of a mass of complex and incoherent experiences on when *they* have to work.

How, then, can we find out the effects of such experience?

Notes

1. Bettelheim, B and Rosenfeld, A. *The Art of the Obvious*. London, Thames and Hudson, p.7, 1993.

2. Chukovsky, K. *From Two to Five*. Berkeley, University of California Press, 1963. Writing at the time of Stalin's massacre of the millions.

3. James, A and Prout, A (eds.) *Constructing and Reconstructing Childhood: Contemporary Issues in the Sociological Study of Childhood*. London, Falmer Press, 1990.

4. Aries, P. *Centuries of Childhood*. New York, Knopf, 1962.

5. Elias, N. *The Civilising Process*: Vol.1, *The History of Manners*, Vol.2, *State Formation and Civilisation*. Oxford, Basil Blackwell, 1978 and 1982.

6. Haste, H. Growing into Rules, in Bruner, J and Haste, H (eds.) *Making Sense*. Children's Construction of the World. London, Methuen, 1987.

7. Piaget, J and Inhelder, B. *The Child's Conception of Space*. London, Routledge and Kegan Paul, 1956.

8. Donaldson, M. *Children's Minds*. London, Croom Helm, 1978.

9. Borke, H. Piaget's views of social interaction and the theoretical construct of empathy. In Siegel, L and Brainerd, (eds.) *Alternatives to Piaget*. London, Academic Press, 1978.

10. Shands, H. The Hunting of the Self: Toward a Genetic Affectology. In Modgil, S and Modgil, C (eds.) *Toward a Theory of Psychological Development*, Windsor, NFER, pp.61-89, 1980.

11. Donaldson, M, op cit.

12. Light, P. Context, Conservation and Conversation. In Richards, M and Light, P (eds.) *Children of Social Worlds: Development in a Social Context*. Cambridge, Polity Press, 1986.

13. The answer is E and 7; the sealed envelope and the 1st class stamped envelope.

14. Bruner, J and Haste, H (eds.) *Making Sense: The Child's Construction of the World*. London, Methuen, 1987.

15. Dunn, J. *The Beginnings of Social Understanding*. Oxford, Basil Blackwell, 1987.

16. Geertz, C. *Local Knowledge: Further Essays in Interpretative Anthropology*. New York, Basic Body, 1983.

17. Butterworth, G. Some Benefits of Egocentrism, in Bruner, J and Haste, H, op cit., pp.62-80.

18. Feldman, C. Thought from Language: the Linguistic Construction of Cognitive Representatives, in Bruner, J and Haste, H, op cit., pp.131-146.

19. Kuzmak, S and Gilman, R. Young Children's Understanding of Random Phenomena. *Child Development*, Vol.57, No.3, pp.559-566, 1986.

20. Siegal, M. *Fairness in Children: A socio-cognitive approach to the study of moral development*. London, Academic Press, 1982.

21. Piaget, J and Inhelder, op cit.

22. Piaget, J. *The Child's Conception of the World*. New York, Harcourt Brace, p.56-60, 1929.

23. Kajan, J. *Change and Continuity in Infancy*. New York, Wiley, 1971.

24. Bandura, A and Walters, R. *Social Learning and Personality Development*. New York, Holt, 1963.

25. Gesell, A; Ilg, F and Bates, L. *The Child from Five to Ten*. New York, Harper & Row, 1946.

26. Luria, A. *Cognitive Development: Its Cultural and social Foundations*. Cambridge, MA, Harvard University Press, 1976.
Leontiev, A. The heuristic principle in the perception, emergence and assimilation of speech. In Lenneberg, E and Lenneberg, E (eds.) *Foundations of Language Development: A Multidisciplinary Approach*. New York, Academic Press, pp.43-58, 1975.

27. Brown, G and Desforges, C. Piagetian Psychology and Education: Time for Revision. *British Journal of Educational Psychology*, Vol.47, No.1, pp.7-17, 1977.
Bruner, J. *Beyond the Information Given*. London, Allen & Unwin, 1974.

28. Rotman, J. *Piaget: Psychologist of the Real*. Harrocks, Harvester Press, 1977.

29. Voreche, J. Conclusions in Modgil, S and Modgil, C, op cit., pp.765-787, 1980.

30. Egan, K. *Education and Psychology: Plato, Piaget and Scientific Psychology*. New York, Teachers College Press, 1983.

31. Erikson, E. *Childhood and Society*. New York, Norton, 1963.

32. Noel. 1983.
Bee, H. *The Development Child*. New York, Harper, 1978.

33. Shakespeare, W. *As you like it*, Act II, Scene VII.

34. Kohlberg, L. The Development of Children's Orientations Towards a Moral Order. *Vita Humana*, Vol.6, pp.11-13, 1963.

35. Speece, M and Brent, S. Children's Understanding of Death: a review of three components of a death concept. *Child Development*, Vol.55, No.5, pp.1671-1686, 1984.

36. Webb, C. Young Children's Views of Social Behaviour. PhD University of Huddersfield, 1998.

37. Wilson, J and Cowell, B. *Children and Discipline*. London, Cassell, 1990.

38. See later chapters.

39. Siegel, M, op cit.

40. Cullingford, C and Morrison, J. Who Excludes Whom? The personal experience of exclusion, in Blythe, E and Milner, J (eds.) *Exclusion from School*, pp.130-148. London, Routledge, 1996.

41. Cullingford, C. *Children and Society*. London, Cassells, 1990.

42. Cullingford, C. *The Inner World of the School*. London, Cassell, 1991.

43. Vygotsky, S. *Mind in Society*. Cambridge MA, Harvard University Press, 1978.

44. Halliday, M. *Learning How to Mean: Explorations in the Development of Language*. London, Arnold, 1975.

45. Searle, J. *Speech Acts*. Cambridge University Press, 1969.

46. Chomsky, N. *Language and Mind*. New York, Harcourt Brace Jovanovich, 1972.

47. Bruner, J and Haste, H, op cit.

48. Geertz, C, op cit.
    Tajfel, H. *Human Groups and Social Categories*. Cambridge University Press, 1981.

49. cf. Leontiev, op cit.

50. Mortimore, P; Sammons, P; Stoll, L; Lewis, D and Ecob, R. *School Matters: The Junior Years*. Wells, Open Books, 1988.

51. Tizard, B and Hughes, M. *Young Children Learning*. London, Fontana, 1984.

52. cf. Jesuits' designs on influencing very young children.

53. Shakespeare in *The Tempest* significantly accepts both.

54. Jones, S.

55. *The Tempest* Act I, Scene II.

56. Smith, F. *Understanding Reading: A Psycholinguistic Analysis of Reading and Learning to Read*. New York, Holt Rinehart & Winston, 1971.

57. cf. *King Lear*.

58. Ornstein, R. *The Psychology of Consciousness*. New York, Harcourt Brace Jovanovitch, p.20, 1977.

59. ibid., p.21.

60. Kelly, G. *The Psychology of Personal Constructs*. New York Norton, 1955.

61. Bruner, J. *Beyond the Information Given*. London, Allen & Unwin, 1974.

62. Egan, K, op cit., pp.88-89, 1989.

63. Quiggle, N; Garber, J; Panak, W and Dodge, A. Social Information Processing in Aggressive and Depressed Children. *Child Development*, Vol.63, No.6, pp.1305-1320, 1992.

64. Dodge, K. Social Competence in Children. Chicago University Press, 1986.

65. Baddeley, A. Human Memory; Theory and Practice. Hove, Erlbaum, 1988.
    Underwood, G. *Attention and Memory*. Oxford, Pergamon Press, 1976.

66. Beck, J. Worlds Apart: Readings for a Sociology of Education. London, Collier Macmillan, 1976.

67. Quiggle, et al., op cit.

68. Vygotsky, K, op cit., 1965.

69. Paivio, A. Mental Imagery in Associative Learning and Memory. *Psychological Review*, No.76, pp.241-263, 1969.

70. Scarr, S. Biological and Cultural Diversity: The Legacy of Darwin for Development. *Child Development*, Vol.64, No.5, pp.1333-1353, 1993.

71. Ibid. and see the subsequent debate.

72. Barrett, S; Abdi, H; Murphy, G and Gallagher, J. Theory-based correlations and their role in children's concepts. *Child Development*, Vol.64, No.6, pp.1595-1616, 1993.

73. Catron, T and Masters, J. Mother's and Children's Conceptualisations of Corporal Punishment. *Child Development*, Vol.64, No.6, pp.1815-1825, 1993.
    Howes, P and Marman, J. Marital Quality and Child Functioning: A Longitudinal Investigation. *Child Development*, Vol.64, No.5, pp.1044-1051, 1989.

74. Bourdieu, P. *Distinction: A Social Critique of the Judgement of Taste*. London, Routledge and Kegan Paul, 1984.

75. Selman, R. The Growth of Interpersonal Understanding: A Developmental and Clinical Analysis. New York, Academic Press, 1995.

76. Kahneman, I; Slovie, P and Tversky, A. *Judgement Under Uncertainty.* Cambridge University Press, 1982.

77. Wellman, H and Hickling, A. The Minds 'I': Children's Conception of the Mind as an Active Agent. *Child Development*, Vol.65, No.6, pp.1564-1580, 1994.

78. Schwanflugel, P; Fabricius, W and Alexander, J. Developing Theories of Mind: Understanding Concepts and Relations between Mental Activities. *Child Development*, Vol.65, No.6, pp.1546-1563, 1994.

3 The first academic discipline: evidence

The experience of young children has a clear effect on their subsequent development, attitudes and abilities. This is clearly recognised and clearly outlined not just in the research literature but in more public surveys and commissions.[1] How these effects work, and how they manifest themselves is, however, a relatively untouched question. It is as if the compartmentalisation of stage theories affected the approach to research. There is a great deal of admirable and painstaking exploration of very young children's sense of the social world at the time when they are beginning to be articulate and able to demonstrate their intellectual and social abilities. This research points us back to a time when children are able to carry out all kinds of feats without necessarily being able to explain or demonstrate them.

Once children clearly have a mind and voice of their own and can articulate their thoughts and perceptions research interest ironically enough seems to wane. There is plenty of research going on concerning older children but the focus is rarely on the mind of the growing child. It is as if once the young person is recognised as a free and able agent all attention is turned away from the child to the teacher, from the inner workings of the individual to the effects of various kinds of treatment. One of the characteristics of the research on children aged three, four and five, is the constant realisation that there is a distinction between the experiments that can be tested, and the ability of the child to go beyond all limitations. The excitement in the research lies, in a sense, not in discovering what the child can do but in discovering a method which can articulate it.

This is understandable. Research is an exciting academic pursuit in which the task itself can become more interesting than the discovery of new truths. There is considerable pressure on the individual researcher to show what a clever person he is. Academic esteem and success, as well as funding, depend on it. There is also considerable pressure on researchers to give those who fund research the answers for which they are paying. It is therefore no surprise that the delights in the original experiment should be so strong, as with the delight in statistical techniques, that the consequences, the meaning of the results, are forgotten. It is part of human experience to be so enamoured of the task in hand that the minutiae outweigh the overall vision, and the setting of the discipline itself is so powerful that it creates a small world of its own. Besides, many researchers dare not speculate too much, and the word 'truth' has an old fashioned air.

The research focus therefore is primarily on what is demonstrably researchable. In the early years the emphasis was on finding factors and variables that could be isolated, in showing the boundaries and parameters of set tasks. Thereafter the focus tended to be on the variables that affect the individual, the greatest of these being the teacher. Whatever can be measured and controlled is of prime scientific importance, and the inner workings of the mind do not easily fit such a category. About teachers and teaching styles, about classrooms and schools, about effects and effectiveness, about the curriculum and what it should entail, there is a burgeoning literature. Indeed, one can argue that the same desire to classify and categorise, the same fascination with stages drives on such research. What exact style of teaching makes a difference? What are the stages of attainment that should be demonstrated into the hierarchy of knowledge that is the National Curriculum?

About the response of the individual to all these stimuli there is comparatively little.[2] The psychological literature seems as a body to jump from early childhood to problems. It explores all the 'difficulties' of adolescence, and the traumas of the disaffected. It seeks to present preventative methods, incursions of outside influence, to discover what difference they make. Whilst there are always exceptions to this general emphasis, the tone of the research is nevertheless telling. It suggests that the one voice which is missing is that of the individual, him or her self.

It is widely acknowledged that children are rarely listened to, but the acknowledgement does not lead to action. Again, at one level, this should be no surprise. The notion of being seen and not heard is one on which all the psychological and administrative energy of the education system is based. Some might even wonder whether anyone is properly listened to beyond the outcomes of the ballot box. Listening, paying attention to the thoughts and emotions of others is considered an individual rather than a collective act. On the one hand we have many lucid accounts of children's abilities and thinking skills.[3] On the other we keep them silent, and pay little attention to them. Even books ostensibly about listening to children are more about the researchers and their research.[4]

People generally do not know how to listen to children. They naturally interpret what they hear with their own meanings and find them amusing to their adult inferences. When people do listen to children they do not necessarily know what to do with the consequences, they do not know how to act on what they hear. For it is like being confronted with completely new evidence. It is like change. New evidence is sooner and more easily rejected than absorbed. And when absorbed it will sooner be transformed into something other, more fitting, than effect a change.

The emphasis on the stimulus rather than the response, on the teacher and what is taught rather than the pupil and what is learned, is natural. It is the result of the combination of self-absorption and mechanics. There is a search for ways of making a difference, for isolating the variables which work. What seems like a desire to create behaviouristic and objective competences are in fact driven by personal need. Thus teachers are naturally absorbed in their own teaching. That is the focus of outside attention. The learning of their pupils is judged as nothing more than outcomes of the teaching, standards against which the teachers, as individual human beings, are measured. The image of teaching is, after all, a very powerful one. It is of someone with knowledge, pouring what is known into the empty vessels that are laid out in rows before her. Given such a strong hold of this traditional image it is no surprise where the attention of researchers lies.[5] But this traditional stance deeply affects teachers themselves, as well as being reinforced from outside. In one study to research the effects of group work, teachers were asked to ensure that the pupils worked with each other without looking automatically for help and instruction from the teacher.[6] They were told that they could seek information from books or from each other and only in the very last resort turn to the teacher. The results were interesting. The progress the pupils made was rapidly increased. But the teachers felt guilty. They felt they were not doing their job.

Teachers feel they are there to teach and their professional interest lies naturally and humanly enough in themselves. Besides they are also the ones who are being measured, whose competencies are being assessed. The success or failure of children is a judgement on the teacher. The voices of children in this cacophony of inspectorial judgements is easily lost. Or perhaps they are only ignored until such time as their voices are another weapon of measurement.

Whilst there are many reasons that could be presented for the lack of attention paid to the human voice it is nevertheless still a puzzle. There seems to be a cultural inhibition against certain modes of consciousness; that one can learn, that people might change, that something educational could make a difference. We have already mentioned the superciliousness that finds in the supposed limitations of children the last refuge of the superior adults.[7] But it is as if that egotistical idea of the self-made man were combined with all the complex arguments that suggest that it is impossible to hear any other voice because it is impossible to believe it.

We live at a time when, at a number of levels, we are self-conscious about language. We hear politicians. That should be enough of a comment in itself. But the study of language, not as a means of communication but as a system of thought in itself, has dominated philosophy for more than a century. There was a time, before the rise of state education, when language was considered to be the means of conveying ideas. But then language became formalised as the vehicle of thought itself. The formalisation of the study of language itself suggests a mistrust in what is conveyed by it.[8] The arguments of different philosophers at first suggest that the meaning of words is built up purely through the circumstances or the games in which the words are used, rather than the idea that a word can convey an objective meaning.[9] The plausibility of this - or at least the notion that everything is not exactly what it seems when it comes to what is said - relates to the early and the continuing realisation of the difference between truth and falsehood. And yet, when else do we have to connect with our inner worlds but language? How else are we to explore and communicate?

That there is a problematical relationship between language and thought, as between truth and falsehood, cannot be denied. But for all kinds of reasons attention has been paid to language as potentially false rather than ostensibly true - even if we use language every day to convey meaning. It is after all far easier to study language for its own sake then for what it conveys, easier to see it as an instrument than as a means to a clear end. We can play games with language. To trust what we hear seems naive. This has meant that the very notion of listening to what people say seems to be academically unrespectable. We cannot be seen (or rather heard or read) to be listening since that seems to be an unphilosophical act. And thousands of words are written about their own unimportance. This means that *not* listening to what people say, and not taking it seriously, has a philosophical edge.[10]

To convey anything complex has its difficulties. That there should be a certain amount of the arcane or the impenetrable is almost inevitable, and each discipline is bound to develop a specialist vocabulary as a kind of shorthand for particular concepts. The tradition of linguistic philosophy, whether the 'Oxford' one, or that of the French school, has led to greater understanding of the difficulties of communicating. But we should draw a distinction between complicated language describing complicated ideas, and jargon. The attempt - as here - to make clear what is bound to be as complex as any human being means struggling to find the right words in order both to do justice to the richness of the material and to communicate. It is a far cry from using language not to describe or analyse reality but to create it. There are times when one has the impression that the conclusions to which some of the French philosophers come is that reality is only in the mind of the creator of language, and that anything of hermeneutic significance cannot be shared by anyone else. The irony of the fact that they write about this at great length should not be lost anymore than the robust response of Dr Johnson to Bishop Berkeley's not dissimilar notions of the world only existing inside the mind of the beholder.[11]

The problem with this suspicion of, and fascination with, language as a means of communicating the fact that nothing is communicable outside language itself is that the emphasis becomes an academic one, it becomes an interest that is all absorbing. The same shift away from exploring external reality to finding new terms to explore self-conscious ideas about it affects research methodology. The more one thinks about the difficulties the more difficult it becomes, until anything like a 'truth' becomes impossible.[12] The fascination lies in the intellectual game being played. As Lieberman is quoted as saying:

"Nonsense (when all is said and done) is still nonsense. But the study of nonsense, that is science."[13]

The reasons, then, for being suspicious of what people say are many. The natural distrust of politicians is supported by an academic interest in sophisticated imprecision. The superiority felt towards the utterances of children is joined by the awareness that to listen carefully and to understand takes time. The awareness of the possibilities of falsehood -

significantly something learned early - should not, however, obscure the pragmatics of truth. One of the most influential of linguistic philosophers underlines the fact that people *do* say what they think; that even within the attempted lies there are, in linguistic terms, a ninety percent of truth, and that to mistrust what people say is sillier than to accept it.[14] Austin even went so far as to point out how foolish it is to neglect the perceptive comments of children. And yet the study of children's use of language centres not so much on what they say or what they mean but on the mistakes they make, on language acquisition rather than on the linguistics of thought.[15] The types of insight presented by children are not always those which are expected or sought out by the adult listener. This is not due so much to the lack of anything to communicate but the lack of recognition of what is being communicated. We have noted how experimental tests can exclude children's understanding.[16] We should also note that we need to understand what children are saying about the world, about their semantics and not just their syntax.[17]

The approach to children's experience and their description of it should be both a sensitive and a pragmatic one. But the latter adjective has already been taken over as a word that describes something academically specific. 'Pragmatics' refers to the relationship between signs, or language, and their users. It is an attempt to give a human dimension to linguistics, a reminder that beyond syntax and phonetics and beyond semantics as a study of the relationships between signs and their referents, people are using language to say something. Language is not just a formal object but an instrument "that is used in the interest of getting the work of the world done and not in the interest of abstract science".[18] The more attention given to the study of language for its own sake, the more we realise the division between the academic and the real.

We should not, however, underestimate the strength of the academic discipline, the pull of intellectual superiority, the thrill of finding methological faults. Nor should we lose sight of what is now deemed to be an old-fashioned concept- the truth. Because there has been such an emphasis on academic methodology, almost a self-enclosed, hermeneutic 'game' - modernism, perhaps? - there is bound to be a reaction of which we see many signs in many different disciplines. The alternative approach to language in 'pragmatics' suggests a turning away from cause-effect psychology and simple causal theories, and a recognition of the difference between 'caused' and 'intended' behaviour.[19] Instead of testing theories through a series of experiments, the emphasis is more on interpreting people's actions and their meanings.[20] Instead of explaining natural phenomena the idea is to interpret human ones.[21] Despite the walls put up between different disciplines, to protect their own interests and integrities, the sense that understanding should be grounded in real experience is growing and has been over a number of years.[22]

There are still difficulties to overcome. The fascination with techniques will always clash with holistic views of understanding, or explorations of evidence. There is, after all, a psychology to research methodology as there is to any other human endeavour. The scientific method involves a limitation of enquiry; and the essence of the good experiment is successful exclusion.[23] The problem is that with such a profusion of evidence that constitutes the human experience it is impossible to isolate every variable; exclusion itself creates falsehood. The desire to create evidence which is valid and reliable is essential. But sometimes those results which are recognised as valid are merely those which fit in to an already established set of concepts; and this only changes when new evidence which does not fit is so overwhelming that it cannot be excluded.[24] It has long been recognised that the separation of research traditions and disciplines means that valid evidence can easily be ignored. No single tradition, be it quantitative positivism or qualitative ethnography is enough in itself.[25]

The recognition of the importance of empirical evidence and its validity can always be countered by the acceptance of potential or actual fallibility. One cannot understand one without the other. Truth is defined by the possibility of falsehood. But then a fundamental choice has to be made, between seeking the truth or discovering falsehood. The fact that research is carried out by people implies a matter of interpretation and possible fallibility. This interpretation might come at an early stage - setting up an hypothesis - or at a later one, in the analysis of the results. There is bound to be interpretation, but just as we need to learn to accept pragmatically that people say things they mean, so we need to accept the rectitude and the discipline of making the evidence presented as valid as possible. The other route into obscurity, a withdrawal from interpretation, is academically attractive but itself a type of game; admirable and clever, but not necessarily helpful. Bourdieu points out the separation, the hidden condition of all academic activity, as well as the crucial role of the observer. The problem is that a preoccupation with what is supposed to be objective interpretation can lead to the collection of dismembered and meaningless facts. Bourdieu quotes an anthropologist who records 480 elementary units of behaviour in twenty minutes' observation of his wife in the kitchen.[26] He could have given many more examples.

The acceptance of the researcher as interpreter parallels that of the respect for the integrity of the subject; the individual being who is the location or 'habitus' of thoughts, expressions, perceptions and actions in the particular conditions of his or her own environment.[27] In seeking out the essential facts that link the individual and the shared human experience we need to accept both the simplicities of interpretation and the complexity of the reality from which it is drawn. We are warned against the 'Ricardian Vice', of establishing simple relations between aggregates that then seem to have causal effects, when the really important findings remain hidden.[28] But the battle of methodologies, and the difficulties of scientific or humanistic evidence has long been with us. In classical Athens, and in the sixteenth century, there were always those who would dismiss as irrational confusion what others would recognise as intellectual profusion.[29] We are concerned with accumulating evidence and reflecting upon it, on accepting all its richness, and realising that this is a necessary stage, rather than attempting to fit everything in to pre-set scientific formula. Everyday common sense thought, for all its richness and variety, is also a well organised collection of theoretical positions.[30] People have stories to tell and ideas to convey.

The problem in trying to understand the inner thoughts and workings of the human mind is not unlike that facing any historian. For an historian there are two almost paradoxical difficulties; incompleteness and profusion.[31] However many pieces of information are gathered there is always the sense that something might be missing. What, after all, lies behind the 'don't know'? or in all the unreturned questionnaires? Given infinite time then all possible data could be gathered.[32] But what then would we do with it? The historian accepts that he cannot cite every document or give a voice to every being caught up in historical events. The search for validity depends on interpretation and trust, on seeking out all the available evidence and in making it coherent. There is a profusion of material, but by itself it remains incoherent; it has no voice. The historian is trusted to give evidence a shape, trusted to respect the sources and never to be inaccurate, but out of the mass of material to present its meaning. It is the evidence that comes first and then its interpretation, rather than the presentation of an hypothesis and then choosing the evidence that justifies it.

There are many books written on different research methodologies and their limitations.[33] There is probably more time and energy spent on writing about research methods than there is in actually carrying out research. This is partly because of the contemporary habit of tendering competitive bids for money, which means that at least nine tenths of researchers have wasted a great deal of their time. But it is partly because of the fascination with the subject. Tensions and discriminations abound. Quantity and quality, grounded theory and experiments, action research or participant observation; there are countless possibilities for argument. There is not any method which escapes attack. Any conclusion which is unwelcome is treated not a rebuttal of the ideas or refusal to listen but with an attack on the methodology. A dislike of what is read is them justified by a dismissal of the evidence. But the real underlying battle is more subtle. The question is the way that research is motivated. Is it essentially to discover something new or is it a psycholinguistic or statistical display? The temptations to present evidence in such a way that it cannot be attacked are strong. The defensive, self-protective instincts often dominate. The defensive stance lies in the language of the statistics, in the impenetrability of jargon or in the complexity of the presentation. Again, the temptations and the difficulties that underlie research could be the subject of a whole book, but the point is made here because it has led to a tendency to rely on quantifiable methods since they appear less open to interpretation, less open to attack.[34]

Quantifiable methodologies only *appear* less open to attack. They are, of course, subject to the same accusations of bias, or in the case of Sir Cyril Burt, deliberate distortions. But there is still a tendency as we emerge from the narrow positivist tradition to look at qualitative evidence, such as what people say, as 'soft'. This means that a lot of potential evidence has remained untouched, as being either too obvious or too complex. The tendency to be dismissive is supported by the fact that most people think they know the answers to profound questions even before they think about them. Why are people prejudiced? It seems easier to come up with an instant answer - usually citing a demonstration of prejudice rather than an explanation of it - than to consider it with an open and a curious mind. The other difficulty is that many people feel instinctively that all the answers to the important question - why? - are also unknowable.

There is a potential source of understanding empirically how people think and what they think about themselves in relation to others. The data is rich and analysable, so that shared characteristics and explanations for their occurrence are made manifest. Such evidence is of attitudes and opinions, prejudice and understanding, stereotypes and typologies, about knowledge and the sources of knowledge. It includes an emotional as well as intellectual mind-set. It gathers in all the different levels of 'culture'. Such evidence should arise naturally. Whilst it is, like any evidence, susceptible to statistical analysis, since it includes, at one level, concrete knowledge - "hard" fact - it isn't gathered deductively to support an hypothesis. Hypothetical deductive models seeking out causal attributes tend to come to nothing.

What then is the best way to obtain data which sets out to map the inner worlds of human beings? No amount of participant observation or ethnographic anthropology can do more than give coherence to the outward, the visible signs of cultural iconography. No amount of causal inference can do more than give complications to simple assumptions. The only way to understand the workings of social concept of mind is to enter into communication with it - to use language. It is possible to measure how long people appear to be working academically through observing how much time is spent on a task; but to find out what they are learning is a different matter, and can only be learned within communication.

There are two strong academic traditions which have quite naturally explored the inner lives of people. The first is the literary-historic. It could be argued that we know more about the intricacies of the mind through the explorations of it made through drama, poetry and novels than through large scale social surveys. Certainly we have a more subtle awareness of the mind's delicate susceptibilities, the undermining of emotions, the tricks of attitudes and prejudice. And if we want to see how an accumulation of evidence can give a sense of understanding of peoples as well as individuals, we only need to look at historiography; how historians collect and sift primary evidence, how they learn to make sense of it so that out of a mass of evidence can emerge a generalisable truth. In history, the most real facts are the outcomes, the judgements that derive from collective evidence.

The second academic tradition, which explores mind sets through interviews, is that of psychotherapy. Whatever the tradition that is employed, from basic counselling to psychoanalysis, the essential research tool has been that of language; in helping make explicit thoughts and experiences that lie dormant, making clear attitudes that are only half understood. The irony is that the technique is employed to explore ideas that are supposed to lie too deep for ordinary articulation. Why then should it not be used to uncover those ideas that do not suffer from the same obscurity or obfuscation?

The question then is not which is the best way to explore mind sets but which is the only way. The interview method will always elicit rich data. As linguistic philosophers remind us, people cannot help speaking the truth - *almost* the whole truth, *almost* nothing but the truth - even when they wish to avoid it. But precise definitions of falsehoods do not enter our province. We are concerned with subjects who have nothing to hide, who do not even guess what the interviewer wishes to know, who is free to explore ideas without self-consciousness. The concentration is not on the interviewee - either as a person or as a subject. It is what the interviewee has to say.

Semi-structured interviews rest on three important premises. The first is that the interviewee should feel comfortable, that there should be time to explore ideas and that there should be no sense of threat. The second is that the interviewee should not guess, or try to anticipate, what the interviewer is interested in recording. There can be simple closed questions included in the structure of the interview, but the essential information will derive from open answers. The third premise for semi-structured interviews is that they should involve some form of internal monitoring. The ultimate validity test comes in the analysis, but a return to similar questions in a different context ensures that the answers are not influenced by associative trigger effects, and that there is an internal consistency to the main framework of the answers.

Interviews can give data of a kind that is most sought after in research on effects. They can provide us not only with knowledge but the sources of knowledge. Traditionally this has been the most difficult evidence to research: what is the effect of a television programme? If one makes an isolated stimulus, like a programme, a starting point, it is very hard to prove a response. But the interviewee is a complex memory bank that is often aware of when and where something has been learned, as well as what has been learned, when something was seen, as well as its impact.

Without exploring the mind sets of individuals nothing substantial in the way of evidence that explains attitudes and behaviour can be done. We await still the accumulation of information that derives from such research, to deepen and strengthen, as well as to go alongside what has been learned about the human mind in other disciplines, not in a parody of deductive science, but through open, qualitative, inductive analysis of information in its authentic state. And yet there seems to be an avoidance, almost an antipathy to such empirical evidence. Why?

Everyone talks and can be understood. This seems trite compared to the erudition displayed in scholarship or in the obfuscations of language so cleverly exploited by politicians. The very fact that language is shared by all makes it suspect. A subconscious mistrust of what all people have in common, guided by natural superciliousness, suggests that the very use of language as surface is nothing more than a skin covering the real workings below. Interviews are complicated because of the ambiguities of language but the seeming simplicities of the technique suggest that the statements that people make, and what can be learned from them, should not be taken only at face value but should also be treated seriously. Of course language is complex. That is why it is such an important source of information, not only because it reveals thoughts but because it has many subtleties. It deals not only in the obvious but in irony and ambiguity. It can be treated as 'story' and as 'discourse'. It can be seen to a delineation of a point of view, and as much an expression of the subjective as of the formal. Those who carry out interviews discover that those most inclined to tell untruths are those most aware of doing so; those who are in positions of responsibility describing their jobs. They behave as if they had to make a case. Those who ordinarily describe themselves and their experiences have nothing to hide.

But we are aware of the possibilities of misinterpretation even in those who seem to be the most frank. There is always the potential of untruth, conscious or subconscious. When Brabantio says to Othello that Desdemona "has deceived thy father and may thee" he refers to an obvious deception.[35] But what of the levels of self-deception in Othello's own language? Such gorgeous rhetoric, such gestures of the theatrical! There are times in which one wishes to accept all that he says because of the power of the music. At other times one can see nothing but the apparel of the self-absorbed. Words can deceive but they always communicate something.[36] They can convey truth and they can explore truth.

The question at stake is what is the truth, the whole truth and nothing but the truth? The law is rightly concerned to make these distinctions but the distinctions can be marginal in the context of the raw fact of experience which only language can describe. When people speak of themselves and their relationship to the society in which they are embedded, they are more aware of one than the other, or the formal relations of the generalisable world than their own thoughts, but when they talk of themselves from their sense of their own experience they convey eventually those cultural standards that are the mould of society. What we hear is the power of experience which is not just individual and not just collective, but by the force of the utterance something shared. Brecht begins one of his plays by making the rhetorical statement. "Hannibal crossed the Alps ... By himself? What of the people and the elephants? Alexander conquered the East. Without an army?"[37] Historians make the individual the symbol of the many. But it does not mean that the many, the individuals, the forgotten, do not also exist. They share the same collective experience.

There are as many different types of interview as there are kinds of listening. At one extreme is the survey, with someone asking simple questions against a check-list. This might seem a method more analogous to the questionnaire against which people have to respond against fixed statements; yes or no? But they are interviews nevertheless; asking questions and getting some kind of answer even if, for all the numbers involved, one has grave doubts about the validity of the answer. At the other extreme are the interviews conducted by psychiatrists and psychoanalysts, delving into the depths of the subconscious, of brushing the surface aside to stir up the depths, as if the surface was an impediment to real penetration. But interviews can also probe that cultural middle ground of shared values and experience, not placed against stereotypical reactions, but exploring at length what people remember, what they have experienced and what they think about it. Such interviews attempt to give a voice to the reality of experience.

There are many ways of carrying out interviews. One can look for differences.[38] One can ask one opening question and keep silent whilst the person talks.[39] Some believe strongly that the interviewee should be kept constantly reminded about what he or she has said so that they can change their minds, and re-write it.[40] Some argue strongly for group interviews which reveal consensus views and when the subjects can challenge each other - to show off or verify data.[41] The technique used to gather the evidence from which this book derives is that of semi-structured interviews. Whilst this is not the place to enter the debate about conflicting accounts of reliability, especially in the light of the arguments above, it is important to say something about the methodology out of respect for the subjects and for the validity of the evidence.

There were some essential ground-rules for these interviews. Firstly, they were carried out with individuals. In any search for inner feelings and attitudes confidentiality and anonymity is paramount. It is impossible to have other people overhearing, correcting or judging what is said. If the information is going to be passed to others in a position of power, like a teacher or a prison governor, it is as contaminated as the evidence given by a chairman of a company to a journalist. It immediately acquires a different kind of use. The interviewee must be assured that anything said will not be passed on or misused. This is the everyday ethic of the counsellor and eternal ethic of the confessional. These interviews do not, however, suppose that there must be dark or hidden secrets revealed. What they do respect is the integrity of the individual to say what he or she wishes, in such conditions that they have confidence. Confidentiality and anonymity are essential.

If the context of the interview is a private place, the tone is just as important. The subject needs to be free to say anything he or she pleases without criticism or surprise. This is less easy than it sounds. Whilst children generally make good and natural interviewees, this depends not on their age but on the subject. Adults will talk freely if they do not think they are being assessed for what they are saying. The conditions of these interviews are essentially different from the job interview or the viva. The subject, therefore, is not one that is interpreted as testing their knowledge. The difficulty arises because if the individual suspects that the interviewer is a teacher - or even if she is not - there will be a desire to please, to say what is wanted. The experience of young children is that virtually all the questions they are asked are 'closed'. The answer is either right or wrong. The open question - what do you think? - is as rare in school as veal cutlets for lunch. Even with students at University a simple question like 'How are you today?' will elicit suspicion and hostility. What does he want? What does he want me to say?

Children are not naturally defensive but they have learned by years of experience that teachers only ask questions to test them, and to check on their knowledge, not because they have any curiosity about their answers. It is therefore a great relief to be asked questions by someone who is genuinely interested in what they say. It is possible to research children's thinking by recording what they say to each other whilst they are carrying out tasks. This too is revealing but does not result in anything substantially different. If the listener has no designs on them, and does not reveal what motivations lie behind the questions, then the children will say what they think and feel. They will not then try to impress or to shock. The temptation to play a kind of game with the interviewer needs to be quickly overcome. It is important to be sensitive to this issue so that some fundamental mistakes which could contaminate the evidence are avoided. The BBC, in a survey designed to ensure that nine o'clock was a suitable 'watershed', asked children what time they went to bed. Their answers were predictable, and wrong. Had they asked what programmes they had watched the night before they would have had evidence which was verifiable, and very different.[42]

In order to create the conditions in which children feel at ease with the interviewer and the interview there are two further general rules that need to be followed. The first is that the interviews need to be long enough to let the subjects pursue issues in depth. This puts some researchers off. Interviews take time both in the carrying out and in the analysis. The results might be so rich and so consistent that a few interviews will outweigh a whole pile of statistical data, but the thought of the preparation and the transcribing is at first daunting. But there is no other way of probing the mind, of letting the person speak. Length is not recommended for its own sake. But it does enable the same idea to be returned to, to be explored further. It also allows the interviewee to come up with his or her own ideas. Length merely means there are no artificial parameters, no sense of urgency that leads people to say things to get them out of the way. The psychological impatience of the interviewer in a hurry can have the same effects as the harassed tutor interrupted by a student. This must be avoided. There must be time.

The second rule which underlines the delicacy of the atmosphere is that there should be something of a 'placebo'; the interviewee should not know exactly what the interviewer is after. This is, at one level, more controversial. It has been argued that the interviewee should know exactly what is being elicited, to the point of giving the transcript back for amendments. But is this more ethical? It makes the interviewee into an accomplice or fellow researcher. It also puts him or her on the defensive as if all that is said is no longer confidential but a public statement. This is exactly what the semi-structured interview wishes to avoid. The 'placebo' is there to allow the interviewee to explore any ideas rather than labouring under the constraint of expectation. The whole attention, unlike participant observation, is on the individual and what is said, without any pre-suppositions. The placebo can ostensibly be either an opening general question about interests, or an opening gambit simply asking the subjects to talk about themselves and their experiences. It is not really significant whether the questions to be asked are seen or not. There is no reason for the interviewee not to know beforehand the type of questions to be asked. Sometimes they wish to see them. The whole idea of a placebo is that no hypothesis about the answers is projected. The interviewee is not being deceived. But nor is the researcher deceiving him or herself. What is *not* explored are the avenues of prearranged logic, the groves of expectations. Key words are neutral not defining ones. There is no desire to prove a point of view or seek it out.

The term 'semi-structured' does imply that there is a framework for the questions if not an agenda, hidden or not. It means that the interview remains formal; confidential and relaxed but also professional. There are honest and open questions without the side effects of trying to please or horrify. What is sought is what the person wants to say, not what we want to hear. Nevertheless there is a subject. The reason for this is that the interviewer might wish to return to particular points that are made, and because for the sake of consistency there should be as few gaps in the transcript as possible. If we wonder about the unreturned questionnaires we should also be suspicious of those who did not answer a particular direction of questions. If one is to extract information that is consistent, a line of thinking they all share, one must be certain that this consistency does not exclude some, who might be supposed to think the same, but should not be presumed to do so. Some formality of structure, then, is necessary. It also helps the interviewer, and this leads to a more informal atmosphere. The interviewer is also anonymous; not a teacher, possessing no formal power. Nor is he or she expected to come up with solutions or advice. To such a person it is easy to talk, and for many, a unique experience. There are no reasons not to tell the truth.

The truth in these circumstances is both obvious and subtle. Much of what is revealed is easily understood in terms of content, belief and attitude. But it also reveals depths that are not at first apparent. The open questions will be bland and seem like the kind asked at 'warming up' sessions but they can later be found to have interesting connections to what follows. The general structure of the questions creates a framework which ensures consistency but within it will come probing questions and follow-up questions. One of the forms of an internal 'triangulation', a verification of evidence, is to ask the same question more than once, in a different context. Inconsistencies or subtle distinctions are then detected and the false trail of instance associations avoided. Asking one question without any chance of a supporting one can mean that evidence is overlooked or not detected. For example, when children around the age of eight are asked to say whether they think that the messages of television advertisements are true or false their immediate answers could lead to quite the wrong direction and draw a false conclusion. The younger ones say that the advertisement is essentially true since the product is clearly available in the shops. But then they go on to point out that the messages that are conveyed are not just true since they are exaggerated, biased and often plain stupid. Older children will immediately point out the falsity of the claims - 'the best', 'better than' - and the wild fantasies that surround the messages. But on reflection they will also concede the reality of the product lies in its existence, despite the exaggerated claims made on its behalf; is a true fact.[43] Just one question and you get an answer. But you do not always get the whole truth.

The interviews, with individual subjects, were carried out in private, in reasonably comfortable circumstances - eg. in a room not constantly interrupted - and recorded verbatim. The presence of a tape recorder if ever a problem is soon forgotten. The interviewer, clearly not part of the school staff, if the interviews are carried out in school as they mostly were, was both formal and sympathetic. There was no sense that she - again for the majority of the interviews this is the accurate term - had any personal or emotional interest in what the interviewees were saying. All the conditions were such as to make sure that the transcripts were uncontaminated by any foreseeable mistake; like the psychological desire to please or to shock; to defend a position or present oneself in the best light possible. Even such a description of the avoidance of potential mistakes shows what a defensive position interviewers are in. There is still a need to make a plea, despite all the philosophical logic on their side, for the efficacy of interviews as a way of gathering evidence. Language is our most basic and refined means of communication. 'I have to use words when I'm talking to you'.[44] And it is only through words that we are able to explore the inner thoughts of people, their interpretations of events, their understandings and their memories.

The evidence that we are here exploring is concerned with the thoughts of individual people. It is empirical. It is attempting to uncover something hidden. This is itself very unusual. Most research, for many reasons, is concerned with policy, with making changes with action, not with the evidence on which action and policy should be based. It is a characteristic of human nature that money should be spent on putting things right, on changing things, without knowing what the results should be. The real need is not only to listen but to have the patience of genuine curiosity to discover and verify what is there. It is to the indifference of the majority, the satisfaction of the few, and the despair of many, that so much money is spent in such a lavish way on schemes that are doomed to fail, when a little reflection would make us realise that there are matters that could be genuinely improved did we but try.

Interviews can discover significant truths, but it must be acknowledged that such an open statement is not popular. It comes across as too simple, given the need for instant policy decisions, for instant solutions and for instant personal gratification. Interviews can be both simple and obvious as a research technique. But they are as complex in reality as they seem simple in outline. However refined and carefully constructed a questionnaire, and however subjected to factor analysis, there are bound to be limitations in the evidence. Of their usefulness there is no doubt. For certain types of information they are essential. But if the desire is to explore the attitudes, the assumptions, the cultural scaffolding of the mind, then there are other more subtle techniques necessary. There are, after all, other means of learning about the human experience than the positivist tradition.[45]

The ethical issues underlying this type of research centre on the respect for the dignity of the individual and for the integrity of the results. All research is based on interpretation and there are many dangers in this. The first is that this evident fact is not even acknowledged. This is not to suggest that all research is subjective. The whole point is to come to a conclusion which is valid. But in order to achieve this it should be acknowledged that the possibilities of being led in the wrong direction by following false clues are always present.[46] In many research designs there is a clear indication of what is being sought. What seems like scientific logic can be as biased as any other interpretation which is not a priori.

There is a deep-seated part of human nature that will fit new material into an already existing belief.[47] Most people know what they want the truth to be. They will therefore find exactly what they want within the evidence that is brought before them. There is, indeed, a collective will to enlarge the research diaphragm - the 'tradition' - rather than to change it or challenge it. This drives much of the research that tries to justify policies. The attractions of finding what is provable, if meaningless, can overcome the empirical evidence on which policy should be based. It is always possible to find correlations between, say, left-handedness and the taste for potatoes, but it is not always helpful. Such an example is, however, not far-fetched to one who wishes to prove the detrimental or positive side effects of either left-handedness or the love of potatoes.

The ethical issues in any research are many. In interviews they centre on the integrity of the interpretation, and the awareness of the dangers of overlapping distinctions between the illuminative example and the generalisable insight.[48] The issues which are not covered are as potentially important as those which are. This is why the interviews are semi-structured. The 'don't know' response which can mean anything from ignorance to refusal must also be taken into account. But the underlying issue in the interviews is the respect afforded to the subject. This is not just a matter of anonymity and confidentiality. It is dependent on paying due attention to what is said, of treating it seriously, of allowing the responses not to be led, or to be treated as answers to closed questions, but as statements that come out of spontaneous but reflective thought. All important definitions must emerge spontaneously from the interviewee, rather than imposed upon them. There are therefore levels of answers. They range from obvious tastes and attitudes to more defined statements of experience and sources of influence. The interviews allow for follow-up questions and for the same question to be asked twice. But they also allow the interviewee to say what he or she wishes. The whole focus is on the statements made, and not on the questions themselves as would be the case with a structured questionnaire.

The samples from which this research derives are many. Originally the core sample - those used to illustrate the consistencies of response - was 160 children aged between six and nine and another 120 children aged between five and eleven. But the whole book is influenced by far more data than that. It is impossible not to remain aware of the implications of other research, or children's attitudes towards their experience of school, or their reflections on society.[49] The research then reported limited itself to establishing the empirical evidence rather than on seeking out all the implications. Since then there have been a number of research studies of a qualitative kind that have influenced what is reported here. There have been interviews with school leavers and the unemployed, young criminals and truants. There have been as many interviews with young children in school, and on holiday - with those who show no tendency to 'drop out' of normal society as well as those who do.

The core group of interviews with the children around the ages of seven and eight are therefore informed by much wider evidence. They illustrate the desire to find a sample which is representative of society as a whole, to avoid any bias towards the abnormal. This was to double-check the distinctions between those experiences which all had in common, those attitudes which they all shared, and experiences which differed because of the circumstances. In the computer analysis which was carried out this spread of background was a significant factor. Whilst the interviews were mostly carried out in schools in rooms in which they could not be interrupted or overheard, this was mainly to make sure that the sample was representative. The sample can be divided simply between boys and girls, and over a spread of ages, with a concentration on seven and eight year olds. But the experiences of which they speak are not *just* about the present circumstances. Valuable information about early childhood can be gained through the reflections of adults. These children, however, were still in the middle of coming to terms with, and understanding, their experiences and still learning the techniques of adaptation. They had not necessarily learned the art of denial of evidence.

There were three ways of ensuring that the sample represented a wide range of backgrounds. One was to select children who came from inner city areas, defined by the DHSS as low socio-economic circumstances, children who lived in suburbs and children who lived in the country. It could be argued that at the levels of experience we are discussing here such distinctions are not necessary. But it is important to establish in the sampling whether this is so. If there were not such care taken in the representative nature of the interviews it could have been argued that whatever views expressed were bound to come from those living in rural bliss, or those living in the more threatening ambience of socio-economic deprivation. The habit of denial of evidence would have centred on this aspect of methodology first. There is no easier way of dismissing evidence than to attack the results as a freak of sampling. Besides, we are concerned to establish the commonality of the human experience, the extent to which certain attitudes are shared, whatever the circumstances. Other background variables were also included to represent a cross-section of society. Fifteen percent of the children came from minority ethnic groups. Ten percent came from private schools.

Each individual voice was taken into account. There were no a priori assumptions made about what each person might say. The results might have led to great and deep distinctions between the outlook of those from deprived backgrounds and those who had more fortunate circumstances. Cultural and monetary factors might well have had such an influence that the attitudes and reflections expressed would have seemed like the experiences of different worlds. Had there been such distinctions then the conclusions would have been very different. In past experience differences between people have not been as significant as those things they have in common.[50] And yet there is a yearning in many to seek out differences - class distinctions or ethnic divisions. The yearning for simple cultural explanations is strong. This does not suggest great respect for the individual; but if there were to be such distinctions they would stand out clearly.

The theme of this book is the human experience as a whole and not that of a particular group. It is therefore important to acknowledge the wide representation of the sample. What makes the findings significant is their consistency. Clearly the ideas are not dependent purely on one (or many) samples. The quotations illuminate and demonstrate the way in which the ideas emerge. But the consistency is not just that of a common human inheritance - relationships with parents, and with siblings, with core intellectual and emotional experiences. It is not just that of styles of coping and interpretation. The consistency includes even those experiences that might be deemed to be more a matter of surface - towards the town and countryside, or towards traffic and pollution. Of course one can never completely separate the surface from what is within. What seems as superficial as skin is an integral part of experience. The children witness symbols of richness and poverty and develop their attitudes towards them, but they also experience and understand the consequences of being poor or being rich. Whilst their interpretation of money as a means of exchange might vary, and their knowledge of precise rates of exchange be hazy, they know about its power.

In the interpretation of the results there were different levels of analysis. The first was the content analysis looking for any inconsistencies or exceptions and carrying out cluster analysis taking into account the background variables like gender, location, and age, and certain themes that emerge in the following chapters; like attitudes towards the rich and poor, towards their parents, siblings and themselves. This analysis of 27 different variables, to see if certain sections of the cohort expressed markedly different attitudes than others towards different themes, was carried out using an SPSS computer package. It would have been significant if we had found inconsistencies. But what is demonstrated is the consistency of the overall findings. One could give an account of the chi-squares, the contingency coefficient and the significance of each variable but all we would be doing is supporting in statistical terms what could as easily be expressed in words, and easier understood.

The first level of analysis therefore was to discover the variations or lack of them, any signs of development according to age, or any gender differences. It was to ensure the validity and reliability of the statements made. The second level of analysis could also be said to be of content. All the children mentioned certain themes. It should be made clear that these subjects emerge from the answers and not the questions. When the transcripts are analysed as they are again and again, certain themes emerge from them. These are the essential themes and interests, the concern raised by the children, whether it be the lack of space in their bedroom, their quarrels with siblings or their experiences of the homeless. The third level of analysis reveals the subsets within the themes, the particular images or incidents that inform their attitudes. If, for example, the children were talking about countries around the world and all mentioned Africa, they would share a vision of Africa, an association with poverty, a negative image. Within that would be subsets of information, the housing, the flies, the food. The fourth level of analysis would be the reasoning that lies beyond their subsets of information. In the case of Africa, for example, it might be the hot weather and the droughts, or the preference of the inhabitants for their style of living, or the lack of development. All these would, of course, make a coherent whole in which the fifth level of analysis, the clues to the sources of influence, personal experience or secondary information, would be embedded. The images of starvation presented on television and in Oxfam advertisements would be a clear source for attitudes towards Africa.

Only then, in the sixth level of analysis, as in the first, would there be a double checking for differences: would there be any clues in the tone and style and approach to understanding themes like poverty or colour according to whether the individual was educated privately or in the state system, whether he or she came from a minority ethnic group or whether he or she had experienced severe deprivation. For whilst we acknowledge the universality of the human experience, and whilst we respect the individuality and idiosyncrasy of each one, we are trying to explore *how* people become as they are, that middle ground of culture, that tension between personality and circumstances. It is the way in which individual circumstances as well as shared information affects people that is of interest, and there is no doubting the variety of experiences. Thus the sixth level of analysis seeks out the distinctions between the types of circumstances.

The seventh level of analysis does two things. It looks at the style of expression, the tone of voice, the emotional range behind the statements, the ways in which there might be speculation or a change of mind, the significance or reluctance in pursuing a theme and the measures of personal defensiveness. But the last level of analysis also pays attention to the ways in which all the 'levels' make a coherent whole. That there are levels including that of context, is clear. But it is the way that they are embedded in each other, the way in which they form a unified whole - both in themselves and in relation to each other - that provides the real evidence. We are seeking to uncover the usually hidden experiences, by giving people the chance to communicate without defensiveness and without knowing the audience. This means that the recordings and the transcripts are treated with respect. The analysis must have regularity and consistency. And that means reading the interviews over and over again so that patterns emerge from the text rather than being imposed on it.

The quotations used to illustrate the findings are chosen to do just that. They are exemplars. They have two characteristics. The first is that they are typical of the others. They are not chosen as being extreme examples that demonstrate perfectly, or unusually well, the arguments in the text. If the majority of statements on a theme are expressed laconically and only occasionally heavily elaborated then the example given will be short. But the chosen quotations also demonstrate, when possible, the 'embeddedness' of ideas. The separate attitudes are interwoven with each other. Even if one particular piece of evidence is being presented - like fear of poverty - that quotation will not necessarily be separated from a different theme - like witnessing the homeless even if the latter is not at that time the subject of the argument. Thus there will be evidence of children making certain statements that support the argument of quite different chapters. The quotations give, without the need for additional comment, additional evidence.

This should obviate the need for massive quotations. Again, there is controversy about how much raw data should be presented, and how. There are those who argue that every single transcript should be presented, which would lead to the book being five times as long and which often prevents those who advocate this from carrying out research. There are those who argue that any quotation should not be at all selective since every single nuance of expression could have significance even if such significance does not help the argument: "Well ... er ... erm ... well ... I think ... well ... I would say ... you know ... well ... its like this ..." One can see the reason for both arguments, the stress on validity and reliability. But the real point in making these judgements of selection is that the material presented only speaks for itself up to a point. The argument is in the main text, and the quotations are exemplars. The historian after all is not expected to present every piece of primary evidence. If a manuscript of the 16th Century found in an archive demonstrates at length the duplicity of Granville in his dealings with the Netherlands is it necessary to reproduce the whole of it?[51] The truth of Gibbon lies in the style and commentary as much as the sources.

The significance of the quotations is that they constantly remind us of things we seem to have missed. They show the range of interests, and the activity of the human gaze. They demonstrate the awareness of issues supposedly the domain of adults. They show the ease with which these ideas are handled and expressed. They also suggest that so much more material lies hidden and ignored.

There is of course an underlying reason for this, and explains why time needs to be taken in explaining the methodology. By the end of the book, the reasons for human defensiveness and conservatism should be clear, and they should explain some of the motivations that underlie the research. But the research traditions that normally focus on the human psyche themselves can as much obscure as well as illuminate. Qualitative research, that is concerned with cognitive social and emotional development in individual learners, is rare compared to more quantitative studies that deal with matters like resources and organisation, or the social class of entrants to universities. The positivist paradigm with its emphasis on what is quantitively measurable has been pervasive. It approaches 'problems' in the main line of the empiricist tradition. It is functionalist whilst borrowing from phenomenology.[52] It has certain hypothetic deductive characteristics. It proposes an hypothesis to account for the problem (rather than letting the evidence be looked at first), it deduces from the hypothesis that certain phenomena should be observed in given circumstances (isolated, quantified and repeated), and then it checks the deduction by observation. Explanation is equated with prediction; the method of 'falsification' is used for testing claims of truth.[53] There is here already a contradiction. In deductive models our knowledge is often limited to what is necessary for a certain event to occur rather than to what is sufficient, which it cannot predict. Rather than dialectical reasoning the method relies firmly on formal logic, eschewing anything that does not confirm it.

Any hypothesis put forward depends on striking up a theoretical position that arises out of the previous literature. This maintains the importance of the tradition and upholds it. It explains the continuing influence of Piaget. The assumption is that the only way to approach research is through a consensus of existing methods. There is an essential conservatism in positivist methodology. Explanation is seen in terms of prediction and falsifiability. There is little question of the 'meaning' of test measures. For example Eysenck's 'extroversion/introversion' dichotomy is made synonymous with observations since being subsumed within a class of 'variables', whereas they are clearly socially informed theoretical concepts. The point is not, however, to attack the theoretical traditions of research, nor point out their weaknesses - again, there are whole books on that - but to affirm that there are alternative ways of making discoveries, of uncovering the 'truth'.

What we are trying to establish is that the ground rules of human behaviour might not (or do not) fit into the assumptions we make about them, assumptions themselves based on the way that people adapt to conditions, and the way they find comfort in certain intellectual traditions. Types of personality, fitting into one or another cluster of characteristics, might seem plausible and interesting but they are based on the unexamined assumption that nature is characterised by regularities, that the personality of each individual is not so much a unique assemblage of traits but that these traits are so grouped to make human types who are classifiable. Learning styles and personality inventories might seem to give answers, but they might also be as arcane and ungeneralisable as believing in star signs. The crucial difference in approach is that between finding what is measurable - like a 'personality factor' - and what emerges from a profusion of evidence until it becomes a characteristic.

Let us take an analogy. There is a great reliance in many organisations on personality inventories. Respondents answer simple questions. The analysis of these seem to indicate validity and reliability, although no-one knows exactly why this should be so. Using such measures saves time, and certain people are eliminated from carrying out particular practices - like being an air-line pilot. But whatever their efficacy and constant testing and retesting for correlations of internal reliability they leave people at another level the more puzzled. To take one example of a self-esteem scale, which has been tested for reliability and validity over many years: it depends on being able to circle one of four responses on the Likert type score from strongly agree to strongly disagree.[54] (Again, whether there should be a neutral mid-point, i.e. a four-point or five-point, six-point or seven-point scale is a source of argument for many papers.) The kinds of questions posited are like this:

"All in all, I am inclined to feel that I am a failure."

Those ticking or circling 'Disagree' or 'Strongly disagree', will be deemed to have satisfactory self-esteem. This depends on an instant response. The trouble is that the more you think about the question the more difficult it is to answer. Suppose someone asked in an interview about such views of personal success and failure. It is clear that very different results would emerge. But even the person presented with the scale must ponder on the complexity of the question. A failure? Against what criteria, given the profusion of experiences. At home? At work? At which moment? The more thoughtful, and the more thought that goes into it, the more difficult it is to give an unequivocal answer.

"On the whole, I am satisfied with myself."

The self-esteem scale seeks out those who will answer as blandly and positively as a politician. But in the actual social world is such self-satisfaction prized? There is the saving grace of 'on the whole' as in 'all in all' and yet if one really scrutinised one's own achievements, failures and successes, would anyone be satisfied?

What we do know is how children answer such a question when they reflect upon it. They do not necessarily follow the rules of 'adolescent self-image' that the scale seeks to detect. It seems to create a whole world of its own, of binary opposites, of groups and clusters of characteristics. There is a whole world of alternative explanations. It is the world of quite different possibilities that is being explored here. A new approach does not necessarily lead to new outcomes, but it does not exclude the possibility.

It must be made clear that qualitative research, the attempt to discover truth, is not 'unscientific'. There has been so much fascination with what is termed 'hard' data, quantifiable and deductive, repeated and re-emphasised, that whatever does not fit its paradigms is often considered 'soft' or worthless. This has led to some tragic misinterpretations of the human condition. Those who are caught up with the tradition of academic controversy will no doubt seek out dilemmas and hypotheses; rocks on which to break the evidence. But there are many aspects of experience that will not succumb to experimental methodology. One should not need to apologise for the fact that human beings cannot be summed up in a Pavlovian study of rats, or that they do not behave with the predictability of a chemical. Nevertheless there are matters to be learned: there are many characteristics held in common. What we are trying to elicit here is an argument that arises from discourse, to make the best use of what evidence is clearly before us. When studies are carried out that give examples of what people think they tend to be treated as if there were mere 'anecdotes'.[55] Researchers seeking to explore the real complexities of people have to protest, to argue that their studies are systematic, that quotations support conclusions drawn from carefully documented study.

Those who seek out the truth should no longer be apologetic, even if they ever were. The reiteration of the mistakes of the past is an almost inevitable part of the human context. What remains puzzling is its institutionalisation into habits and practices of research. What we are trying to achieve here is the power of surveillance, of an all-seeing gaze, letting every detail play its part.[56] The research, the understanding, is based on inclusion, not exclusion. It seeks to discover and inform, not to demonstrate. The temptations of the arcane and the impenetrable are many, but the excitement of finding the unexpected outweigh them.

Sometimes the aim of research, even into people, is to exclude all complexities. But as in historical truth, a complete account of an event as it really happened is never really attainable, leaving aside the stories of each participants and their pasts. Historical truth in that sense is impossible; but truthfulness is more important.[57] As Erasmus said: the important thing is not how much you know but the quality of what you know. There is a discipline in its own right of attempting to understand the human condition in terms of learning. The idea of this, of learning (and teaching - what we can do to enhance this) as a central discipline to 'Education' is still new. There still remain the conflicting academic boundaries that compartmentalise and withhold understanding for the sake of specific autonomy. When so many careers are dependent on exclusion and exclusivity this is no surprise. But then to contain all human knowledge and awareness in one field is impossible. The traditional subject boundaries will fall not from conflict but from modesty and the embarrassment of riches.

The first academic discipline and the oldest is the discovery of the world as a whole. It is the discipline each young child faces, and it is a 'discipline' in this sense. Order must be made out of the mass of information or it remains inchoate and unrealised. That order is personal. It is not just something imprinted on the brain. The individual cannot overcome it. There is always that tension between the experience and the reaction to that experience, between the fact and the interpretation. Disciplines attempt to create a complete world in themselves. Reading physics or chemistry, one knows the rules, even as they change. The purer the subject, the less contaminated by the complexities of reality, the more academically respectable it is. Young children are thrown into a new discipline. It is vast and complex, terrifying and unformed. And yet it has its own secret logic. That development of learning, the synthesis from a mass of information until it is logical, personal and controlled, is what children individually undergo, for the most part without help and without support, because we do not realise what they need, or are incapable of giving it.

It is a typical response to the demands of learning not to pursue an understanding of the whole but to specialise and set up boundaries. If the information is too great it cannot be controlled. But the first academic discipline is to choose which are the most relevant facts in a vast array of information. Thus the imposition and the interpretation of the individual mind, ever watchful, ever seeing, and as yet ignorant about what to ignore, is as significant as all the experiences that are presented.

Notes

1. eg. The national commissions of enquiry chaired by Sir Claus Moser and Sir Christopher Ball.

2. There are, more recently exceptions, eg. *The Inner World of the School, Children and Society.*

3. eg. Meadows, S. *The Child as Thinker: The Development and Acquisition of Cognition in Childhood.* London, Routledge, 1993.

4. Weber, S and Mitchell, C. *That's Funny: You don't look like a Teacher: Interrogating Images and Identities in Popular Culture.* London, Falmer Press, 1995.

5. Bennet, N. *Managing Learning in the Primary Classroom.* London, ASPE, Trentham Books, 1992.

6. It is interesting to mote how some languages, like German, contain words which have no immediate or exact equivalent in English, like 'Didaktik' or 'Erziehung'.

7. Tyler, S. *The Said and the Unsaid: Mind, Meaning and Culture.* London, Academic Press, 1978.

8. Wittgenstein, L. *Philosophical Investigations.* Oxford, Basil Blackwell, 1953.
    Wittgenstein, L. *Tractatus Logico-Philosphicus.* London, Routledge, 1961.
    Austin, J L. *How to do things with Words.* Oxford University Press, 1962.

9. Derrida, J. *Of Grammatology*, trans. G Spirah.

10. He gave him a kick and asked if he was imagining the pain.

11. There is of course a subject here, like 'Wirkung' or response.
    Iser, W. The Act of Reading: A theory of Aesthetic Response. London, Routledge, 1976.
    There is also an analogy to be made between the 'law' and 'justice'; the two do not go always go together, and have their clear distinctions. The same is true of the suspicions of a word like 'truth', as if it were such an unobtainable goal it is hardly worth pursuing.

12. Quoted by Schama, S. *Landscape and Memory*. London, Fontana Press, p.134, 1996.

13. Austin, J. Philosophical Papers. Oxford University Press, pp.183-4, 1970.

14. Camerata, S and Leonard, L. Young Children Pronounce Object Words more accurately than Action Words. *Journal of Child Language*, Vol.13, No.1, pp.51-65, 1986.

15. Borke, H. Piaget's View of Social Interaction and the Theoretical Construct of Empathy, in Siegal, L and Brainerd, C (eds.) Alternatives to Piaget. London, Academic Press, 1978.

16. McTear, M. *Children's Conversations*. Basil Blackwell, Oxford, 1985.

17. Tyler, op cit., p.xi, 1978.

18. From P J Bruner onwards. Bruner, J. *Towards a Theory of Instruction*. Cambridge MA, Harvard University Press, 1967.
    Bruner, J S. *Beyond the Information Given*. London, Allen & Unwin, 1974.

19. Shotter, J. Social Accountability and Selfhood. Oxford, Blackwell, 1984.

20. Giddens, A. *The Consequences of Modernity*. Cambridge Polity Press, 1990.

21. Baddeley, A. *Human Memory: Theory and Practice*. London, Laurence Erlbaum, 1990.

22. Ornstein, R. *The Psychology of Consciousness*. New York, Harcourt Brace Tavonovich, 1977.

23. This academic conservatism is rather like Carlyle's view of history where any change needs to be resisted until it proves itself inevitable.

24. Hammersley, M and Atkinson P. Ethnography: Principles in Practice. London, Tavistock, 1983.

25. Bourdieu, P and Passeron, J. *Reproduction: In Education, Society and Culture*. London, Sage, 1977.

26. Bourdieu, P. Distinction. *A Social Critique of the Judgement of Taste*. London, Routledge & Kegan Paul, 1984.
cf. Doyle's analysis of classroom activity. Doyle, W. The Use of Non-verbal Behaviour: Toward an Ecological Model of Classrooms. Merrill Palmer Quarterly, No.23, pp.179-192, 1977.

27. Bourdieu, P. *Outlines of a Theory of Practice*. Cambridge University Press, p.98, 1977.

28. Schumpeter, J. *A History of Economic Analysis*. London, Allen & Unwin, 1984.

29. Toulmin, S. *Cosmopolis: The Hidden Agenda of Modernity*. New York, Free Press, 1990.

30. Geerz, C. *Local Knowledge: Further Essays in Interpretative Anthropology*. New York, Basic Books, p.75, 1983.

31. eg. Ford, F. *Europe 1780-1830*. London, Longman, 1989. The Sources.

32. As attempted by the now ignored and forgotten 'Mass Observation'.

33. eg. Robson, C. *Real World Research*. Oxford, Blackwell, 1993.

34. Like those of Sir Cyril Burt whose falsification of evidence was kept obscure for many years.

35. *Othello* Act 1, Scene III.

36. The critics also show how language can be interpreted by their reaction to it, from Bradley's nineteenth century reading of Othello as genuine tragic hero, to Leavis's later impression of Othello as self-deceiving bombast.

37. *Galileo*.

38. eg. in cluster analysis.

39. du Bois Reymond, M. *Neue Yugend Biographie? Zun Struckturwander der Jugendphase*. Oplanden, Leske and Budrich, 1990.

40. Spradley, J. *Participant Observation*. New York, Hold, Rinehart and Winston, 1980.

41. Lewis, A. Group Child Interviews as a Research Tool. *British Educational Research Journal*, Vol.18, No.2, pp.413-421, 1992.

42. Cullingford, C. *Children and Television*. Aldershot, Gower, 1984. "What is a watershed?" is itself an example of a 'closed' question. There is only one answer, not a metaphorical one of the common understanding, but the line separating the waters flowing into different rivers or river basins.

43. Cullingford, C. Children's Response to Television Advertising: The Magic Age of 8. *Research in Edification*, Vol.51, pp.79-84, 1994.

44. Eliot, T S. *The Dry Salvages*.

45. Bahktin, M. *Speech Genres and Other Late Essays*. Austin, University of Texas Press, 1986.

46. As in the 'garden path' theory where people anticipate what idea will follow next.

47. See *Conclusions*.

48. Sanderson, P and Cullingford, C. The Ethics of Interviewing Children. *Children and Society*. Forthcoming.

49. eg. Cullingford, C. *The Inner World of the School*. Cassell, 1991. *Children and Society*. Cassell, 1992.

50. eg. Cullingford, C. *Children and Television*. op cit.

51. And can one not see the truth in Motley's comment on him "if it had ever been possible to find the exact path between right and wrong, [he] would have found it, and walked in it with respectability and complacency."
Motley, J. *The Rise of the Dutch Republic*, Vol.1, p.340.

52. See Open University 3rd level course: *Methods of Educational Enquiry*. Baldamus, the Ruling Paradigm. see Owen.

53. Kaplan, B and Warner, S. *Perspectives in Psychological Theory*. New York, International Universities Press, 1960.

54. Rosenberg. Self-esteem scale.

55. Dunn, J. *The Beginnings of Social Understanding*. Oxford, Blackwell, 1988.

56. Foucault. *Power/Knowledge*. New York, Pantheon, 1980.

57. Thomson, J I. *Lectures on Foreign History*. Oxford, Blackwell, p.1-2, 1959.

4 The life of the world to come: the identity of the self

Young children look at the world with an intelligent eye. Their mental abilities, and their analysis of social relations, is demonstrated to have developed so early that it is only the limitations of experiments that prevent us having an even greater insight into what happens during the years of infancy. The abilities are well established. But what is the consequence of this gaze? How much do they comprehend about what is going on around them? How do they interpret what they witness? And how does all this affect them?

Young children must create an explanation for themselves. That they have a theory of mind is apparent. But what about their theory of personality, and their theory of the relationship between themselves, as individual beings, and the world in which they find themselves? For they have their own theory of life long before anyone explains it to them. The excitement generated by the study of young children is that of seeing the untutored powers of the mind in grappling with reality, both physical and mental. It is as if adults were overlooking on a process of learning, amazed outsiders themselves witnessing rather than helping the process. The great difficulty is that for adults any theoretical position, or understanding, let alone the demonstration of this fact, depends on language. The fascination with the physical demonstrations of understanding, as in Piagetian experiments, derives from the sense that thought is inarticulate, but it also dominates the thinking of those who study children when they are articulate.

The rapidity with which children learn language, once they have established for themselves the rules of syntax and phonology, demonstrates their need to give expression to their ideas. Increases in vocabulary around the age of eight amount to significant new words (and therefore ideas and concepts) everyday.[1] If people kept up this rate of semantic acquisition the vocabularies we would possess would be richer than any dictionary. Of course most people learn to live within a restricted vocabulary, relying on the familiar and the well used, in terms of ideas as well as words. But children not only have the capacity for rapid learning but a need for it.

They are driven to make sense of what they see and develop their own theoretical concepts. They are never passive.

At the same time that infants are learning, at their own individual pace the art of physical manipulation and control, they are also becoming accustomed to their own individual identities. One of the first matters to be learned is the singularity of the self, the shock of the personal. This is not to suggest that the development of the personality appears egocentric; they are concerned not only with self-mastery but the manipulation of other events, seeking attention, and deriving gratification. The personality develops as much through gazing at the world, looking outwards as well as within. Children are not merely drawing attention to their own needs and waiting for responses, but are learning how to do so. They not only react to what is physically present, but are aware of absences. They quickly learn that there is a real world which remains there even when they are not in it. They have no sensory illusion that the whole world centres entirely on them. The distress of crying is a realisation of absence as well as of need. Infants of three-and-a-half months are able to represent and to reason about hidden objects.[2] They know when an object should appear and doesn't. They are learning about the rules of the physical world, objectively and precisely. And they are developing their own personal abilities to analyse it.

One of the most important concepts for young children to master is the distinction between those events which are predictable and those which are not. They need, for example, to have conceptual insights about natural growth, and the difference between the perceptual appearance of, say, animals and the transformations that they undergo.[3] Lawful and non-random change is distinguished from events just as they occur. In other words children by the age of three demonstrate the ability to predict and to understand natural laws which go a long way beyond their own sensory perceptions. This is why they understand so early both abstract concepts like truth, and the physical actualities of the world, like mutability and death. Nothing is left hidden, and even if it is left unexplained, all is examined, and even before it can be easily demonstrated, understood. The world is an actuality, there is an objective reality and this cannot be removed from the attention of young children. What as adults we take for granted and learn to ignore as insignificant has a dramatic effect on young children. For they ignore nothing, needing to develop the conceptual framework that enables them to relate to all they hear and see.

Much has been written about the patience and the energy of the very young in either looking at pictures, learning psychomotor skills, or developing their sense of the world of meaningful sound. The attention paid to an object of interest, like the leaves of trees as the pram passes beneath them, or the colours of a picture that covers the blank wall, will be profound and unremitting. What children want to do is to understand and be able to take their full part in the world. This is true of their physical reaction. Their frustration at not being able to hold an object is as obvious as their desire to master the ability. When babies of around four months learn how to give signals to gain rewards, like turning their head right, left and right to get the light turned on to be given some milk, it soon becomes clear that what delights them is not the reward (they may refuse the milk) but the mastery of action, getting something done.[4]

The ability to master psychomotor skills is paralleled by the understanding of concepts; young children do not merely perform but think about what they do. They are aware of the conditions which affect perceptibility, as well as developing their sense of seeing and hearing, smelling and touching.[5] They have necessary theories about perceptual conditions and the relationship between physical and mental processes. They also realise that objects, events and meanings can be represented in multiple ways. This leads them to see that different people may have contradictory representations of the same event.[6] Once they have understood all this they have achieved a sophisticated perception of the complexities of the world. Seeing that people have a point of view of their own means that children are acquainted with the difficulties of learning and being misled. They cannot always trust what they see and hear.

Whilst young children gaze outwards and see the intricacies of the world they are also the more conscious of the self. This is a necessity and the two perceptions, inward and outward, go together. There is no gradual shift from autism and perceptual egotism to the understanding of the social world, nor is there moulding by the external world of the individual. The two are in continual tension for one cannot have any self understanding without insight into the distinctions of points of view. Opinions and shifts of emphasis, and the complexities of changing relationships are what mark out the identity of the individual.[7] The ability to hear themselves and understand others is not limited by any cognitive deficit. They not only see but understand and this has consequences. All these findings from the research that has taken place in recent years underline the necessary and common abilities that all children have in common. It is an inevitable and necessary part of the human experience, without which no 'normal' individual would survive. One should then ask what happens to all these abilities as they get older?

There are some aspects to the mental life of young children that are different to that of adults. One clear difference lies in the sheer intensity of thought, and the constant accumulation of new evidence, as opposed to learning to fit anything newly experienced into pre-ordained ideas, and the ignoring of fact. But this also has consequences in terms of what is most important in young children's theories of mind and of themselves. They are, firstly, very aware of the process of thinking. Whereas adults conceptualise thought as a constant stream of consciousness, young children believe that the mind can be free of thought for stretches of time.[8] This is not so much a misconception as an insight. They make the clear distinction between thinking and not thinking; they know when they are using their powers of concentration to such an extent that they assume that there must be times when they are not doing so. After all, they are constantly engaged in making the distinction between those perceptions which carry meaning and those which do not. At the same time that they are aware of the functioning of their own minds they are conscious of the accumulation of knowledge. For this reason young children before the age of eight place the greatest significance on memory. It is only later, after the age of ten, that comprehension and attention are defined as distinct from memory.[9] By then children have learned that hard work and achievement are separated and that new evidence can be treated conceptually in the same way as previous experience. They realise that they have adapted to the habits of adult thought, even if they are lazy habits. For younger children all information is fresh, and so the ability to remember it, to store it and recall it, is significant.

The importance placed on memory and on the powers of conscious thought gives a further clue to the psychological development of the individual, and the relationship between personal experience and being part of a greater consciousness. The hierarchy of experience is paralleled by a hierarchy of action.[10] The individual is self-conscious but also self-activating, but the way the mind is formed depends on the social and linguistic habits of the community, so that personal being is also part of the social inheritance. But it must be stressed again that the social structures are not simply pressed into the template of consciousness. They are examined and analysed. Other people's behaviour is consciously looked at for clues of motivation, and falsehoods or misconceptions are as clearly understood as acts of kindness and reason. If three and four year olds know about false beliefs and deliberate deceptions, and see others lying or manipulating, they must also account for this.[11] They not only learn about society through their own interpretations but see other people's inter-personal relations.[12] They watch how people treat each other as well as how they themselves are treated. Whilst physical knowledge seems easier to acquire than social knowledge, which is more arbitrary, the latter is just as significant in terms of learning and more significant in terms of long lasting effects.[13] They witness bad behaviour long before they enter the social world in which teachers are given the authority to control it.

The stress that has been placed on young children's understanding of falsehood and false beliefs derives from the fascination with outlining their ability to have a theory of mind. But the implications of this discovery are profound. Young children not only demonstrate understanding but their awareness of an imperfect world. It is sometimes suggested that all the traumas of childhood are to do with unfulfilled personal needs - both emotional and physical. But to emotional insights and disappointments must be added the awareness of a society which includes many examples of violence and depravity. From the beginning children know they can be hurt. They know about the possibilities of being abandoned. They all experience the sense of loss, emotional deprivation, whether inadvertent or actual. But they also see people's behaviour to each other. They see fighting or bullying or arguments or the impoverishment of their personal circumstances. But they also hear of and see the same phenomena at second hand in terms of society at large. The news is not hidden from children. They might not assiduously follow newspapers, but the images of war and poverty, linked to their awareness of people's mendacity and potential personal violence are constantly before them. They are aware of the flaws in the world. When asked an innocent question like 'could the world be a better place than it is?' they are adamant that it could, or should be.

It would after all, be illogical as well as untrue, to see the world as an innocent Eden, full of unremitting happiness. Signs of individual suffering and symptoms of depravity are what fill the pages of newspapers and seek our constant attention. The capacity to be shocked remains, as in the most extreme cases of cruelty whether at Dunblane or in Bosnia-Herzegovina, but the personal state of shock which accompanies the first realisation of what is happening is far more sharp than the almost resigned acceptance of accumulated evidence. After a time horror becomes theoretical, abstract. The repetition of bad news makes it more distant rather than more shocking. But the first time, the first realisation or witnessing of horror has an effect which goes deep into the levels of the traumatic. Understanding the implications of the fact of war, of killing or bombing, has a profound effect to those who see it, and survive, as well as to those who are forced to be part of it. What we cannot measure is how deeply the individual is affected.

We do know that children are clearly aware of the reality of war, and that it is a symptom of human nature as well as the human condition.

> In all the wars and everything, you know ... they're knocking all the homes down ...   *(girl 10)*

The sense of being at a loss in the face of such facts 'all the wars and everything' contrasts with the possibility (for others) of being 'safe'. Such safety is, however, defined by this girl as 'where there's no people around'. It is as if any people 'involved' have the capacity to make war. What is interesting is the way that the list of headlines - of murders, as well as wars, of violence to property as well as to the body - are all linked to a general sense of the human condition. One way to contain or control such information is to see it as part of a pattern. Thus every single reported event is not only a shock but a symptom. Children, as well as adults, understand the way in which they need to cope with all the 'terrible' events that are reported. It is the sheer accumulation of fact that has to draw a general conclusion:

> I think people keep showing all the terrible things that have happened on the television and I think most families are looking at it and realising how terrible it is but I don't think there is anything you can really do to stop it. The ordinary programmes have got all the divorced people and people going on and taking drinks and drugs.   *(girl 10)*

'All' the terrible things that have happened make the headlines as opposed to the everyday depravities and domestic traumas. What is most significant, however, is the sense of helplessness. The only way to 'stop it' is to hide from it psychologically, not to watch the facts on television. The underlying sense that this is how people are remains. It is domestic misbehaviour writ large. Whilst it might seem distant at first glance, it also relates, albeit in an extreme form, to the child's perceptual framework of the everyday.

The relationship of a general or distant disaster - it might happen there but never here - to the everyday realities is always kept in mind. Children talk of wars and rumours of wars. But what they know about them is that they affect people personally and deeply. The sense of the inevitable - 'the countries is always fighting' *(boy 11)* - is matched by the vivid detail of the imagery through which wars are presented. They are no longer hearsay but made explicit through pictures. Those events, like wars or diseases, that might not seem like an obvious or immediate part of their lives are nevertheless related. The awareness of what they are told, or what is presented on the news, is linked vividly with their imaginative experience

> Well, there's the fear of AIDS, which isn't all that big at the moment. There's the drugs, which is bad, and I'm never going to take any. I never want to. Sometimes I've had an idea that people might smuggle drugs. They could smuggle drugs in packets of glucose because glucose looks like cocaine. I was a bit put off by that.   *(boy 10)*

The personal reflections are sophisticated links between reactions to the reporting of news and awareness of the implications - 'I was put off by that' 'which isn't all that big at the moment' - and the actual detailing of events that make them real. There is, beneath the distancing of generalisations, a continuing personal reflection on the issues, which includes the awareness of the malleability of what is reported, which subject is fashionable - "big at the moment" - as well as the ability to enter into the experience of the protagonist or those close by or become part of the complex mental construction process of the child's world view.

How, then, do children cope with this realisation of an imperfect world? In one sense it is not unlike adults in that they get on with their daily lives and ignore it. But there is a limit to ignorance. The world in which they are growing up is not just a world full of distant violence or potential violence. It is one which impinges on their daily consciousness. One of the themes most often mentioned in their descriptions of the world, to underscore why it could be better than it is, is the possibility of sexual violence.

> Now girls cannot go out in case there is a man waiting for them. There's so
> many people getting raped.   *(girl 11)*

> The world could be a better place if there wasn't so much sexual violence.
>   *(boy 11)*

The facts are that violence is not just an abstract or distance concept but an
extreme and palpable form of what they witness themselves.[14] There is a
link between the petty teasing and the more ruthless bullying, and between
the physical violence that they see in the playground and the threat of the
larger world. There is never any sense of a world of perfection as depicted
occasionally in the nostalgia of autobiography when perfect moments are
woven into a seamless whole. After all the imperfections of the world are
obvious and everyday and do not need to be made manifest on the news.
The world could be a better place even in terms of what is not the
responsibility of mankind. The weather causes floods or droughts. In a
perfect world would there be so much uncertainty, or even chaos?

> The climate goes up and down. One day hot, one day cold. You never know
> what day it's gonna be tomorrow.   *(boy 8)*

The notion of a world of innocent perfection in which the sun constantly
shines in the imagination of the child is impossible.

No-one is deceived into thinking that the world is perfect. There are
close links, as we will see, between the large events that come to symbolise
human depravity and the everyday, domestic suffering to which we are all
witnesses. Whilst young children learn the art of distancing the great
events, of making them into a routine background - the news is not their
favourite programme - they are also deeply affected by them. They help to
form their sense of human nature, and their understanding of themselves.
The personal desperations are linked to those of others. And signs of the
imperfect nature of man, from falsehood to fighting is a diurnal occurrence.
The possibilities of being deceived, or let down, or of sudden change are
what link the external fears to the everyday. What makes children most
insecure is the sense of the unknown and the helplessness that goes with
it.[15] This insecurity is not just one that affects young children but remains
with them throughout the years of school, links to their perception of the
world at large and is continued in the uncertainties of adult life. They can

never be certain about what might happen. This is one of the reasons that the cry 'it's not fair' is so widespread and so significant. The cheap reply is 'life's not fair'. Children know that, but the knowledge does not displace the personal sense of anguish and of helplessness. It might be so but it ought not to be.

The desire for fairness, however, is not just a reaction to the unexpected, the realisation that terrible events like war or rape could happen, but a sign of the need for some kind of authority. Children are keen on rules and seek to have a form of discipline imposed on them.[16] This is not because they are defined in the Piagetian sense as moral primitives, having external rules as a prelude towards personal understanding, but because they see rules as a collective acceptance of authority necessary because of the flawed nature of human beings. When authority is placed in the hands of the teacher this is a result of a combined will that there should be a structure to social interactions. The arguments over friendship and over the group to which they belong or from which they are excluded are all very well in the everyday definitions of relationship but they belong within a larger structural sense of a society. Children are good at rules, and can invent rules for games. They realise that for any transaction between people there need to be agreements to which both parties adhere. Rules are therefore important.

But rules are also important because of the nature of people; they are not only the necessary agreement over games, but the fear that without rules there would be trouble. The experience and observation of young children leads them to the view that human beings are generally, and in some cases extremely, prone to do bad. This is not to say that they are seen as evil by nature, nor does it suggest that there is anything uncomplicated in the generalisation. After all most people will make a judgement about other people's behaviour without including themselves. To accept the fact that people can be bad is to acknowledge a distinction between good and evil: to discriminate is to suggest the possibility of something different. Children put forward consistently the fact of bad behaviour, including their own. They see it at school and through the media. What concerns them is the fact that this is so, not the theological explanation. That at least some people are bad is clear. That there is a propensity towards their being so is also apparent.

What is interesting about children's views of human nature is their explanations about it. They do not merely label but have their own psychological reasons for the propensity to harm others. Their theories are usually a mixture of the genetic and the environmental. Given the conditions in which people live it is not surprising to children if people break rules and damage others. At the same time it is clear that there is a kind of malicious pleasure in doing harm, that it seems to be a deep-seated attribute in some to be unkind, to molest or hurt, as if there were an almost natural habit. The psychological explanations are as many and as varied as any adult attempts to understand the human psyche and how it is formed. When one tries to sum up the children's views about *why* people are as they are, particularly why they are as bad as they are there are several propositions that symbolise the collective thought of all.

The first explanation for bad behaviour is to do with their upbringing. 'Because they are spoiled when they are young' *(girl 8)*. Both at the time and on reflection afterwards there is a consistent judgement, presumably arising from their own experience that laissez-faire attitudes by parents, whilst seemingly attractive at the time, are corrupting.[17] The assumption is that young children need discipline. The sense that there is a need for formal control, to overcome a natural tendency to be naughty, is very strong. What is so interesting about this theoretical position is that it matches their sense of the propensity to be bad - assumed to be universally shared - with the belief that it could be controlled. The responsibility therefore lies with parents and with society. Young criminals, looking back on the experience of their early years all regret the lack of discipline. Whilst this is clearly not the only factor that was missing in their lives, the sense of the lack of outside control is very strong. To be able to do whatever they wanted seemed to be attractive at the time, and they acknowledge that fact. But they consistently regret the lack of firm control because it subsequently appeared to them not as brute discipline, nor as attempts to please and placate, but as a lack of personal attention. 'Go away and do what you want' is not a sign of appreciation or of kindness but indifference.[18]

Of all things that children most fear it is the lack of concern, the lack of interest by others. The matter that most affects them is the lack of a healthy dialogue. They struggle to make sense of the world, and mostly talk to their peers in doing so. But they long for that interest by them in parents and other adults that shows itself in energy and attention to detail. This is symbolised for children by control and by rules. The real problem lies partly in human nature and partly in its treatment. The proposition is quite clear:

> Sometimes it's not their fault. It's their parent's fault or friends who try to lead them on.
> *(boy 10)*

There are psychological explanations for bad behaviour. The influence of others is perceived as being very strong. When children describe their relationships in the school, and their own attitudes towards bullying they recognise their own susceptibility to influence and their own weakness. They know that most behaviours might appear natural but are unnecessary. There are times when the nature of the environment seems paramount:

> They can't help having something wrong with themselves. They live in an unpleasant house.
> *(boy 10)*

Being as sensitive as they are to the circumstances in which they find themselves children very quickly learn how fragile they are in the face of influence. This does not mean that they think of themselves as by-products of the environment. But they acknowledge how they are influenced by it, and see it as an explanation for at least part of what goes wrong. They pick out the social psychological mechanisms for it. This is not the only explanation they give. They also see themselves and their peers as having a strong need to be kept in control, weak and easily influenced as they are. After all, the other explanation for bad behaviour is the pleasure it can give, and they see, and try to explain, the way in which some of their friends do harm, and the reasons that lie behind the stories of depravity on the news. There is also a circumstantial explanation for behaviour; - a natural propensity to be bad.

> If people do not get punished they keep doing bad things.
> *(girl 10)*

Children make it clear that upbringing is important, whatever the temperament of the individual. They might be amateur theorists about the psychology of learning but they are not unsophisticated. Being closer to the experience they keep a just balance in their minds between personality and circumstances. They do not show any naive optimism about people's natural good nature. On the contrary, they witness the importance of events that shape other people's lives and the contrast between the temptation of helplessness and the need for firm order and control. Their belief in rules is not, as Piaget and Kohlberg suggested, an absence of moral integrity or subtlety but an acknowledgement that people react according to circumstances and that a constant experience of the laissez faire leads to anti-social behaviour, since it is contrary to the normal experience of being in society. Children have a fairly bleak view of human nature. They see too much depravity in the large-scale and too much meanness in their immediate experience not to assume that strict controls are necessary. This generally accepted fact about the need for controls and punishments is based on the belief that it both helps the individual to learn what matters, and prevents outbreaks of what they might otherwise get away with

> because they are not punished a lot when they are really bad.   *(girl 8)*

Crime and punishment; a balance between natural tendencies and necessary controls. What makes children's views of the psychology of behaviour interesting, is their judicious mixture of the recognition of human nature, and the influence of circumstances. Their advocacy of rules and punishment might seem to suggest a conservative belief in the natural tendency to evil that needs curbing. But their own experience also suggests that they themselves and their friends could learn differently. The shock at what is bad derives from the fact that it is not inevitable or necessary, just natural, given the opportunity and the indifference of society. The melancholy pleasure in doing harm is recognised as a temptation that some people cannot resist.

> They just want to cause trouble and be spiteful.

But it is inevitably balanced by a psychological reason

> Some children have been through a rough patch themselves, so they take it out on other children. It makes them go through a rough patch just because they've gone through a rough time at home.   *(girl 8)*

Bad behaviour is not condoned, but there is an attempt to explain it. They recognise the censor links and generalise about the epistemology of crime.

Attempts to analyse and explain behaviour reveal how closely children monitor their experience and observe that of others. It is not enough for them just to describe. In Kohlberg's outline of the stages of moral development - which suggest that children are essentially thoughtless and amoral until the age of ten - all the emphasis is on description. There is no attempt to explain why people behave in certain ways, no reasoning about the causes of delinquency. These children, on the contrary, are engaged every day in trying to understand *why* people behave as they do, why there is unfairness, why friendships are broken and why there is teasing and bullying. They are not blind to all forms of behaviour.

Nor are children unaware of their own faults. Far from blaming all bad behaviour on other people, as if they themselves were uniquely innocent, they recognise and accept that they too can be at fault. In this, perhaps, they are more honest than adults. There is always the temptation of the pharisees, to think of oneself as perfect as is possible, whilst other people's faults are glaring. But whilst young children have a disconcerting view of how they see people behaving in society, they also recognise this as an immediacy. The generalised image of the world as a whole, with particular cases of outstanding brutality is related to the nearer and just as real world of fighting and bullying, teasing and lying. And the children see themselves as part of this world, not distant from it. A lot is made, in surveys of bullying, about the percentages of pupils who are either victims or bullies, but in a way this is meaningless, since all children play some part in this.[19] Whilst there is no doubting the distinction to be made between the extremes of behaviour, there is not a child who does not recognise that he or she has also behaved unkindly to other people. Nor is there a child who, in making moral reflections on the world, has not experienced personally the crafts of lying and disobedience.

The recognition of their own imperfections and bad behaviour is consistent, but as in their judgements of other people's behaviour, they are aware of the complex psychology that surrounds it. There are always explanations for the way people behave - the way they were brought up, problems at home and temperament. When they examine their own behaviours they are aware of two strong underlying emotions - moodiness, or 'grumpiness' as they often term it - and reaction to provocation. They sense the unpredictability of moods, of sudden incursions into their inner worlds by chaotic, sudden or extreme feelings. When they are in a bad mood they realise that they can cause the argument that leads to a fight or initiate a bout of disobedience. When others are in a 'mood' they start to tease or provoke, and then the temptation is to react rather than ignore or control. When parents or teachers give an order or make a suggestion there is always the temptation to disobey or ignore it.

Children are fully aware of the complexities of moral behaviour, the small distinctions to be drawn between inadvertent hurt and deliberate unkindness, between different levels of lying, and the difference between knockabout fun and fighting, ritual and aggression. It is perhaps because all forms of interaction are so physically vivid - whether fighting or the refusal to talk to someone - that children are so much more aware of moral ambiguity and the distinctions between guilt and fear, as well as the difference between ritualised and shared aggression, as in a crowd of hooligans and individualised violence. They also have a hierarchy of faults in which lying is more significant than fighting. Children do not see themselves as being 'good', although they quickly recognise that it is important to try to be so. They possess an almost fascinated interest in the distinction between guilt and shame. They quickly learn that there is a moral world: there are no signs that they do not realise from within the battles between doing good and doing evil. For they are clearly and explicitly caught up in the *emotions* of guilt and unhappiness. They know the advantages of lying, but are absolutely clear about its immorality, even whilst they blatantly continue to lie. Such ambiguities are at the heart of social understanding.

There are many ways of being bad - 'playing about in class', 'bad temper', 'don't obey'; but whatever the instance, they all share the recognition of their own limitations.

No, I'm not always good. I don't think one can be good all the time.   *(boy 11)*

This is widely shared. The provocations and the temptations are too great. They know themselves to have flaws. This is a far cry from the idea of innocence. By the time they realise their own weakness they will have experienced many forms of subtle disobedience with their parents. And they know that they will always see the possibilities of doing bad things whether they eschew them or not: 'Because I sometimes get temptated' *(girl 10)*. When someone catalogues faults, it is not out of a sense of bravado, but simple recognition of the fact.

I'm naughty. I lie. 'Cos I punch. And I beat up my mates. Like David. We usually have fights. I lie so I don't get into trouble. So the other person gets into trouble.   *(boy 8)*

Fighting and lying, the two hang together. One overlaps the boundaries of play and relationships. The other is the manipulation of the personal response to the world of social rules and intentions. Often the reasons for bad behaviour are given as temperament.

I wish I could have more patience and not argue so much.   *(girl 9)*

The consequences of temperament include an acceptance of acknowledged personal fault. Anger, bad temper and impatience are all recognised as emotional leads to behaviour problems; they are never neutral.

Sometimes I throw things even if people are there, like last night I threw the chair really badly and I nearly hit the TV and I dared to throw it through the window or something. 'Cos I get really angry sometimes ... some people don't really like me or be nice to me or anything.   *(boy 8)*

To admit anger is not to excuse or condone bad behaviour; it reinforces the way that individuals are not neutral: they do not formulate a moral code which is such a clear set of rules that there are no ambiguities. Good or bad behaviour is developed in relation to other people; it is not an abstract concept. Other people are either those from whom children would want to have authority thrust upon them, parents and teachers and adults generally, or those with whom they are in more ambivalent interactions, their siblings and peers.

There are different levels of bad behaviour. Some children suggest that they themselves, whilst naughty, are not as bad, or as extreme as others; naughtiness is shared by all, but to different degrees.

Naughty, yeah, when I start fighting with people like Stuart or John ... yeah, friends. 'Cos sometimes like I do something and they come over and start. I've started in a few ... But I don't swear or spit or bully ... swear at teachers or kick 'em ... you can get done for kicking or spitting at 'em ... since I hit him over the back with a hammer, and he had a bruise down there ... I just went to bed and watched a video. I felt mad and everything.

'Cos if there wasn't [rules] there'd be fighting every day.   *(boy 9)*

He suggests that he does not break the basic school rules - does not swear or spit or bully. He also confesses to bullying despite the assertion. It is as if there were both different degrees of bad behaviour - swearing is worse than fighting - and personal motivations which make one's own behaviour more understandable than that of others, where the temperamental background would not be as significant as the explicit physical effect. But there is also recognition of the tendency to fight. He does not suggest simple innocence, as if he merely responds to provocation.

One of the most significant distinctions to be made is between provocation and response - 'she started it'. They all feel caught up in a series of relationships in which they both observe the varying behaviour of others and are caught up in them. They observe such a volatility of behaviour that there is a sense that there could be outbreaks of violence at any time and that it is important not to be the one to start it - to exhibit self-constraint. They observe other people:

> They're OK but I don't like them so much. 'Cos they always chase me and everything. So I chase them back and go and play with my friends again ... Sometimes they be horrible to me. Sometimes they don't be that nice to me. Just hit me and start chasing me.   *(girl 7)*

It is the sense of unreasonable attacks, something that seems to be unexplained as well as unexpected, that is the most difficult to understand. Friendships and enmities are all part of the tempestuous world of childhood - in which people fight back, or tease. But the concern is not so much with the behaviour as with the motivation; who started it and why.

> Them two just had a fight. Because one of them thought that ... one of them thought that someone else, the other one stuck her tongue at her. And I'm not sure what happened - who did it or not because they're in a different class.
>   *(ibid.)*

In the experience of difficult relationships the rules of conduct are the more important because they are necessary. Children recognise that there is a constant temptation to be 'stupid'. Even those who deem themselves to be comparatively gentle and kind, and who attempt to keep away from trouble know there are moments when they themselves behave badly. The same girl:

Sometimes I jump on her as well ... and then sometimes on purpose I go on her bed and say that I accidentally rolled off ... Both of them slap me a lot and hit me a lot ... just get told off and just get mad and go to their bedroom ... they just go and they just feel mad and cross and just watch TV ...

And when I be bad to my mum ... Might do it by accident, but I won't do it on purpose.   *(ibid.)*

Children sort out all the different strands and compartments of experience into a chaotically causal order, reflecting far more closely the actuality of experience than some easily assembled 'agenda'.

There is such a thin line between the 'accident', the irresistible little push or teasing, and the deliberate 'starting' of a fight. This girl shows the inner contradiction of what is deemed to be an 'an accident' of going on her sister's bed - in other words a falsehood. But she likes to think of herself as less naughty than her brother and sister because she sees the consequences of their actions. These lie not as significantly in the punishments they receive - being 'grounded' or sent to their rooms - as in the emotional effects of rage and guilt. It is the strain, the anger of bad behaviour, and the humiliation which is so visible:

And they don't feel very well, and I wouldn't like to do ... not feel very well, get told off badly and everything like that ... I wouldn't like that ... And the other people feel really sorry afterwards and they have to say sorry and everything.   *(ibid.)*

There is a close connection between unhappiness and bad behaviour. This is considered to be 'normal'; part of the human condition. It means that the children accept themselves for what they are - driven by moods and emotions but recognising the value of good behaviour. This is not so much a question of avoiding punishment as avoiding guilt. What they do not condone are those who seem to do harm for no particular reason but who seem to derive pleasure from doing so. The 'normal' child might be disobedient, tell lies and quarrel, but he or she will also feel bad about it. There are many subtle distinctions to be made between the different levels of 'badness'.

Some people like whipping me with a branch and stuff like that. And that makes them bad because they're doing something that they wouldn't like to other people. And if they wouldn't like it, the other person wouldn't like it ...

Some people are really, really bad, some people are only a little bit bad. People who are really bad might be good or bad for the rest of their life, or bad people might grow badder or gooder ... Sometimes they do and they don't do it again and sometimes they don't know they're bad and they start carrying on to be bad ... And when they're bad, they're not so nice, and if they're bad they don't know what they're doing to other people. And when they hit one another they be taught a lesson and stop doing it. Sometimes they stay bad, sometimes they go good ... And when they're bad, they get sent off and when they're sent off, sometimes they just don't care if they get sent off and when they're allowed to go they just start doing it again. And sometimes if they start doing it they keep on getting sent off and sometimes ... they still don't care. Some people care afterwards and sometimes people don't tell of each other and they just do it, and the other person starts carrying on, but then they do it and you don't tell of them, and stuff like that.   *(girl 7)*

All the dilemmas and principles of morality are encapsulated here. There are no moral questions left unexplained or ignored. Underlying axioms like 'Do as you would be done by', elaborated at length by Bentham and Mill and others, are the recognitions of the force of social order, the least possible underlying principle of the moral - a sense of equity.[20] Even here there is an distinction between guilt and fear. The people who are 'doing it', 'wouldn't like it themselves'. There are crucial differences between shared guilt, and degrees of wickedness. There is an acknowledgement that people are not branded with one particular attitude, but that they can change - for better or worse. Some might learn from their mistakes. Others might grow more deeply accustomed to their habits. There are some whose social outlook, like that of a terrorist, do not recognise their actions as bad or immoral. There are others who because of their circumstances or the environment in which they have been brought up do not recognise themselves as bad. Criminologists have long pointed out crime as a social description according to the particular moralities of the powers of the time. The whole question of crime and punishment is addressed, with the question of its efficacy and its failure, and the tension between punishment as reform and punishment as a way of removing the irredeemable from society. The influence of the peer group is also taken into account.

In all this the most important moral strain is probably that of guilt. Some people might survive by not feeling anything; they do not 'care'. The children also explore morality not just in terms of actions and outcomes, avoiding pain or punishment but in the feelings that are invoked. They realise there is a personal responsibility in morality as well as a social consequence. They know that when they do something wrong they have a conscience about it. This might make life more painful but it also makes them human. Those who no longer feel any trauma, whose sense of personal pain, and personal morality has been lost, those are the really 'bad'. For the real sanction against wrong-doing is not punishment but guilt.

For children the moral world, or choices between obedience and disobedience, lying and confession, kindness and cruelty, is one charged with emotions. They have not learned the neutrality of complacency and self-justification. In these volatile circumstances it is relationships that are the grounds on which the choices are made.[21] Up to a point all relationships are found to be difficult: how does anyone balance his or her own desires with the needs of other people? Always to be selfish is clearly wrong, but to be utterly self-effacing is also unhealthy. How does anyone balance firm rules, strictly laid down, with the liberties of action and expression? Every relationship tests the central moral ground and the tensions between rules and meanings, between seeking a common standard of shared behaviour, and finding a personal place within it.

> If they do something you just go 'I'm not your friend anymore' and then sometimes you go later on or a couple of days you just be friends again ... My friend Sahib got hurt by H 'cos he was getting angry. They wasn't friends. First, one got pushed over and then they started fighting ... They used to be friends, then they fell out, then they was friends, then they fell out ... it's sad. He tries to tell the teacher but M won't and he gets done ... First I liked him and then he slapped me on the cheek, so I was never his friend again. He just slapped me ... Told the teacher and he started crying. And then I got done because he said that he didn't do it, and then I got done.   *(boy 6)*

One might look on this and think, with exasperation, of the constant troubles and petty annoyances: but for the children involved these are traumatic incidents. Not being friends is to be hurt as much as being slapped. And they do not know quite what to do about it. They realise there are rules but wish to place the authority of imposing them on the teachers. That leads to the shock that society at large can be unfair, make wrong judgements, remain indifferent. Where should they turn after that?

The only place to find succour is in their own understanding. Children are constantly trying to make sense of the way in which personal temperament and temptation needs to be controlled. The battle with themselves and with other people is always there, at least in the background. These quarrels and arguments are not only painful in themselves but are a way of trying to understand social behaviour. Their understanding of society at large derives from these emotionally involved experiments in behaviour. All the time they are trying to find out the boundaries of what is acceptable and what isn't, the emotions they feel and the constraints they should put on them.

> I have to do the washing up, but sometimes I don't, and I'm not allowed to ... I don't know what I'm not allowed to do. I'm not allowed to play with T's things without asking ... Only in the mornings and the night I'm getting really grumpy ... I'm shouting and I get mad and just sit in my bedroom and watch TV and then never come back down again. When somebody's upset them on purpose you could tell them 'it's OK you're nice and you're not how that person said you were - horrible'. Because they don't like them and they're just being a bit grumpy.   *(girl 8)*

This girl knows what denotes good behaviour. She knows not just rules and etiquette but rules of genuine kindness. But she also witnesses people being nasty to each other and recognises that this also includes her. She is just as capable of changing friends, or hitting her brother, as anyone else. Underlying the behaviour are the moods; those which lead up to inappropriate behaviour and those which stem from them. One cannot exclude the facts of emotional trauma from the daily life of children. That they are linked to their moral judgements is clear.

School is, of course, a significant part of social life and a place where the relationship between private friendship and public behaviour is most constantly tested.[22] Children find themselves in the middle of complex social interactions, about which they have to make judgements. They need to recognise the emotional forces that create the tensions; and they have to draw their own psychological conclusions from them. They explain why people are behaving badly:

> She's been through a rough patch. Nearly everyone keeps on saying that she's, mmm, that she looks like the colour of pooh, just because she's black ... she gets a bit frustrated and angry and takes it out on everyone. And, um, she

thinks that they actually try to say to her that they don't like her because she's black. But that isn't always true ... I feel a bit sorry for her, 'cos sometimes when I say I like her, she doesn't believe me. Like, well, when everyone is being horrible to her, she says 'No one likes me, I haven't got any friends'. And I say 'I like you, Nabila, you're my friend'. 'I know sometimes we fall out with each other but I'm still your friend'. And then she just walks off in a huff and says 'You're just pretending. I know you don't like me because I'm black' ... maybe she feels that no one likes her at all ... they just want to cause trouble and be spiteful. Some children have been through a rough patch themselves, so they take it out on other children. It makes them go through a rough patch just because they've gone through a rough time at home.   *(girl 8)*

Here we have the attempts to reason out why people behave as they do, in the distinction between 'spitefulness' and 'a rough time at home'. Personal friendship has a larger social dimension, with issues of causes for behaviour and being called a liar, but perhaps for a reason, linked with frustration and anger. It is as if the psychology of bad behaviour were being explored, as well as *the* emotional range of suffering. The distinctions between the permanent: acts of kindness, acting like a friend, feeling sorry for someone, trying to help - and the temporary: arguments, quarrels and 'falling out' are constantly having to be made. Personal morality is squeezed out of experience rather than rules.

Rules are, however, considered a necessary part of experience. This would not be the case, quite logically, if they could not be broken. They are in place to keep order in a turbulent world. But they are also symbols of agreed morality. They have no meaning unless people believe in them. What rules are supposed to present are agreed certainties; those behaviours that are based on moral as well as on social judgements. Children are from an early age aware of rules being broken, of imperfections and difficulties. There is at no detectable stage symptoms of moral optimism in the sense that all is good, stable and certain. This is shown in the understanding of falsehood and deception. Children can never quite trust all that they see. To the side of every gesture is the shadow that it might be deceptive. This recognition of falsehood is matched by the ability to use deception, just as children's understanding of bad behaviour is a personal, not just a judgemental one. Even two-and-a-half year olds were found to be capable of employing a range of deceptive strategies.[23] The researchers were looking for a theory of mind, but what we can see is the early awareness of the ambiguity and the uncertainty of the world. This uncertainty is part of the intellectual and emotional precocity of children.

The sense of fairness and unfairness is strong because the possibilities of suffering are always apparent. One of the earliest surprises for young children is detecting other people's falsehoods, of witnessing lying. One of the earliest shocks is not being believed. The sense of pain, of deep insecurity when the rules of fairness are flouted or ignored can last for ever.[24] Deliberate falsehood, or inadvertent deception is part of the fabric of the world and is painful. The awareness of lies and deception is not, therefore, just theoretical but emotional.[25] It is also sophisticated. Lying is something all children understand. It can seem small - like pretending to have washed hands before a meal. Or it could be, as it has been to all children at one stage or another, a major false accusation by someone else of having done something when innocent, and taking the blame unfairly.

> She draws pictures on the rubbers and she goes 'this one's my rubber 'cos I drew a picture on it this morning', and I saw her just adding felt tip colours onto it. So that's what happened this week - she pinched one of my rubbers ... All upset and I went to the Headteacher's and she said 'if she does it again just tell me', so I do ... 'cos she's scared of the teacher telling her off and she'll just lie to her and say that she didn't do it - it's just me playing tricks on her. And she goes 'this is my rubber - I dropped it under my seat, although my rubber rolled over there under your seat'. Sometimes they might have done something bad to somebody that they know they shouldn't do and not admitted that they'd done it.   *(girl 8)*

The experience of the laws of society - innocent until proved guilty and a belief in the right of the individual to lie in order to escape punishment - is mirrored in the early lives of children. It pays to lie, to cover up what has happened. Often children get away with it. But false accusation, the passing of blame, throws lying into a new dimension. The recognition of the individual's point of view turns into exasperation when there is a major conflict or disagreement over a fact. Lying about behaviour is considered as heinous as the behaviour itself. But then lying is a complex and sophisticated trait. It encompasses genuine self-deception and moments when 'white' lying can even be good.

> Yeah, on birthdays. You might lie like 'keep out of the kitchen - mum's burned the frying pan and it smells' and then you just tell them and lie to them

and he goes 'oh, right'. And then you get all the party things put up and then 'you can come in the kitchen now, it's all gone away'. And there were nothing there really. *(ibid.)*

To this girl lying can be justified. It is also useful.

When I've done something to my friends, I just feel as though I'm gonna get into trouble so ... In the end somebody finds out, but they forgive me for not telling the truth.

The complexities of truth and falsehood are one of the profound uncertainties of any society. No one is immune. These uncertainties affect young children. At a time when people might imagine that everything was immutable and inevitable, doubts and difficulties already play their part. This covering over the awkwardness of the early years, this treating of childhood as a time of bliss is another symptom of the shared human condition, of seeking in nostalgia what cannot quite be found in the present. Part of the restructuring of the past as a coping mechanism is the sense that there was once a time when matters were simple. The sentimentalising of the picture of childhood - naiveté, innocence, self-centredness and optimism - depends on the nostalgia for an idea of freedom without responsibility and the notion of absolute security. The rationalisation of this nostalgia has been to conceptualise childhood as a period of unbounded optimism, full of hope and belief in the future. Research in autobiographies and in recollections suggests that this is not the actual case.[26] There are many partial accounts and there are many fantasies to be recalled. But these are fantasies in the face of difficulties. They recount the ways in which young children have come to terms with their condition. The honest autobiographies recount the good as well as the bad, but they point out that those good moments seem like relief from the often more common traumas, difficulties and uncomfortable longueurs of early life - like a summer holiday that is subsequently portrayed as boundless in time when it was a small, if important, part, of the year. The good moments and the bad are both deeply engraved in the mind. What is less well recalled are the daily conditions, the everyday stresses as well as the moments of pleasure. It is the detail that is missing. The great events will always be remembered, but what were the small ones like? It is the small events that influence the constructive power of children's minds.

It is the uncertainties of childhood that are so easily forgotten. When people are asked to remember in detail their own childhoods (which they are able to do with a clarity which can seem surprising when one recollects that no-one in normal circumstances has asked them about it) - the more troubled aspects come to the fore.[27] The sense of uncertainty and the difficult emotions, the lack of control and an abiding helplessness rise to the surface of the memory. The sense of change - so rapid in childhood - links to a sense of the uncertain. Nothing is static. This means that none of the children believe they are in the best possible place at the best possible time. The sense of relativity and arbitrariness is strong, 'for the world is only what people make it and anywhere else creatures would be the same' (girl 11). Indeed the nostalgia that appears so strong in adults also affects young children. Worrying as they do about the future and conscious of the implications of death, old age is not thought of with any sense of the positive, and they are more likely to think that their best times are already behind them.[28]

> I'd like to be changed back into a baby again, because whenever I go to my friend's house, which has a little toddler or child that's one or two or three years old or something, I love the toys that they play with because I always like playing with the musical tops.   *(girl 8)*

> I am not always happy any longer. I was happy when I was younger.   *(boy 10)*

The feeling that things were better in the past is, of course, a mental construct. It is a sense of escape, a sense of wish fulfilment. Children, like adults, have to accept the age they are. On the whole they are realistic enough to take it for granted, knowing that playing with toys, however nostalgic it makes them feel, is an escape, a daydream. There are moments when they would like the power of older people, or be in different circumstances. They certainly admire the subtle differences that make heroes of those who are just a few years older - but not beyond a few years. But this is all a matter of understanding the difficulties of being themselves. It appears to them as if that were that only escape, others of a different age do not share their own traumas. Older children than themselves seem more polite and controlled and calm. They never quarrel or fight or have difficulties ... Younger ones seem free of any burden of relationship. Or so it seems. Any other time, past or future, seems preferable to their own. Children have to accept the conditions which includes their age and ageing. None of them describe themselves as in a state of bliss. Self-awareness would hardly allow it.

The uncertainties of life lie largely in relationships. There are many facts which seem immutable. Physical realities whilst always in a state of organic or temporal change seem comparatively reliable. It is the individual and other individuals who need to cope with change, within themselves and between each other. The most potent effect of the uncertainty lies (and ends) in the sense of loneliness. Of all the long-lasting and final senses of emotional deprivation, loneliness, the sense of loss and of personal meaninglessness, is the strongest. It affects young children too. Naturally they understand it as a concept, and they both experience it and perceive it.[29] Those who are most aware of it in themselves are also those who have learned about it in the hardest way; by the experiences that lead to differences in behaviour. The difficulty is that the person who seems to be alien, who appears to be different, is the one more likely to be ignored or ostracised. The experiences that lead to feelings that cause people to react and give added re-enforcement to other experiences seem like a never ending cycle. Once locked in to it, it is hard to be released. Being found lonely is to be found miserable and leads to being shunned.

The sense of loneliness has a number of levels. It can be a feeling of deprivation, of isolation, of having no-one to talk to. It can also be a feeling of not being liked, of having enough people around but no-one to relate to. In the one extreme there is absolutely no-one physically near; in the other the more people that there are the more emphatic the feeling of isolation. Both lead to emotional traumas, either those which can be overcome and those which will inhibit permanently the ability to make normal relationships with others. The emotional movement of young children from crying with an urgency for contact to a sense of passivity and dejection is one often repeated.[30]

If there is no response to needs desperation is replaced by despair and even positive responses are then rejected. The feeling that no one cares is succeeded by the feeling that it is not worth anyone caring. Thus the loneliness feeds on itself and makes the individual almost expect rejection. Loneliness can be having no-one around.

> I like to play lots of games and I don't like it when my friends are off and ill, so I don't have anyone to play with. *(boy 8)*

But this is a state which seems circumstantial and can easily be rectified even if it is heartfelt. More significant is the sense of loneliness which derives from social isolation.

> If I ever had to leave this school, 'cos I might have to go to -... My mum says I don't really have to move but I might do. It makes me sad but I have been to hospital once. That made me a bit sad and nervous 'cos I've never been before.
> *(boy 7)*

> Other things that make me quite sad are when people leave me out of games and they don't really play with me much.
> *(girl 8)*

The sense of exclusion, of being 'left out', can have minor or major consequences. It is something understood by all and needs to be taken seriously. It is commonplace to take exclusion and truancy, like bullying, as comparatively rare events, the extreme end of social problems. But the sense of isolation and loneliness, within a family, and outside, affects all children; not just a majority. What becomes in the end a physical manifestation, excluding themselves, staying away, making alternatives, starts as a feeling that all share. The desire to be liked, to be appreciated, to be able to join in, is not automatically responded to, or met. This makes children the more self-conscious. They are aware of others and their point of view. They are also intensely (and un-egotistically) aware of themselves.

One of the most basic examples of their self-scrutiny and their discontent with what they see is their feelings about their own looks. There is an ontological insecurity about their physical appearance. They have to put up with what they are, but this does not mean that they take it for granted. Looks might seem ephemeral but they are a signal for 'difference'. We are not here talking about fashion, about being shaped like a model and responding to the constant advertising of the superficial, nor of the adolescent *sine qua non* of attraction. This sense of discontent with physical defects or imperfections is a result of what they happen to look like in a more general way, a sense of puzzlement that they are who they are, and other people react to that. When students were asked to remember their childhoods they could recall distinctly their concerns with their lack of control over physical circumstances: what they looked like, what they were forced to do and the places they lived.[31]

There are two forms of self-consciousness. Both are to do with being not part of a 'norm'. Long before there is any pressure to stand out - through talent or beauty - there is a pressure *not* to be different. One is the looks that might draw attention from others - a physical fact like being tall or wearing glasses. The other is the way they speak or their names, more ordinary mannerisms. Whilst both overlap, one is more immediate, a type of marker. It can be a simple matter of the hair, not a style chosen by the individual but the way it happens to be.

> It feels, it seems funny 'cos you know my mum has straight hair and I keep on asking her why can't I, why haven't I got straight hair? Well my dad's you know has those fuzzy hairs like ... and I've got really fuzzy ones and it sticks up and I hate having my hair washed. I want it to be straight, but my mum says I look lovely like this. My mummy says 'I have to pay sixty pounds to get it like you and it just falls out in the morning.'   *(girl 7)*

Long before the pressure of fashion is born they worry about difference. Whatever the encouragement and cajolings of the mother - the details are clearly recorded - the fact is that the curly hair, inherited from her father, is 'different'. It is a point of comparison and comparisons, different relationships and differences are all part of the emotional turmoil:

> One thing I wanna change is my hair. Because it always gets knotted. I'd rather like it curly. I'd rather like it like my friend Laura's, because it never gets knotty.   *(girl 8)*

The self-consciousness of children and their comparability makes them begin to detect their world in terms of differences. They would prefer not necessarily to be themselves even whilst trapped by their own personalities. If only they say they could swap one attribute for another - always an impossible dream and recognised as such - 'I wish I didn't have freckles' *(boy 8)*. Of course there are some discontents that could easily be put right - 'My hair. It's a bit too long. It looks better when it's shorter' *(boy 8)* - but these are symptoms not of the designer idea of looks but a slight discontent, something they wish were different. Some are worried about their teeth, having to wear braces, or about having to wear glasses - 'Well you haven't really got your natural self'. These might so easily be dismissed by adults as mere slights, ephemera on the world stage of personality. Or they might turn to means of putting things right, chemically or physically, or emotionally by putting up with it. Adults do not recognise the strain of personal relationships and self-consciousness in children.

The discontent that children express about their looks is but a symptom of something deeper: it encapsulates in a physical way how they see their own lives in relation to the rest of the world. Nothing is perfect and they are aware of it. They see their limitations. In the place of that unaware ambitions of self-centredness some people like to reconstruct as their own childhoods, what we see in recognition of the fact and a critical scrutiny of it. Underneath the given of their eyes and ears and teeth and hair are the facts, the inheritances of their own personalities. If only they were blessed with different abilities: or much more significantly with a different temperament. Temperament, the ability to be happy or content, is put in terms of personality.

I wish I could have more patience and not argue so much.   *(girl 9)*

I would like to have the personality to make people laugh.   *(boy 7)*

I would like to have a personality that makes a likeable person.   *(girl 7)*

I would like to be the sort of person with lots of friends.   *(boy 10)*

If only they were different, they dream, whilst knowing perfectly well that they are as they are. They see others shining with humour and happiness as if the world were easy for them whilst inwardly they know of all their discontents and unhappiness. This they see as the plague of their 'personality' rather than the circumstances in which they find themselves.

Some form of discontent is shared by all children. The way it manifests itself varies, since there is so much to choose from. They could be having difficulties in their relationships, or in their work at school. There are bound to be times when all of them, and not just the few, are victims of bullying or being 'picked on'.[32] But the discontent goes deeper than that. It is true that there are many complaints about circumstances; where they live or lack of money. But these are a symptom of the realisation that things could be different. The sense of the arbitrary that surrounds their consciousness, that they happen to be where they are and happen to be who they are is very strong. It is this ontological insecurity that pervades their sense that things could be different, and by implication, better. All children fantasise, even if they fantasise in different ways.[33] Some might wish for better possessions. Some might wish to become rich or famous when they are older but most wishes go deeper than that. They long for different circumstances, for changes in the home environment, for more power over their own lives. They do not fantasise simply to have money or a glamorous career. They wish that some of the real problems they face could be different.

Clearly the more difficult the home circumstances the more acutely will this discontent be felt. But it is an insecurity shared by all children, not only those whom one would expect to exhibit a sense of disorder or disjunction. All children share an awareness of the darker aspects of life, and know about homelessness and poverty even if they do not experience it. All children have real knowledge of moments of unhappiness that seem temporary, but which arise out of a deeper layer of uncertainty. The longing for security goes deep, because it is not something that is felt, lightly. There are only moments with forgetful security - is part of the experience of childhood. A general insecurity arises not only because they are not happy all the time, or because there are moments when they hate their circumstances, or failure at school, or quarrelling. It is more the a sense of discontent with what they look like. It is, more profoundly, who they are. Saying *why* they are unhappy is more difficult. It is far easier to cite arguments with friends, or braces on teeth, that give voice to the deeper insecurities, especially when so much mental energy is spent on learning how to deal with it, how to cover it up or accommodate it. When children are asked, for example, if they know of the ways in which they can make themselves happy, the immediacy of their answers suggests that this is something which is customary. They daydream, they fantasise, they play to distract themselves. As something which is dreaded nears, so children lose themselves in games to take their minds away.

Play has more than one dimension. It is a sign of being engaged with making sense of the world, of simulating reality, of learning about rules and imagining what it would be like to be an adult. It can, like stories, be a parody of the world as they see it. But play also functions as escape. It has the quality of a dream. However much of it is based on the realities of the world, as all dreams are, play is also a way of manipulating the world, of having power over it. If the circumstances are difficult the temptation is to turn away from them. This turning away mentally is a typical response. If there is a difficulty that is a lasting or semi-permanent one, like the loss of a father, or the death of a close friend, then the child cannot permanently dwell on it. There will be moments when they learn to deal with events by ignoring them rather than being caught up in the darkness of depression. Of course there will be those who will be deeply immersed by events and permanently scarred. But we are dealing here with the everyday, with the normal rather than the pathological.

If there is escapism, there must be something from which they wish to escape. This is characterised by the sense of relativity. Children not only learn to accept that they are as they are but realise this is entirely due to the chance of where they happen to be. Their acceptance of their parents is not uncritical. There is no sense of that benign or simple egotism assumed by Stage theorists. The sense that an individual is in the best of all places at the best possible time is one that is developed later.[34] There is certainly no sign of such moral egotism in children. Whether there was once a time of uncritical optimism I do not know. But the sense of the arbitrary, the unsatisfactory, is strong in children today. Their circumstances could be altered for the better. The environment is imperfect. There are threats in the broader world and more immediate threats at school. At one level the sense of the unsatisfactory is with the environment.

> Where I live is untidy, boring and doesn't look pleasant. Where I live is boring.
> *(girl 7)*

At another level the sense of the unsatisfactory - 'there's not always anything to be happy about' *(boy 10)* - is more self-directed. The sense that they could have happier dispositions or more satisfactory circumstances can go deep.

> My mum keeps on saying I'm sort of like different.
> See, when I have assemblies I like running away.
> They're boring. Don't like myself.
> Q: Do you like anything about yourself?
> A: No.
> Q: Nothing at all?
> A: No.

Q: Pardon? You'd like to be a horse?
A: Yeah. 'Cos they're nice creatures. They're nice animals.
Q: Do you like being you?
A: No. I never do anything when I go home. I just watch telly.   *(girl 8)*

Swift is clearly not the only person to prefer horses to people.[35] Nor is this the only girl to like horses. But the sense of unhappiness and self-hate is stubbornly pervasive. The sense of boredom, so often expressed, is a sign of this discontent. Assemblies are 'boring'; television is 'boring'. When children read comics they are aware that they do it out of boredom.[36] Boredom and discontent, finding something with which to be distracted, are closely related.

The sense of being bored is a pervasive one in childhood and can only be explained through its root cause. On the face of it, one would have thought that boredom is absurd. There is so much to do, so much to be experienced. Whilst there will be times at school when work is boring, the pleasures of play should seem to be all embracing and unending. But they are not. To dismiss something as 'boring' is to express a dislike, not only of the circumstances but its effect on the individual. It is an unhappy feeling to be helpless in the face of something that is disliked. But boredom arises from discontent, from not knowing what to do. Boredom is a sign of the mind, the gaze being turned off, being shut down. Boredom is a kind of escape, a type of superficial fantasy. Undergoing a television programme or the repeated and repetitive sensations of a comic are both signs of a desire for instant and superficial distraction.

Discontent and fantasy, boredom and games are closely interrelated. They are all part of the battle between uncertainty and the longing for security. Fantasies and desires, wishes and escape are all the other face of discontent, the alternatives in a muddled environment.[37] They are as much a part of the fabric of children's understanding as anything else; they are part of the means by which children come to terms with their lives. Suppression of what is experienced is paralleled by fantasies; but fantasies in the end also draw attention to the actualities. The more clearly is a wish expressed for an alternative the more clear it is that there is a contrast, a tribulation a discontent with the actual case. For the distinction between reality and fantasy is always clear, however much one overlaps the other.

Discontents are the soil on which fantasies grow.

> I don't like being me. I want to be in a different school ... I want to be in a different school ... I want to be a person, like, richer than I am.   *(boy 8)*

When adults think back on their childhood they remember their fantasies, their secret worlds, and sometimes mistake those for the reality, imbuing childhood as a time of uninhibited imagination, unconstrained by the reality of external events. These children express clear wishes but these are in a kind of contrast to their description of the everyday events in their lives at home and at school. The desire for an idyllic environment is a fantasy of control, of escape.

> I wish I lived in a cottage with roses growing up the wall, with a pretty little garden.   *(girl 11)*

The love of the countryside, of open spaces, is widely shared. It partly symbolises a longing for escape. But it also suggests a deeper psychological urge to be free of the chaotic and responsible actualities of the everyday. The fantasies are also mixed up with worries, especially when they are about their own futures.[38] On the one hand children think how pleasant it would be if they had power and money and did exciting jobs. On the other they realise that such fantasies must be tempered by realism. It is a desirable dream to become a 'footballer' or a 'millionaire' but these are clearly nothing more than fantasies.

> I like to think about being a good footballer.   *(boy 7)*

> I love to imagine myself in the future and famous, but this always leads me to feel worried.   *(girl 8)*

> I like to think about what it would be like to be a millionaire.   *(boy 8)*

Enjoying the thought of success is distinct from asserting that they will be successful. Thoughts of their futures include those fantasies that they would like to see come true, but there is always the shadow of a more pragmatic and prosaic reality.

> It's important if you are really good at the violin, you play in the concerts and get lots of money and things that. I want to play in concerts in my spare time

but be a rally, um, racer. It's more likely that I'll be a musician 'cos I don't really know as much about cars as I do about music. *(boy 8)*

For some people playing in concerts and becoming famous does become a reality. But these children realise how slender are their own chances. They would 'love' to be this or that, but see themselves, almost invariably, in less glamorous circumstances. They are aware of the importance of work and of talent. They do not have any uncritical or comfortable assumptions of their own careers. Some jobs, as depicted on television, appear to be 'fun'.

I'd like to be a business man, a computer consultant like my dad ... I won't be a spy. No way. But it would be fun. I might be in the Army or the RAF. But I expect the very most likely job I'll get is something ordinary like a business man, something like that. *(boy 8)*

The glamour of certain jobs - like detectives depicted in films - is known to be quite unlike the actuality of being a policeman.[39]

Just as everyday life contains the juxtaposition between dreams and reality, so do their speculations about their own futures. All the children know that one day they will be responsible for themselves and will have to make a living. They know that there is a difference between types of job, that some are more rewarding or fulfilling than others. One of the jobs that appear to be attractive to some girls is that of teaching.

I would get any job there was. This is my favourite job I would want to do. I would want to make - well, there's two jobs. I'd like to be a teacher and I'd like to make clothes and dresses for when people get married and also I would like to be someone who makes cakes. I've always wanted to be a teacher because I want to write on the blackboard and I would like to teach people. I think it would be nice being a teacher because I get to go out in the middle of school. Teachers go out, when we have some dinner ladies and lunch ladies, to get their own lunch. *(girl 7)*

Their own futures are constantly on children's minds. They are aware that they will enter the adult world and undergo lives that are not unlike those of their parents. Most of their fantasy play is centred on their observation of adult behaviour and adult roles. The work on gender stereotyping concentrates on the fact that boys and girls easily associate doctors with male role models and nurses with females, but overlooks the fact that behind the stereotyping children are revealing their consciousness of careers, of jobs, and of being paid. Whilst it is easier to place certain jobs like doctors and nurses into the actions of play, since other jobs are less interactive, there are a host of possibilities within reason that children become aware of. Thus making clothes and baking, of writing on the blackboard and being allowed out of school at lunch time are also visible signs of both work and play.[40]

The underlying sense of realism is that children know that there are great disparities both in rates of pay and in job satisfaction. All children are aware of the nature of work and of the possibilities of doing something humdrum. They are also aware of the chances of not finding employment. But whilst they speculate on the future they realise the relationship of the future for their immediate lives.

> You'll get a better chance of getting better jobs if you learn better things. I want to be in the RSPCA when I'm older. 'Cos I love animals and I want to keep them and if you go into the RSPCA I think you would be able to. My step-mum wanted to be in the RSPCA but she wasn't clever enough. If I'm clever enough I should be able to. *(girl 8)*

> It means you can get a good job, which means you get lots of money. And that means you can have nice things. It makes you do well. Which is good to do. 'Cos then you get to do more things which makes your live a bit happier. It's important to learn things 'cos then, 'cos if you don't learn anything then you won't know anything for your job. 'Cos you have to have a job, and then you won't know, you won't get anywhere. And you won't have money to live. In the short run it's very hard, but in the long run I'm going to lead a happier life if I work hard for it. *(boy 8)*

Working hard or being clever. The future depends on what goes on now. It might be 'hard' but all children see the purpose of school as preparing them for jobs. A good job is clearly connected to having 'nice things'; not having a job at all - a real possibility - is acknowledged as a disaster.

Children's sense of their own futures, like their pasts, affects their present. They do not live for the moment, even if they live for moments - of bliss or fantasy. Sooner or later the actual circumstances, the consequences of their action or inaction, and the reality of the world as it is intrudes on their consciousness. Whilst the uncertainty of the present is clear it is one that is partly affected by the future. Children see themselves in context. This context is the world as presented to them, and detected by them, a world which includes ambiguity, hope as well as despair, success as well as failure, and the possibilities of fulfilment as well as its denial. The daily tribulations of school are felt the more strongly because it connects to what might happen to them when they leave. The analysis of the world to come is one which mixes up aspirations with quiet desperation; it is one that is meticulously realistic in the ironic ambiguities of emotion and finance.

> You'd grow up to get a good job and earn quite a bit of money. You wouldn't get that good a job and you'd end up quite poor.
> If I learn quite a lot and learn how to read and write properly, I think I'll have quite a good life. Like being a builder or a computer maker. Archaeologists would be a real lot of money.
> Well I wouldn't mind to be an archaeologist or in the army, but I would like to be in the army more. Because, one, you can discover things from the past and in the army you feel quite special 'cos they help people from dying, protecting them.
> Problems about jobs because sometimes they don't get enough money.
> *(boy 8)*

It would be unnatural to be devoid of a 'fantasy' about the possibilities of the future, becoming an archaeologist or a veterinary surgeon. But such possibilities, like fantasies, always bring with them the opposites. There is a need to earn money, and the threat of not having enough, of being poor.

Attitudes towards the future show a connection with to the present. The future is part of the context, just as the international world is part of the environment. Children are not isolated either in space or time. They are aware of their own pasts and have a sense of nostalgia about it, but they can also project this 'nostalgia', this 'Sehnsucht' on the future:

> I would like to have two nice children and I'd like nobody to get hurt in my family and I'd like to have a long life and a happy life ... I like the fact that you'd have children to keep company and to help. *(boy 8)*

> I'd live in a smallish house like this and I would have a husband, but I don't know who. It's a real secret. He's called Michael. And I try to hide from him because he used to be my boyfriend when I was in the infants and it's been a

long time since then, so I try to hide from him. But he has seen me lots of times.

He's seen me a lot of times and I'm gonna ask my mum tomorrow if she could say, well, that my daughter loves you, and she wants to know if you love her and can you go to her and say.

I would have a husband and I would have two children. I would have them. I don't know if it will happen but I would like to have a girl and a boy. I'd call them like Amanda and something else.   *(girl 7)*

It is too easy for some to interpret the analysis of children as containing more of a hint of the absurd. But this arises out of the supposedly ironic juxtaposition between what children say and what they are supposed to say. How many people's aspirations, when they dare to evoke them, would include the idea of having a family - keeping them company and having a settled home. The future and the present are all bound up in each other, the combination of an actual person, and actual name and an actual house with the sense of distant but possible security. Speculations about what is yearned for are based on the realities of what they know. One girl talks of having just one child because 'if you have two then they might start arguing like me and Sarah do' *(girl 8)*.

The future is not seen in terms of unproblematic bliss. It is also packed, like the present, with threats and with tribulations. There are those who predict the possibility of 'getting into trouble', and those who understand the temptations of crime. There are those who dread old age and dying. The reality of the everyday is as much part of their future - 'the normal people who walk their dogs and stuff' - as it is of their present. 'Normality', after all, is also something for which children yearn. They might feel that it is like a fantasy, but as in their everyday lives it is a need. The consequences of adult life are around them with the clarity of meaning and effect.

My mum and dad haven't split up yet or anything like that ... there's quite a few that I know ...
Q: What's your life like then?
A: Oh, that's a hard question. Sometimes it's fair, sometimes life is not fair.[41]
                                                                      (girl 8)

The judgements thus need to be made about social circumstances combine the objective, seeing things as they are, and the personal, being affected by them. There is nothing that does not connect. Judgements about morality and punishment are linked to the sense of what people are like. These insights into human nature are linked to themselves. They understand a variety of feelings, both temporary and long term, feelings which affect them and their judgements constantly.

If we had to remind people of the connection between inner emotions and their tensions with the world that adults take for granted we would only have to raise the question of embarrassment. In the face of one glance it would be possible to think of the shame of embarrassment being one that because it is so often based on a *social faux pas* is merely a trivial manifestation of convention.[42] But at a second glance we have to remind ourselves how heart-felt embarrassment is.[43] It contains just that dysfunction between the inner and the outer, the personal feelings and public exposure that cause anguish in children. As they seek to find out the ways of convention and how to adapt to the deliberate ignorance that maintains social behaviour, so they are excruciated by their sense of the inappropriate. A parent makes a joke, or does a pretence, and the usual proprieties of behaviour are broken. The shame of it is powerful. It might not be long-lasting but it highlights just that struggle between the private and the public, the understanding of a personal place within a shared convention, that is the daily ritual of learning in children.

The rules of social order and the conventions of morality, feelings of guilt and shame: these are all understood, if not always articulated, by children. Their struggles to create meaningful relationships - with peers, and parents, with those in authority and with the vast authority of reality - are constantly embodied in judgements and in pain, in trying to understand what is fair and what personal feelings contain. Moral transgressions and social blunders, embarrassment and ridicule, are all at one with the sense of helplessness, the guilt of being stupid, and the shame that inevitably comes when you are confronted with the point of view of others. People might learn how to clothe themselves with protection but children have no such hiding place. Before they learn how to justify themselves or ignore judgements, they realise that they, as individuals in a complex whole, have faults or limitations, or, even if they do not, are disliked or despised, hated or spurned. There are no exceptions. The discontent is both realistic and social. It is realistic because it rests on an analysis of the world as a whole, a world which includes unhappiness and unfairness. It is social because the events that happen are volatile and unstable, and depend so fundamentally on the ephemeral nature of other people's feelings. At the core is no automatic bliss. Childhood does not consist of the optimism of fantasy fuelled by ignorance. It is the time when the world is seen as it is.

Notes

1. Miller, G. *Spontaneous Apprentices: Children and Language*. New York, Seabury Press, 1977.

2. Baillargeon, R and de Vos, T. Object Permanence in Young Infants: Further Evidence. *Child Development*, Vol.62, No.6, 1991.

3. Rosengren, K; Gelman, S; Kalish, C and McCormick, M. As Time Goes By: Children's Early Understanding of Growth in Animals. *Child Development,* Vol.62, No.6, pp.1302-1320, 1991.

4. Papousek, H. Individual Variability in Learned Responses in Human Infants, in Robinson, R (ed.) *Brain and Early Behaviour*. London, Academic Press, 1969.

5. Rosengren, K and Hickling, A. Seeing is Believing: Children's Explanations of Commonplace, Magical and Extraordinary Transformation. *Child Development*, Vol.65, No.6, pp.1605-1626, 1994.

6. Flavell, T. Developmental Studies in Medicated Memory, in Reese, H and Lipsitt, L, *Advances in Child Development and Behaviour*. New York Academic Press, 1970.

7. Davies, B. Children Through Their Own Eyes. *Oxford Review of Education*, Vol.10, No.3, pp.275-292, 1984.

8. Flavell, T; Green, F and Flavell, E. Children's Understanding of the Stream of Consciousness. *Child Development*, Vol.64, No.2, pp.387-398, 1993.

9. Fabricius, W; Schwanenflugel, P; Kyllonen, P; Barclay, C and Denton, S. Developing Theories of Mind: Children's and Adults'

Concepts of Mental Activities. *Child Development*, Vol.60, No.6, pp.1278-1290, 1989.

10. Harré, R. *Social Being: A Theory for Social Psychology*. Oxford, Blackwells, 1983.

11. Hala, S; Chandler, M and Fritz, A. Fledgling Theories of Mind: Deception as a Marker of Three Year Olds' Understanding of False Belief. *Child Development*, Vol.62, No.1, pp.83-97, 1991.

12. Haste, H. Growing into Rules in Bruner, T and Haste, H (eds.) *Making Sense*. London, Methuen, 1987.

13. Furnham, A and Stacey, B. *Young People's Understanding of Society*. London, Routledge, 1991.

14. The fact that they take on an adult tone in describing news items and reactions to them suggests that their parents and teachers, with their iterative warnings, reinforce the sense of danger rather than replace it.

15. Grixti, T. Ambiguous Shades: Consciousness and the Images of Fear. *British Journal of Educational Studies*, Vol.31, No.3, pp.198-210, 1983.

16. Watt, E. *Authority*. London, Croom Helm, 1982.

17. Smetana, T. Parenting Styles and Conceptions of Parental Authority During Adolescence. *Child Development*, Vol.66, No.2, pp.299-316, 1995.

18. Cullingford, C and Morrison, J. Who Excludes Whom? The personal experience of exclusion, in Blyth, E and Milner, T (eds.) *Exclusion from School*. London, Routledge, 1996.

19. Cullingford, C and Brown, G. Children's Perceptions of Victims and Bullies. *Education 3-13*, Vol.23, No.2, pp.11-17, 1995.

20. See Mill, T. *Autobiography*
    and the maxims of Tupper
    and see Hazlitt's analysis of 'fear and guilt'.

21. Hartup, W. The Company they keep: Friendships and their Developmental Significance. *Child Development*, Vol.67, No.1, pp.1-13, 1996.

22. See Chapter 6.

23. Chandler, M; Fritz, A and Hala, S. Small-scale Deceit: Deceptions as a Marker of 2, 3 and 4 year olds' Theories of Mind. *Child Development*, Vol.60, No.6, pp.1263-1277, 1989.

24. Waksler, F. *Studying the Social Worlds of Children - Sociological Readings*. London, Falmer Press, 1991.

25. Hala, S et al., op cit.

26. Burnett, T. Destiny Obscure: Autobiographies of Childhood, Education and the Family from the 1820s to the 1920s. Bennet, A. *The Way of All Flesh*. London, Allan Lane, 1982.

27. Waksler, op cit.

28. Goldman, R and Goldman, T. Children's Sexual Thinking. London, Routledge & Kegan Paul, 1982.

29. Cassidy, T and Asher, T. Loneliness and Peer Relations in Young Children. *Child Development*, Vol.63, No.2, pp.350-365, 1992.

30. Spitz, R. The Importance of the Mother-Child Relationship during the first year of life. A synopsis in five sketches. *Mental Health Today*, Vol.7, pp.7-13, 1948.

31. Waksler, op cit.

32. Cullingford, C. Children's Attitudes to Bullying. *Education 3-13*, Vol.21, No.2, pp.54-60, 1993.

33. Winkley, L. The Implications of Children's Wishes. *Journal of Child Psychology and Psychiatry*, Vol.23, No.4, pp.477-483, 1982.

34. See Cullingford. C. The forming of Culture and Identity. Forthcoming.

35. The Houyhnhnms and the Yahoos in *Gullivers Travels*, last book.

36. Cullingford, C. Why Children Like Comics. *Research in Education* No.54, pp.108-109, 1995.

37. Klein, M and Riviere, T. *Love, Hate and Reparation.* London, Hogarth Press, 1953.

38. Simmonds, T. *Psychiatric Examination of Children.* Philadelphia, Lea and Feber, 1969.

39. Cullingford, C. *Children and Television.* Chapter 5, pp.177-188, Aldershot, Gower, 1984.

40. Cullingford, C. *The Inner World of the School.* London, Cassell, 1991.

41. She goes on to explain all her tribulations.

42. Ricks, C. *Keats and Embarrassment.* Oxford University Press, 1974.

43. Ferguson, T; Stegge, H and Damhues, I. Children's Understanding of Guilt and Shame. *Child Development*, Vol.62, No.4, pp.827-839, 1991.

5 Home life: the significance of others

Parents bear an enormous responsibility whether they want to or not. Of all relationships, that between parents and children has the most lasting effect. When one traces back the influences that have made lives happy or sad, successful or not, fulfilled or disappointed, the most significant is that of the parents. At some levels this influence can be comparatively slight, as in tastes and choices. These are in themselves important and interesting, but the profound effect that parents have lies far deeper than questions of cultural taste. The most crucial relationship of all is the earliest one of a child and an adult. The quality of later life depends on the quality of that relationship.[1]

Parenting is a difficult task because the effects on children are often inadvertent as with an overheard or misunderstood remark. This means that whilst parenting can be understood and learned - although this fact is usually neglected - and whilst the difference between good and bad parenting is the difference between fulfilled and destroyed lives, it is difficult ever to be absolutely perfect.[2] This needs reiterating since the evidence in the book comes from children's experience of their parents, and their accounts of the actual effects of parents. This is the empirical case; whilst it has many and profound implications this is not a book concerned with giving advice. Of books that tell parents how to behave, or which stress the importance of the early years of childhood there are many. They give advice according to current fashions - stressing in turn discipline or freedom, keeping to strict rules or relying on love. There are times when parents are advised to keep to exact times for feeding, and wait until the minute hand at last arrives on the hour prearranged according to the book, whilst the baby screams. There are times when parents are told to rely purely on their instincts and not to listen to advice including presumably the book that they are reading.[3] But we are concerned here with how children see their parents, and the quality of the relationships rather than the habits and arrangements of the home.

The responsibility of parenting is so great and so lightly taken on that it is no wonder that one such book is entitled *The Good Enough Parent*.[4] This

147

is an indication of the complexity and the importance of the subject. One does not wish to be a counsel of perfection, for sensitive parents feel guilty enough already, but young children scrutinise their parents in such a way that it seems that all depends on it. Some parents do not seem to know how to make relationships.[5] This is better than exhibiting obvious indifference, but it can have as devastating an effect. Childhood is an extremely sensitive and difficult time and the place of parents is crucial. This much is universally acknowledged, but the relationship between the kind of parenting and children's subsequent development has been described rather than explained. This is partly because of the attempt to study parents rather than children's response to them, creating typologies of parenting rather than ways in which children react. The two approaches do arrive at some similar conclusions but it is by the study of the children that we see how influential is the tone and the nature of the relationship.

From children's points of view there is nothing more intense than their early relationship with the closest adults. Saying 'adults' rather than 'parents' is to make an important distinction. Because parents feel so strongly about their children and are so emotionally attached to them, it is easy to assume that natural ties are enough. The emotional bond is two way but there is an important difference. The young child views his or her parent with need and intensity but also with objectivity. That adult who is conveying cultural values and ideas as well as warmth and food, is a distinct other, and not merely an extension of the mental world of the child. The adult is scrutinised and assessed as well as loved. It is parents who tend not to see their offspring objectively. They are so emotionally attached to their children that they see them almost as extensions of themselves.

Part of the intensity of the relationship with their parents is the fact that it is not just a matter of emotional bonding. Children are constantly learning from the example they see. Parents demonstrate behaviours and attitudes as well as emotions. The desire to be loved is recognised, but it is a love that is exhibited in action. Wanting to have a close relationship with parents means that nothing is taken for granted.

> Maybe mummy and daddy think that I'm a bit too old to have cuggles and kisses and hugs. But I like having a nice cuddle sometimes. 'Cos it makes, sometimes when I have a cuddle it makes me feel loved and cared for. Which I am, even though sometimes I think I'm not. Well, what I meant by saying that is, I do not think they care about me, but maybe just sometimes I don't feel

that they do. But they probably do. And sometimes I don't like getting told off that much. But sometimes I think I deserve it. So I don't always feel sorry for myself. Sometimes I do, but not all the time.   *(girl 8)*

The desire to be loved, to rest in emotional security is the desire for a close relationship, for parents to provide more of an interest in them as individuals, rather than a physical stability. At one level nothing is taken for granted, for the desire for assurance is not always forthcoming. The desire to feel loved and cared for is the more intense for the realisation that not everyone is granted that privilege. In even in the most 'normal' of households there are moments of rejection - of being told off, of feeling unwanted. The outward physical sign is a kind of assurance, an assurance of interest and a personal relationship.

This intense desire for a close emotional and intellectual relationship, and the recognition of the proximity of insecurity means that the behaviours and attitudes of parents have long term effects. The extent to which parents (or significant adults) can express and demonstrate curiosity and interest in the children makes a longlasting difference to their subsequent development. Emotional warmth is not enough. The occasional gesture of concern only underlines what is otherwise absent. The intellectual relationship between adult and child is one in which two features are strongly represented. One is an interest in the mind and ideas of the child; the ability to listen and converse, to ask why as well as to answer. It is this sense of being a person, a matter of interest to others, that gives the real sense of security. A consistent intellectual curiosity in the individual is the strongest sense of comfort. For it is out of that interest that the second feature arises. This is the sharing of interest in other things, and other people. The dialogue is not just about the 'me' and 'you', nor just about warmth of feelings. It is the shared curiosity about the world at large.

One of the earliest and most profound facts that children have to learn is the sense of themselves, their own theory of mind. They are seeking the assurance of the objective identity, not only understanding themselves in relationship to others, but in being recognised as having their distinct place. Egotism, in the way that Piaget describes is, as a type of autism, comes later. For young children look on the world not as a series of personal attachments but as something objective, to be scrutinised, studied and learned. It is because adults play such a crucial part in children's understanding of the world that their influence is so strong. At one level children develop and understand despite their parents. But their need for a critical dialogue to make understanding the more readily available means that they can look at the social and physical environment with confidence rather than suspicion.

Parents are often described as care-givers. This arises out of the belief that the feelings of love, the emotional attachments that parents feel, are enough in themselves. If this were so, early childhood would be relatively untroubled. If human beings did not think as well as feel, attachments might be enough. As it is, we recognise the crucial difference parenting makes - even if, as a society, we do little about it. Parents' belief in their own effectiveness - a sign of intellectual curiosity about the relationships that are the definitions of families - enhances their ability to make a difference to their children.[6] What parents do and what they do not do is central. The intensity is felt on both sides, but as in real love, it is exhibited in an almost disinterested concern for the other. Love is not a selfish bond, a desire to extract emotions from others but a sense of a relationship.[7] There might not seem to be conflicts between child's and the parent's point of view. That comes later. But before conflicts emerge there are clear differences of opinion, of inference and understanding. Children's awareness of false beliefs arises out of their sense of a separate identity, of the idea of a point of view.

The way in which young children tune in to the emotional needs of adults, and their sense of adults as 'others' - with their own agendas, and moods and peculiarities to be negotiated, is clear. It starts very young, for children see the perspectives of others, responding to different emotional expressions, long before the end of the first year.[8] Children learn the rules and parameters of arguments even before they have the verbal capacity to exploit them. They witness the distinctions of points of view in those around them; siblings, parents and other adults.[9] It is because of their understanding of the difference between dialogue and argument, and because of their grasp of the parameters of the individual mind, as well as the importance of relationships, that children are so profoundly affected by their parents quarrelling. This draws attention to the insecurity of the environment, the arbitrariness of where they are placed. Their sense of the objective, their scrutiny of circumstances makes them understand how many separate lives are being led, and how many different home lives, with contrasts of agreement and argument, are possible. Far from being indifferent to what goes on before them or egocentric, children witness disagreements, as between siblings and their mother, and display sensitivity both to the topic of the dispute and the interests of the antagonists.

The relationship, verbal as well as physical, between the parents and child is more important than any particular technique of child rearing, in so far as one can separate the two. The ability to fulfil the demands of being a parent will only be learned by those who wish to develop a personal relationship.[10] If there is a sense of dialogue that is permanent and reliable, traumatic events do not have such a profound effect. Indeed, the ability to create a strong relationship with one adult is more important than the cohesiveness of the marital unit. Whilst witnessing quarrels and divorce has a strong effect on the children, this is more because they have become peripheral to their parent's concerns than because they miss the emotional stability of a placid home life. Parents quarrelling means that their attention is taken up with the partner; the relationship, however negative, is strong and dominates all others. Children are deprived of the intellectual and emotional substance of dialogue, of the sense of their own unique identity. It is for this reason that they feel guilty, as if all that happened were their own fault. Perhaps 'guilt' is the wrong word. It is the way that children try to express their realisation that they are no longer of immediate interest, that they are more of an encumbrance than person. When parents use their children in their arguments with their partners, this sense of children's isolation is the more profound. The very fact that they are 'used' as weapons diminishes their sense of identity. They look at what is happening objectively and intensively, and see a drama being played out in which they no longer have a part.

There are many ways of feeling abandoned and deserted. Most attention has been paid to physical deprivation, but the sense of emotional and intellectual abandonment is probably even more important. After a certain length of time in which the young infant left alone cries for attention until the parent returns there is no immediate sense of comfort even when the parent returns. If the need were simple physical presence, and the warmth of emotion, the return of the parent would have an immediate effect. But it does not. The sense of being deserted remains; and the anger lasts.[11] Just as young children when deprived of physical handling over a long period sink into a decline, as if they suffered from sensory deprivation, so the absence of intellectual handling creates an emotional decline. The hunger for stimulation is not just physical. Intellectual starvation might not be as obvious but it is just as long lasting.

Given the need for attention and the strong reaction to the sense of being abandoned it is no surprise that there should be a theory of attachment, that the 'universal bond with the mother' (sic) should be seen by Bowlby as crucial.[12] This is usually interpreted as an emotional security, as if the provision of a figure of attachment were enough to alleviate stress. The repeated daily experience of model care-giving is implied as being enough in itself, as if the mother-figure were the central need of early childhood. This might be appealing but it is not true. There is much more to mothering than the provision of milk and warmth.

Bowlby's theory supposes that there is one universal law that unites all mothers and their offspring. But the more one studies the relationships between mothers and children the more are cultural differences exposed.[13] The ways in which mothers and children relate to each other reveal how much depends on the language and the concepts that are jointly explored. The 'universal' bond is in fact a more complex intellectual discourse that shows differences of perception. When, for example, mothers in two different cultural inheritances expressed their feelings and perceptions of attachment, and described the ways in which they wished to help their children, there emerged profoundly different outlooks and expectations.[14] The types of relationships described were in contrast to each other, with one cultural group constantly stressing self-esteem and insecurity; a sense of children clinging to independence and autonomy, and the other underlining respect and shame, a filtering through of cultural and shared identity. The mothers express levels of relationship that go far beyond simple physical attachment. It is this, as well as the saturation of different cultural meanings, that is so significant. From the child's point of view it is just at that level - of dialogue, or shared understanding - that relationships are significant.

Children observe, and through their objectivity come to understand. This objectivity of understanding is by no means detached from emotional implications. On the contrary, what children observe includes loneliness and insecurity, desire and passion, anger and mistrust. The emotional aspects of life are as clearly absorbed as the milk. Far from needing little more than attachment children require the sustenance of understanding. This includes the definition of feeling. Very young children understand loneliness.[15] They do not only feel a sense of being abandoned. A two year old stands in the street feeling abandoned, and cries. This is not just for the parent's immediate attention, nor just an outcry of rage and disappointment. It is deeply felt. Loneliness is not a temporary matter but a feeling that can last. The absence of dialogue with adults almost invariably leads to the inability to make relationships with others. Social incompetence, the sense of social ostracism and victimisation, starts early.

Attachment theory does not explain the subtleties of individual differences. There are some children who seem not to be very distressed by a parent's departure. There are also those who are not comforted by their return.[16] Simple comings and goings do not explain the complexities of personal dialogue, through mutual understandings and anticipations as well as through words. That subtle interplay of curiosity in which one person can make up for the deficiencies or limitations of the other reveals that the sense of identity and self-respect, however insecure, is based on understanding as well as warmth. The stress must be on the relationship and not just on the particular type of parenting. This needs stressing not only because it should be clear by now that so much depends on children's formulations of their own ideas rather than assuming that their attitudes are mere reflections of their parents but because there have been a number of typologies of parenting. In so far as they deal with those characteristics which are to do with the interplay between one person and another, they reveal some general truths, confirmed by the children. But there is a tendency to study the observable behaviour rather than the effect; the model to which children are supposed to react.

The most typical typology of parents' behaviour breaks parenting into three models.[17] The first is the detached and controlling 'authoritarian', demanding obedience and using threats and punishments. According to the theory this leads to the child's poor interactions with peers and a tendency to over-react. The second is the permissive parent who has some warmth but is not in control. This is connected to children's low self-reliance and low self-control. The third type is the authoritative, the parent who combines warmth with encouragement; the reason for having rules is discussed but the final authority lies with the parent. This, of course, is then linked with independent outlook and the ability of the child to get on well with peers. These distinctions have a long history and some good reasons for their formulation.[18] They draw to our attention the tension between the 'laissez faire' and the 'controlling', and the subtlety of balancing one approach against the other. As we will see, children have their own acknowledgement of this tension; the support of the parent in letting the child be independent, and the recognition of the need for authority.

The outlining of the three types, when considered from the point of view of children, actually centres on the delicate balance between control and permissiveness, which lies at the heart of the subtleties of the relationship. Children are quite clear that they resent either extreme: the parent who lets them do what they want, and the parent who lays down the law on everything. But both extremes show the same underlying difficulty; the lack of interest in the child as an individual. Extreme discipline obliterates the identity; it assumes that the personality is something to be moulded or controlled, or a person who has no voice and no distinct intelligence. The extreme of the laissez faire is that of utter indifference. The child does not even count. What seems like freedom is soon detected as the convenience of forgetfulness. The interesting insight that children consistently give is that they need that clear relationship. One might have supposed that freedom and indiscipline could be welcomed by some, but there is an agreement that in the end this is a burden, a lack of help, that they find hard to bear.

There is nothing more important than children being able to share their interests with others. This is where consistency and genuine concern are so important. In attempting to clarify the nature of the world they are in children seek from their immediate adults the intellectual companionship that asks as well as answers, explores as well as lays down the rules. But children's own highly developed moral awareness - if not moral action - also seeks to find a framework of authority in which to operate. The parent does not need to assert the rules; the children almost create the parent in the role of rule-giver. They need the parents to demonstrate in a microcosm the rules and norms of society - not because of fear of punishment but because they are concerned with the consequences and the unhappiness of misdemeanours. Children are not good but they have a profound desire to become so. They do not see themselves as innocent, nor do they behave innocently, but they do seek for grace. This is dependent on having people they can trust, who stand for fairness and consistency and to whom they can talk.

There was never any automatic power possessed by the parent. The power of authority in the parent is sought by the children. There was always a sense of negotiation, even when children were seen and not heard. More recently parent-child relationships are characterised by a more familial culture, but this is a matter of a consistent need coming closer to the surface.[19] Long before the articulated negotiations of the middle years of childhood come the explorations of children, testing their insecurities and searching the competence of the parents. There are those who suggest that some of the problems of ambivalent and insecure children are a result of inconsistent maternal behaviour.[20] But vulnerability comes about because there is an absence of any positive relationship. This is not a question merely of leaving the room whilst the baby screams. Some can cope with that. It is more a question of not knowing what to do with an inexplicable, intelligent, inarticulate and observant human being. The bewilderment and the fear of some parents is perfectly understandable.

The personal connections between parents and children are a subtle blend of the psychological and the behavioural. There need to be both internalised and externalised forms of control, personal understanding, intuitive sharing of beliefs and the recognition of set rules, of regulations that are necessary to contain different points of view.[21] Children are constantly seeking consistencies. This includes behaviour and not just a succession of unstructured personal relationships. Children are first and foremost observers: they are witnesses. Relationships come about through dialogue, through seeing what the other person, as a person, wants to say. Children early on learn to understand intentions, as well as the behaviour of others.[22] This arises out of the development of the concept of 'agency', the fact that people have their own wills and generate their own behaviour. The most basic development of language arises out of the need to describe: 'Daddy read'.

Children's objective understanding includes themselves, their parents and their circumstances. They see the relativity of it all: that others live in different circumstances and have different relationships. They can, and have to, accept this. They see their own families as entities and can openly describe what later they would learn to keep hidden. These are the facts.

> My Dad, he used to live in Holland and my sister used to, but me and my mum lived in England ... it makes me remember when my Dad went to Germany and my next Daddy, because my other Daddy died in Germany. I haven't got two Daddies, but my one, I can't remember, but I think when my Mum wasn't married. She married somebody who died but that was before I was born. And then I've got my next Daddy.   *(girl 6)*

This mixture of the laconic and the precise denotes both the acceptance of the circumstance and the objective description of it. Children readily acknowledge that their parents have a past and their own framework of identity. They all see what they have inherited, including a network of relationships, past and present, and the physical environment of the home. There is no embarrassment at the facts, no stumbling to mitigate the actualities. Instead it is the sense of the immediacy of the real and tangible, combined with the feeling of relativity. This is simply how it is, for them. 'My Daddy died' as other members of the family die for one reason or another.

> My dad's mum died of cancer and, well, my dad's dad didn't die of any illness. It was just he wasn't healthy in life. He didn't eat well. He didn't eat the right foods to keep you healthy. He had two heart attacks and then he had a stroke and after that he just died.   *(boy 7)*

Children simply relate the facts, of divorce, or death, and recognise the individually circumstantial aspects of their lives, like the possibility that they might have been brought up in Holland or in Germany. This is part of the objectivity of their accounts of themselves; objective and intense. Their stories are linked to others, even if some of the others remain shadowy figures.

> I have Greek blood, half Greek blood. My father's Greek. But I, I never saw him. I only saw him when I was about six months old.   *(boy 7)*

Children are renowned for relating facts without embarrassment. This is sometimes seen as a sign of innocence and lack of affectation. It might be the latter, for they have not yet learned about projecting an image of themselves. But this objectivity is not a matter of the naiveté. It shows that in their awareness of their circumstances there are many issues that need to be taken into account. Beyond the immediate relationships are extended families and jobs, a lack of money or space, and quarrels as well as pleasures. They describe illnesses and ambitions, the work their parents do and where they work, their qualifications and their limitations. They describe the pain of divorce, of not seeing their absent fathers, or the fear of seeing their parents argue. They acknowledge the physical arrangements as well as the emotional ties.

My Mum's got bad legs. She can't walk upstairs. It's easy for my Mum because she's not in a house with lots of stairs, but it's not so easy because she's got six flights of stairs to go up if she wants to go out. I like playing and working and that. But I like doing things for my Mum. Like make a cup of tea, do some toast for her, go down and get some washing up liquid and all stuff like that. She's got really bad arthritis. My Dad's downstairs and my Mum's in hospital at nights, 'cos my Dad, if he cleaned the floor he's up about eleven o'clock and I stay until he comes up. The shop 'cos he runs it.   *(girl 8)*

It sometimes seems as if it is parents who believe themselves to be 'seen and not heard'. They are certainly seen, in their daily habits, the dealing with the day to day from which children do not feel themselves excluded even if they are left to their own devices. The early stories which young children like are about the reality of diurnal activities: the world of adults as well as their own. Their play parodies adult habits and behaviours. This is the result of observation as intense as that of Gulliver.[23] The capacity to make the tea, to do household chores and take responsibility is as clearly present today as it was before our version of childhood was invented, protecting them from what we feel is the premature responsibility to work and earn their keep. Because we expect different things from children, and dress them in different clothes and give them 'tailor-made' toys, this does not mean that children have suddenly begun to look on the real world as if it were subsumed in their play. Their inner lives feed off the actuality of what they see and hear. Whilst they seem to be absorbed in their own activities they still hear what is said; they note the quarrels or arguments between their parents as readily as being hurt themselves. However strong the emotional bond, the objectivity includes parents.

The quality of the relationship between the child and the parent depends on the degree of interest in each other. The concern for the other person's point of view and feelings, which are demonstrated so clearly by young children, need, to be reciprocated. Nothing is more difficult to cope with than the other's self-absorption, an indifference to the other person that means that there is no sharing of opinion, no refinement of understanding through the interactions of language. It has been suggested that some children are not gifted at this ability to carry out a dialogue, but from these observations and this evidence it could be concluded that the inability to see another person's point of view is more characteristic of the parents than the children.[24] Adults have not only learned how to shield themselves from reality in their desire to cope, but have inherited a culture in which children are seen as having the limitations of pets. In order to have a dialogue with another person you need to be able to take them seriously. Many parents cannot take their children seriously in this way, cannot therefore laugh *with* them rather than at them. The kinds of egocentricity often levelled against children are more often seen in adults, so locked into seeking the fulfilment of their hypotheses that they cannot observe or understand what is so clearly laid out before them.[25] To such a vision the ability to create an experience that has all the virtues of a holy science - excluding all human variables - overwhelms the clear sight of the everyday.

Children have an objective sense of reality as well as an intense need for relationships. Both depend on each other, since sheer warmth, or sudden demonstrations of affection, are not enough.[26] Objectivity means seeing the other as a real person with ideas as well as feelings, understanding the distinction between intention and action. Beneath the stereotypes of the roles of Mother and Father, children acknowledge the essential separation of their lives from their own. They look back years later and recall their mother's drunkenness or their father's indifference. These are not inventions after the event but a realisation of laziness or some other flaw, or limitation, that children had to learn to live with.

> She used to like drink a lot, but she used to drink in the day and that ... my sister used to cook the food and that sometimes and she used ... say when I was about nine she was only about twelve, my mum used to just be on the sofa and that, drunk, watching telly or something.[27]   *(female 19)*

The extreme will always be remembered, together with the capacity to cope with it. But it is not only the outrageous or unusual that is recalled. The same intensity of observation affects the ordinary and the everyday, long before a distinction is made between the ordinary and the unusual. For nothing is ordinary to the observer absorbed in attention to detail. The senses of a child are heightened: to the temperature, the smell of a flower, to the strength of wind, with the clarity of an epicure. For these things are not just exquisite, for their own sake, but as part of the pattern of sensations that build reality. The most sophisticated of the senses is the intelligence, the understanding of what things mean. It is like a prior-perception, a necessary bond to hold all small signs together. The eye that sees and copes with the drunken mother also observes the behaviour of the normal, the arthritis, the disability, the hopes and fears, the aspirations and the realities of the ordinary struggle to survive. Children are not sacrosanct, and do not feel themselves to be so.

One cannot understand the complex forms of mutual understanding between a parent and a child without acknowledging the powers of the observant mind.[28] Without this there would be no basis for dialogue. The need that children express, for being given a sense of their own worth, is not just a cry for emotional support but for understanding. They know clearly that if they are told off, if their parents direct their anger at them, this can be either a result of a loss of self-control, or, on the contrary, out of concern for them. The right balance between concern and tolerance is never an easy one for a parent to strike. But children are quick to perceive the underlying intention of the parent, and forever marked by the distinction between a genuine lack of interest in them, and a desire, however fraught, to do the best for them. What children want to share is the essence of understanding and trust; knowing that there is an expectation against which they can judge themselves.

> They'd still be pleased with me because they always like me. They wouldn't tell me off at all. They know that they always say to me 'As long as you do your best'. I mean they do get cross if I do something scruffy or something. But, if I was bad and I really was trying my best, I know they wouldn't be cross with me.   *(girl 8)*

Security includes intellectual as well as emotional security, the realisation that adults can be as objective as themselves, that adults are not merely driven by 'agendas' of their own.

The relationship between a child and a parent depends upon the relativity of beliefs. One cannot grasp the sense of a 'point of view' and a separate identity unless there is a realisation of potential disagreement, a disparity between one set of wishes and another.[29] There are certain physical facts which are constant, and there are other matters of principle rather than fact that should be so, but are not, like morality and social convention. It is a hard matter to attribute different but justifiable beliefs to other people. It is far easier to label them as deviant. Young children learn to see the completeness and the distinction of other people's point of view. It is adults who so notoriously do not, or have given up trying to do so. It is far more comfortable for them to slip into a warm dressing gown of habitual assumptions. But for children strenuously making sense of the contradictory nature of the social world there is no such easy deliberate ignorance. It is always difficult for anyone to believe that another holds a false belief about a matter of verifiable fact. It is slightly easier to infer that other people hold their own unusual beliefs about matters of taste and value. Children of three are remarkable in being able to see the distinction between the two at an age when the idea of verification is so new.[30] Like adults, they see the distinction between belief and reality; between the facts that will remain facts whatever people make of them, and those which slide lubriciously into the arguments of the self-absorbed. What is more, they learn to understand that people hold their own beliefs in the face of facts. Long before they learn the utility of this device they absorb the fact of it.

Far more important than the ability to understand how the actual state of reality can be represented in different, apparently contradictory, ways is the acknowledgement that there is a distinction between reality and belief, that there are points of view rather than a fixed, immutable and uncontradictory world. This is learned the hard way, by observing the different realities of attitude exhibited in other people's behaviour.[31] Each person presents their belief as universal reality.[32] Out of the conglomeration of what seem to be facts but are not, children build their theory of minds, their's and other people's.[33] The difficulty and the potential for misunderstandings arise because every message, every word has an effect, even if it is unintentional. The speaker can be inarticulate, can desire to say something, but he or she cannot be certain that what is intended to be said is what is understood. Misunderstandings arise not only from faulty beliefs but from incomplete utterances.[34] It is never easy to get the words into the right order, and never possible to say exactly what is meant to be said. The melancholy comfort is that even when, or if, all that should be expressed is in fact expressed clearly and exactly, (if that were possible) the person responding to what is said will understand it in their own way. This is not to imply that it does not matter what is said. On the contrary. Children need to have such a verbal relationship that every effort is made to try and try again to be clear. What is important is the recognition of the attempt - by the person speaking and the listener. Words are the means of understanding and communication.[35] The intention of the speaker and the listener, whatever the understanding, is of central importance.[36] The way one person listens affects the style of the other's utterance.

This implies that in this complex of individual beliefs and personal statements, there is a constant juxtapositioning of points of view, of personal assertion and the rivalry of individual understanding. Nowhere is this more clear than the rivalry, and awareness, between siblings. Much, perhaps too much, is talked about sibling rivalry. The important fact of being in the same family is that the distinction between having an independent point of view and being placed in a certain environment is highlighted in the relationship between brothers or sisters. They learn not only to deal with similar circumstances but that they do so in different ways. They learn not only that relationships, like beliefs, differ, but that there are inherent distinctions to be made between each person, subtle nuances of response according to age and gender.[37] Siblings are not just equal rivals for a place in the affections of their parents but are in the most intense relationship of all: they are in their 'given' circumstances, with their given personalities, trying to discover a way that is unique to them, whilst recognising the separateness of the other point of view in the same circumstances and the same people. It is not rivalry for a single goal, but the juxtaposition of permanent fact with distinctions of personality that is so important.

This is not to say that siblings do not fight for recognition from their parents. In most homes they will receive individual but equal treatment. Whatever they receive they are aware of the others, and their distinction from them. In other circumstances than the home the acceptance of many points of view and many backgrounds and the need for set rules and moral codes are taken as read. The more variety of people the more clearly the need for shared values. But in a home it is as if the values should be taken for granted and agreed. The home is the microcosm of society. It blends age with inexperience, the most delicate of behaviours with the most raw of emotions. It is both a controlled environment and out of control The very mass of people in a public arena means that any outbreak has to be controlled; but the home is a kind of freedom from control. It is the place where the most intense and the most obvious forms of expression are made manifest. There is no running away from the relationship, no real possibility of saying 'I won't be your daughter any more' as you could say 'I'm no longer your friend'. Home is a given, whether it is accepted as such or not, even if it ran away from. The relationship remains. And there lies the rub.

The home is often remembered as a place of ritual and control, of familiarity and content.[38] Once accommodated, it is seen or even becomes a private space, an escape, a place for the personal sense of shared solitude.[39] It is there where one person can be the most 'one' self, with constant physical habits, unobserved and uncriticised by others, or else guarded against judgement by the anticipatory arrangements; the tidy room, the boundaries of welcome. The home is, in retrospect, the arrangements of the extent to which private meanings can become public, the creation not just of a physical but a personal entity.[40] The home, in the mind, stands for a paradigm of shared interests and meanings, a series of constructions of the world in which all members play a part. It seems to consist of a mixture of daily routines, a kind of regulatory pattern - what one eats for breakfast and how - and some highly symbolic moments, like family gatherings or occasions.[41] The home, in the imagination, symbolises the unity of the family, and the security of certainty.

For young children, the home is not like this. Whilst it contains other people, and whilst it is one amongst many to be compared with, the home is far more fraught. It does eventually become a symbol of refuge - but that is what it becomes in retrospect rather than in the early reality of experience. The home marks out the differences of person and place, of shared environments and the point of view. For children it is their siblings who symbolise the tensions of relationships within the home. Parents matter; their interest or indifference is the most essential influence. But they are, in a sense, apart. They are assumed to inhabit a different world. Parents matter, but a great deal of social interaction is learned from siblings; how to by-pass the authority of the older ones, and how to play games together. It is as if being placed in a particular environment with other people were enough in itself to cause difficulties. The fact that siblings so often develop poor relationships with each other is often commented upon. Friends, who can be chosen, are quite another matter. All the strains that friendship and enmities in the large sphere can evoke are placed firmly at the centre of the experience of home.

Sibling interactions provide one of the richest sources for the children's development of a theory of mind, including the uses and misuse of mistaken or false beliefs. The younger children learn a significant amount about social behaviour from[42] the older ones, and take on the shared familial influences that the oldest child so strongly demonstrates.[43] Differences of temperament or outlook are not enough in themselves to create tensions: these arise from the facts of learning, from the testing ground of living together, developing an independent point of view and the social mechanisms of survival. Being the eldest child carries certain privileges and responsibilities, but it does not prevent the similar fight for attention and personal autonomy. At the heart of the sense of 'rivalry' is the attitudes that children and their parents express towards each other, although the sense of the need for personal response is balanced by the observation of other siblings' social ingenuity.

> Sometimes it's just that, well, mum and dad are just saying to me 'go upstairs and play and don't come down'. Like, I never get a chance to go downstairs and see my dad when I come home from school. My mum says 'go upstairs and play'. But then my sister sneakily comes down and then I see she's just going down to talk to them, but then she ends up staying down and not me. Mum and Daddy say 'You should remember things and set an good example for your sister. She's four years younger than you'.
>
> I'm gonna have one child because if you have two then they might start arguing like me and Sarah do.   *(girl 8)*

Arguments abound. They can arise because of 'sneaky' behaviour or a sense of unfairness and injustice. But the tensions go deeper than that. The children all mention the centrality of arguments with their siblings, arguments over space and over toys, as well as the different privileges or expectations of behaviour according to age. They are all, at one level, jealous of each other, whatever their respective ages.

> And sometimes he climbs in mum and dad's bed when I don't want him to and I want to.   *(boy 6)*

Whatever the invocations to 'set a good example', the picture that children present of their homes is never that of peace and harmony. What they are most aware of is the arguing and the fighting, the difficulties of living together. It is as if the home were the first and most important experience of the gang or the group, constantly jostling for power and influence, learning how to avoid as well as create conflict. Children look for friendship outside the home rather than within as if they did not like having other people thrust upon them. The result is tales of fighting, whether with older or younger siblings.

> My brother punches me. He's fourteen. I sometimes beat him up. And he
> sometimes beats me up. Giving my chin kisses. He always just gives me chin
> kisses. He gets his chin and he scrapes it along my cheek.   *(boy 8)*

Whatever the curious form it takes, it seems that few older children can
resist teasing or hurting the younger ones, as if there were a malicious urge
that has to be expressed. Of course the boys and girls all talk of fighting
back; they do not like to see themselves as helpless victims. Indeed, many
of the incidents that children report are of being tormented by younger
siblings, being teased or punched, or having their possessions taken from
them. What we hear are accounts of many quarrels, of people being
'horrible' to each other. Some of the incidents are trivial, but they all give
the impression that the protagonists are all looking for an argument, or a
quarrel. It is like the testing grounds of friendship, the exploration of a
personal identity in a social setting, but one which contains almost the
desire for argument. Quarrels are a central part of the experience of home
life. It is difficult to isolate particular reasons beyond the central fact that
children are learning with difficulty to come to terms with the world and
with the circumstances in which they find themselves. Before they
articulate their resentment towards their parents they explore the tensions
of relationship that are founded on proximity rather than choice, on shared
circumstances rather than a sense of inclusion.

Arguments are about personal identity expressed through factors such
as space and possessions. They are like experiments in behaviour, to find
out what will happen. But they are also outpourings of inner tensions and
the nagging of discontent. Children have not yet learned how to contain or
modify their feelings and ideas, have not yet developed that bland and
deliberate thoughtlessness that can so easily become a modus vivendi.
Quarrelling sometimes seems like an extension of play, but it is also taken
very seriously. Whilst this aspect of their lives appears to seem inevitable,
they do not take it lightly. It has a strong emotional impact, like bullying.

> I've got a brother and sister who I quite get annoyed with. 'Cos they're
> annoying. They do things that annoy me and sometimes they boast a lot. When
> I'm annoyed with my brother and sister I get grumpy inside. When my brother
> gets annoyed, when I get annoyed with my brother and I get all grumpy, I
> don't like the way it makes me feel.   *(boy 8)*

Quarrels are the manifestation of underlying tensions. They cannot be isolated from the daily perceptions of unfairness and discrimination. The children could more easily have described their home lives as havens of peace and security: but it was the difficulties they wished to relate. They described their parents and what they did. And they described the jealousies and the rivalries which seemed to them to be at the heart of the reality of home. It is as if there were an atavistic exploration of personal rights.

The inner sources of the arguments and the more obvious physical grounds for them come together in the concern over space. There is no child who does not wish to have a sense of personal, exclusive space. Far more than the sharing of possessions or affections, the need to share space is at the heart of many difficulties. Having to share the same bedroom is associated with arguments; those who have to, hate it.

> I have to share a room with my sister. She's always talking in bed and when she makes a mess I have to clean it up. I would change my big sister. I want her to be older.   *(girl 8)*

Sharing is 'just trouble'. When the family paradigm is described as the sharing of constructs and expectations of the social world, we need to remind ourselves that it is also an example of the actual social world.[44] It is the first crucial experience of society. Sibling relationships, like those with parents, are described as being very intense to start with and then becoming easier.[45] But this is so simply because the children learn to explore the larger social world which becomes more significant for them. They create more mental as well as physical space for themselves. At the core of experience there hinges the essential struggle with the art of living together, of rubbing up against other people. Relationships are all important but they are also difficult. If this were not so children would not mention the quarrels, or the desire to find somewhere to be on their own. They would be concentrating on the means of gaining access to their parents, and on the shared pleasures of sibling friendship. But it is the tensions of proximity which prevail.

The social science of 'proxemics' deals with the ways in which people relate to each other physically. It explores the interaction between people, how close they get to each other, how much they touch and how distant they wish to be. It explores the behaviour of friends and of anonymous people behaving in particular ways in crowds. The study of the way masses of people behave has been long established, from observing spectators at football matches to the propaganda purposes of mass rallies. At the same time the psychological study of 'inner space' - individuality symbolically addressed in terms of physical closeness or distance - has gained currency in understanding the way in which people can feel about, and be observed to express, their identity in relation to others.

'Proxemics', like so many fields of observation, has, however, rarely been applied to children, although the subject could be deemed to be especially important in the way that children relate to each other in groups within the classroom and in games on the playground. With their need to adapt themselves to group behaviour, and to the demands of controlling many people in confined spaces, children learn rapidly about the dynamics of physical relationships. They are aware of how much space means to them, not just in terms of symbolic value but in actual physical consequences. One does not need to observe their behaviour with each other to notice how space, or lack of it, can be a point of confrontation. Can some children resist poking others when standing wedged in a queue? How much physical aggression manifested on the playground is due to overcrowding?

When children reflect on their feelings about the circumstances they live in, and their environment, it is soon apparent that having enough space to manoeuvre in is important for them. They talk about space within the home and outside it; they associate space with freedom. One of the points of argument they have with siblings is the tensions that can arise from having to share a room. There is no child who actually relishes sharing the same bedroom. The idea might be a novelty, as when a friend comes to stay, or in the fashionable 'sleepovers', but as an everyday reality it is a negative experience. The desire for space then symbolises one of the essential wishes that children share. What they do not like to share is not toys but room.

> I think I'd like to live in a house instead of a flat. 'Cos then you get your own room. I have to share a room with my sister.   *(boy 8)*

> If there was a big house - if we changed to go in a big house, probably I'd have a bedroom of my own. And my brother would probably be moved.   *(girl 7)*

This realisation of the importance of space is part of the analysis of their own circumstances and its comparison with other people. Just as the children have an objective as well as emotional view of their parents so they have a clear idea of the reality of their own circumstances, and the differences that money makes. They have to accept where they live but this does not mean they take it for granted. An accepted reality is not the same as an assumption of ontological content, a blissfully realised fantasy of perfection. Not only do children experience the complex social world of the home in terms of relationships but are both aware of, and influenced by, the physical and symbolic presence; space as place. Many express the limitations of where they live, the immediate environment, or the size of the house or flat. It could be otherwise. Having a room of their own is just one stage in wishing for something other.

> My brother's friend's house, well, it's a big house and it's really good fun. It's good for playing lots of different games 'cos it's very big. I'd like a house because we just live in a flat. 'Cos you get more space to play in. *(boy 8)*

> If my dad had enough money to buy a different home, to buy a bigger home. 'Cos we've got a very small house. *(girl 8)*

Whatever the circumstances in which they live all children express their appreciation of space. This includes the size of house, and the extent of garden. It promotes an idea of the countryside as a symbol of bliss. In the contrast between the rich and poor which marks the edges of their social understanding, palpable wealth is expressed not must in the flaunting of possessions but in the freedom to move. The fantasy of possible perfection is early on expressed as a kind of suburban idyll; of a rose-encrusted cottage (but a substantial one) somewhere out in the country (but not too far from the shops and school) with fields and gardens in which to play (but without too many threatening woods).[46] There might be a hint of the culturally absurd, as if children had taken on the shared fantasies of the collective adult dream, but this clearly expressed set of symbolic preferences arises from a strong desire to find space of their own. They want freedom to manoeuvre, to choose when to be with others, to avoid being crowded in, having people forced upon them in the narrow confines of the corridor. The sense of space - the dislike of playgrounds and certain corners of the school - is felt strongly because of the association with threat, a threat that arises from proximity to other people.[47] The value given to large gardens and the countryside is that of freedom, a sense of the personal identity being unthreatened by others.

The reality, of course, is that they cannot escape from other people. Nor do children simply fantasise about the countryside. They have a pragmatic sense of the pleasures of space, and if it is provided by the social services in the forms of parks and playgrounds, it is appreciated as a utility where they can ride bikes or kick a ball. Space has real value. But whilst children see their own inner and exclusive space as liberating them from the confinements of arguments and the proximity of quarrels, they also attach cultural and aesthetic value to it. Space is a factor that separates the contented from the discontented, but it is also a contrast to the strong sense of urban deprivation. The objective scrutiny of the home sees comparisons, and possibilities, alternatives as well as difficulties.

Relationships within the home are very important. Whilst it is the difficulties with siblings that are to the fore, the way in which each of them relates to the parents is crucial in terms of the style of dialogue and the amount of attention. This varies a great deal. Some relate how well they get on with their parents - some praise the style of parenting, pointing out that they are taken to see interesting things. Others are far more aware of their parents' self-absorption, in the activities which do not include anyone else. In either case parents are acknowledged to be important, whether they argue or yell at the children or whether they are a sense of security.

> I like the things around me. Well, the ones I especially like are my Mum and Dad and the house around me.
> *(boy 8)*

But parents are equally important to those who live with either one or the other. The sense that in an ideal world the family would stay together is very strong; even in the face of the realities of argument. Quarrelling with siblings is a personalising of the arguments that attend their parents. The crucial desire is for a continuing personal relationship. When parents quarrel they are absorbed in themselves.

Parents, whatever the circumstances, are a part of the reality of the environment, a substantial fact, an entity as well as relationship. They are the cause: they are the reason why children are as they are.

'Cos most Mums and Dads you just have a white Mum and Dad rather than brown and white. Well, it feels funny, 'cos you know my mum has straight hair and I keep asking her, why can't I, why haven't I got straight hair? Well, my Dad's you know has those fuzzy hairs ... *(girl 7)*

She wishes she were different, but she also understands the simplicities that cause her to be who she is. It's like talking about having 'Greek' or 'American blood', like unknown fathers in the past. Their families are seen leading their own lives, and described as having particular activities and interests, whether writing or painting, or cooking in a restaurant or emptying bins. They are both an important part of the 'things around me' and people leading their own separate lives, their attention directed elsewhere. The simple facts of divorce, as a common experience are related with the consequent feelings.

I like seeing my Dad a lot. Sad going home from my Dad's to go back to my Mum's. Because my Dad normally takes me out swimming and he buys me a present and stuff like that when I'm over there 'cos I go over there for a weekend. And on Sunday I have to back to my Mum's and I don't really want to go back 'cos I want to stay at my Dad's and my Dad has a dog. *(girl 8)*

As with the 'things around me', the circumstances - swimming, presents and a dog - are seen as important. They actually express in physical terms what is perceived as a personal interest. For when there is no clear relationship then that is made very clear. Many children complain that their parents seem more interested in watching television than talking to them. Very few say that they have conversations about important matters with their parents. The field of argument seems to be over behaviour rather than ideas: which TV channel to watch rather than a discussion of the programme. The glimpses we have of the home is of 'the just watches the news all the time and the weather' and of arguments over behaviour.

At least arguments show a certain kind of attention. What is most feared is indifference. When adults look back on their early experience of the home one of the two most searing of memories is the lack of dialogue, the lack of any personal interest.[48] The sense of being neglected, of being excluded, of being marginalised, is as profound as the witnessing of and suffering from personal violence. The lack of relationship leads to a lack of a sense of self-worth, of an epistemological base. Having food provided, or being spoiled, is not enough. It is the lack of caring, not physical but intellectual, that stays in the mind.

'Parents don't care about them so they don't have a care about anyone else.'[49] This summarises both the sense of what is missing and the fact that children assume that the limitations of the parents will inevitably be visited on their offspring. This recognition that what parents do affects children is one that is made very early. It is not only with hindsight that the significance of parenting is understood. Even whilst they are observing their own parents children analyse the effects they have. Whilst they might not describe the exact influence on themselves they are aware of the general effects of parents. They all know the importance of parental behaviour.

> Like if some parents beat up their kids it could change their life, make them wanna hit people ... if their parents make them goody goodies, when they grow older they'll get fed up with being goody goodies.   *(boy 10)*

This encapsulates a commonly held analysis of the difficulties of parenting, of maintaining the balance between kindness and discipline. Both violence and the laissez faire of over indulgence are signs of a lack of control, of neglect. Children subsequently deeply resent the indifference that signifies a lack of discipline. At the time it might appear to be something to be treasured - to be allowed to run wild, to stay out late, to do what they want. But even at the time children realise that they actually need and want rules, and that their absence is not so much a sign of parental indulgence as a sign of neglect.

> I'd say I was neglected a bit y'know when I was younger. I was neglected. I wasn't bothered about it, you know. I could do what I wanted and that. Maybe some kids would have thought this was great but after like a couple of years ... I guess I was used to it. Neglect, some one who's not warned about, nor cared about, nor given love and stuff like that and support.[50]

What appears at first as 'great', a freedom to indulge, soon becomes habitual and recognised as neglect. Lack of discipline is seen as indifference rather than kindness. Children learn from their relationships with parents and from observing the behaviour of parents. They see the habits as well as the physical attributes being handed down to them. There is therefore both a strong sense of personal autonomy and a desire for some kind of authority from the parent. This is no simple dependency. The idea that parents have complete control, if it was ever so, is one that is superceded by the understanding of far more negotiation. The shift of emphasis to children's rights comes about partly because of a growing recognition of their intelligence, however slowly this recognition seems to surface, and partly because of the communications systems which bring the world of international events so strongly into their presence. We cannot pretend that children escape it. We cannot try to disguise the reality in a packaging of sentiment. Thus children are citizens with a voice of their own.[51] But they still need the guidance of others, and they know this. They might have the 'Allmacht des Gedankens' but they need the assurance of the reality of adults.[52]

The legitimacy of authority is an instinctive part of the mental needs of children. They might not be born 'good' but they have a strong urge to become so. They therefore expect their parents to exert that discipline which derives from legitimate authority; it is the children's wish that this should be so and not a dogmatic parental self-assertion imposed on unwilling infants. The only mitigation of conflicts lies in the recognition of rules, of shared disciplines. This is learned early rather than only slowly unfolded before their minds.[53] There is an early recognition not only that there is a system which operates across different circumstances but that there is a need for a system. Authority might be challenged, or might be negotiated with, but it is a necessity.[54] Its absence is neglect.

The respect which children have for adults, and their parallel criticism, develops very early, and, indeed, increases with age rather than diminishes. Far from the picture of Piaget and Kohlberg which depicts children reacting intuitively to enforced disciplines to which they submit, before starting to think for themselves, they grow into the stronger realisation that authority, properly wielded, is a necessity.[55] They respect the attention. Far from progressing from a morality of adults' constraint towards a more mutual respect which is engendered amongst peers, children grow into an increasing conviction about the necessity of authority and they fear its absence. Those parents who set high standards of expectation and who within that framework encourage the exercise of autonomous judgement remain the type of influence which children seek. What children fear (and later resent) is parental self-absorption, an absence of dialogue, is lack of energetic attention. They can detect, very clearly, when there is no boundary between different types of behaviour, and when there are no rational emotional grounds for the consequences of moods.

> I had a really big fight with my Dad. I kicked my sister in the eye. Me and my brother got told off and my Dad didn't. And he pushed me. He was chasing after me. It was quite funny when I beat up my Dad. But sometimes we only play fights. I smack him round the face and he says 'Don't do that'. Then I grab his feet and then my brother pushes him and then he falls over. And my brother who is sixteen came over. He got beaten up. He got squashed and my Dad ... quite funny. 'Cos if I did have a day at work, and I have a bad day, like my Dad did; he got annoyed with all of us. Even when we didn't do nothing. He got fed up at work and that was all.   *(boy 8)*

Adults are seen as unpredictable, driven by moods, by irrational behaviour, as being not quite in control. Where does the boundary lie between what is acceptable and what is not? What is the distinction between playing and fighting? What is the meaning of the word 'funny'? As in the complex zone of playing and fighting that surrounds the world of bullying, so there is an imprecision of expectation, a condition of arbitrariness and contradiction in which the adult plays the role of another child. Who should have been told off? Sometimes they only 'play' fights. And the rest of the time? The actions are as unpredictable as the moods.

When there is a lack of certainty, or the predictability of authority, then the consequences on the children can be deep and long lasting. They themselves know that they will take on the attitudes and the characteristics of their parents. This can be for harm as well as for good. That uncertain zone of what is false or true, playing or fighting, talking or lying makes a deep moral scar in the minds of children, and emerges in a predictable way.

> They say 'I can't afford it', and things. And sometimes I think they're lying or something. And sometimes they're not and stuff like that. Some people like hurt me, like my Dad sometimes and um, or smacks me. So I get really mad so I do to do things and kick them. Sometimes I used to steal as well, so he used to say 'come on, let's have my money back.' And sometimes he used to take, I had loads of pens and stuff and he used to say 'where's all my money?'. I said 'I can't give you the money back' so he took all my money and I said 'Hey, I only took a few of your money. All that's mine, about that much.' And I only took about one pound fifty, ninety five p. from him, and all the rest was mine. And he wouldn't believe me, so he took all the rest of mine.   *(boy 8)*

Once the boundaries of rules and authority are broken down, then the ambiguities of behaviour are relished. Here is an example of the truth being even more obscure, until all is reduced to personal opinion and personal assertion. Whatever the parents say or do is not believed in. They are called liars and they accuse the father of lying in his turn. That sense of moral security has gone, as if he were conniving in his son's stealing but only quibbling about how much was stolen and from where. This child even recognises that his parents sometimes tell the truth. But that is as unpredictable as his physical reactions. Ambiguity does violence to the mind.

These are glimpses of parents out of control, abandoning the intellectual discipline of concern. They still have relationships with the children; but these are physical rather than mental, matters of argument and assertiveness rather than a shared vision and understanding. The extremes of bad parenting - violence and indifference - show up what good parenting means, what children feel is necessary. The saddest fact of all is that children know that their parents' behaviours carry consequences. As the parents behave, so will the children.

> There used to be lots of arguments in our house. It used to get to me a lot. I didn't like it and I used to start crying and getting all frustrated and then I'd start smashing things up and things like that. 'Cos I couldn't stand me mum and dad arguing you see. I hated it. Me dad used to get up and start arguing with me mum and then they'd start fighting in front of me, and I'd sort of get brought into it and then me dad used to hit me and then me mum would start and Oh God ....[56]

This too, is the experience of childhood. No-one is a passive witness. What is heard is remembered, what is seen leaves a deep impression. But the crucial point - and there are many examples of this extreme - lies in the consequences. The violence that is described does not just damage the victims, does not only sear the minds of the children but is then emulated. With the dispassionate clarity of hindsight, the effects of parents are the most clearly delineated at the most extreme of their outcomes. The desire to be noticed, to have some attention, when the parents are utterly absorbed in their own violent feelings means that anything will be done to gain some response; to a terrible end. What they see enacted they become part of. What they witness they emulate.

He used to beat up me mum and that ... His other woman, got married to her and he's not long beat her up as well ... so like he gave her, mum, a good hiding, over a stupid reason, give her a good hiding. I've been brought up to see me dad hitting me mum and seeing me dad hitting other people.[57]

The consequence of this is clear. The same aggression, the same indifference is inflicted on their children. They know the harm, and yet they emulate it. It is as if the influence were as deep and impermeable as a coastal shelf.

Seeing the inarticulacy of violence is but the extreme end of indifference and neglect. What we see however is the consequence of such witnessing, not only the effect of parenting upon the children but their understanding of its effects. What children desire is that balance of authority and interest, that ability to make a relationship that is based on mutual shared interest and curiosity. Children are not mere appendages who take on and emulate the personalities of their parents: they do not grow into criminals because of genetic inheritance. They learn by what they see. The personality remains their own, but in that early rapid and demanding enculturalisation they learn not only how others deal with the world but how to deal with it themselves. They are aware of what they would like to see: but they also know how deeply the example affects them. Knowing about it is not the same as being able to act upon that knowledge. The frustration lies in the fact that children know what they want to find, and are aware of what ought to be, but are still in a sense helpless in the consequences of other people's actions. Knowledge, which is instinctive, needs to be bolstered by example and action. When this does not happen, the children, with their remaining objectivity growing into adulthood, learn the pain of hindsight. This is a peculiar form of hindsight, learned at the time and stored in the mind. No wonder it needs such unravelling for so many.

Children do know the general ground rules of behaviour, of what ought to be the balance between support and command. Too lax a regime or too rigid a one: both are the pathological extremes of indifference and self absorption expressed in different ways by parents. But they are extreme manifestations of the same thing; a lack of interest in the individuality of the child trying to come to terms with the circumstances of the world. What is sought is the delicate balance of curiosity and firmness.

My Mum lets me decide what to do. She doesn't just go off and say 'Oh you're doing this'. Like, say I was a bit older, some parents say - 'You're going to college and that's that.' And Mum lets me choose whether I, well, she said she'd let me choose whether I'll go to college or not. But I want to go to University and Mum says that's right.   *(girl 8)*

The central realisation is encouragement rather than forcing: it is not will imposed but autonomy recognised. There is no doubt what the parents' wishes are but they have clearly made the individual feel that her own rights are intact. She does not feel she is only a consequence of parents' wishes. The career choices that children make are very much a result of their parents' attitudes towards them, not in terms of the exact career that is foreseen for them, like a son taking over a firm - but in the attitudes towards work and fulfilment.[58] At one end of the spectrum is the fear of being told, assertively, that you *will* do that. At the other end is the sense of the parents not being 'bothered'. What children as individuals seek is that balance of interest and concern, of a point of view which believes and encourages, and an acceptance that each person will find his or her own way.

Like they're not forcing me to do something I don't want to do. But they just try to push me in directions, like they do.   *(girl 15)*

Children see clearly the motivations and the personal lives of their parents. This objectivity does not undermine the consequences. On the contrary it makes the effects the more intense. For whilst they might react against the 'come-on' syndrome, the parental desire to fulfil themselves in their children, they are affected by it nevertheless.[59] The quality of the parents' relationship has a subtle but potent effect; the absence of conflict and the ability to communicate with each other means that the child can be recognised as a valuable individual human being.[60] This does not mean that parents do not have interests outside their children. It means that parents, too, are complete in their own interests, complete enough to share them, to pass them on, certain enough to look beyond themselves. It means having something to share, not just behaviour but ideas. The personality of the child remains what it is, but the intellectual fulfilment depends upon the family environment.[61]

Children are constantly observing and monitoring parental relationships. Whilst they battle with their siblings they are also seeing the ways in which parents are able to negotiate and understand, and the ways in which they share interests. There are definite rules which children recognise. One is the extent of conflict, of implacable and inarticulate enmity.[62] Another is the sense of a complete abrogation of the self towards an acceptance of the dogmatic obedience to some other inexpressible will.[63] Both leave out the autonomy of the child. One is the completely liberal and the other the illiberal. Both are exclusive of the personal.

We constantly see signs of the tension between the controlling and the laissez faire, the desire to mould the child and the desire to leave it entirely free.[64] Neither extreme is successful. Knowing this makes parenting a subtle art, but one that can be learned. It can clearly be done well or badly - and children recognise this.[65] What is delineated through research is already perceived by children. There is a need for the consensus of authority and involvement, that disinterested and firm concern for the individual.[66] The human experience is a very fragile one, given the measure of the middle ground between the shared humanity and the uniqueness of the individual. But its very fragility means that all the problems that we see can be understood and can be dealt with, if there is a will. Parenting can be learned. Children know that. They realise that outside or beyond the personal and the genetic ties are rules of behaviour that help or hinder.[67] Not for a moment does this diminish the uniqueness of the individual. It essentially prevents the unique individual self-consciously failing the test of being fully human.

Those who have suffered bad parenting seek outside help, a large community of understanding.[68] They also realise, with a sense of helplessness, that what they will have learned from their parents will be passed on to the next generation. This, again, seems like something inevitable, but it is also emphatically unnecessary. But one of the curious characteristics of human beings is their ability to know but not to learn, to be aware, as children are, of fundamental truths, and then to ignore them. What is known in theory is not often practised in fact.

Notes

1. See Cullingford, C. *The Nature of learning*. London, Cassell, 1990.

2. Larkin, P.   "Man hands on Misery to Man.
    It deepens like a coastal shelf.
    So get all the advice you can
    And don't have any kids yourself."

"This be the verse." *High Windows*. It is noteworthy that this is one of the most popular twentieth century poems.

3. Spock, B. Baby and Child Care. London, Bodley, 1979.

4. Bettelheim, B. *The Good Enough Parent: The Guide to Bringing Up your Child*. London, Thames and Hudson, 1987.

5. Rickman, N; Stevenson, J and Graham, P. *Pre-School to School: A behavioural study*. London, Academic Press, 1982.

6. Baumrind, D. The Average Expectable Environment is Not Good Enough. *Child Development*, Vol.64, 1299-1317, 1993.

7. Furman, W and Buhrmester, D. Age and Sex Differences in Perceptions of Networks of Personal Relationships. *Child Development*, Vol.63, No.1, pp.103-115, 1992.

8. Dunn, J. *The Beginnings of Social Understanding*. Oxford, Basil Blackwell, 1988.

9. Ibid. p.65.

10. Berelson, B and Steiner, G. *Human Behaviour: An Inventory of Scientific Findings*. New York, Harcourt Brace, 1964.

11. Bettelheim, B. *The Children of the Dream: Communal Child-Rearing and the Implication for Society*. London, Paladin, 1971.
    Berne, E. *Games People Play: The psychology of Human Relationships*. London: André Deutsch. 1968.

12. Bowlby, J. *Child Care and the Growth of Love.* Harmondsworth, Penguin, 1964.

13. Harwood, R; Miller, J and Crizarry, N. *Culture and Attachment: Perceptions of the Child in Context.* New York, The Guilford Press, 1995.

14. Between Puerto Rico and the United States of America.

15. Cassidy, J and Asher, S. Loneliness and Peer Relations in Young Children. *Child Development,* Vol.63, No.2, pp.350-365, 1992.

16. Cassidy, J and Berlin, L. The Insecure/Ambivalent Pattern of Attachment; Theory and Research. *Child Development,* Vol.65, No.4, pp.971-991, 1994.

17. Baumrind, D. Current Patterns of Parental Authority. *Developmental Psychology Monographs,* Vol.4, No.2, 1971.

18. The ABX theory. Newcomb, see ref 64.

19. du Bois Reymond, M; Büchner, P and Krüger, H. Modern Family as Everyday Negotiation: Continuities and Discontinuities in parent-child relationships. *Childhood,* Vol.2, pp.87-99,1993.

20. Cassidy, J and Berlin, L. Op cit. 1994.

21. Barber, B; Olsen, J and Shagle, S. Associations between Parental Psychological and Behavioural Control and Youth Internalized and Externalized Behaviour. *Child Development,* Vol.65, No.4, pp.1120-1136, 1994.

22. Poulin-Dubois, D and Shultz, T. The Development of the Understanding of Human Behaviour: From Agency to Intentionality, in Ashington, J; Harris, P and Olsen, D (eds.). *Developing Theories of Mind.* Cambridge UP, pp.109-125, 1988.

23. In Brobdingnag when he is surrounded by giants whose physical features (and imperfections) are magnified.

24. Richman, N et al., op cit.

25. Donaldson, M. *Children's Minds*. London, Croom Helm, 1978.

26. Heath, S. *Ways with Words: Language, Life and Work in Communities and Classrooms*. Cambridge University Press, 1983.

27. Female. 21.

28. Trevarthen, C. Communication and co-operation in Early Infancy: A description of primary intersubjectivity, in Bullowa, M (ed.). *Before Speech: The Beginnings of Human Communication*. Cambridge University Press, 1978.

29. Flavell, J; Mumme, D; Green, F and Flavell, F. Young Children's Understanding of Different Types of Beliefs. *Child Development*, Vol.63, No.4, pp.960-977, 1992.

30. Flavell, J; Flavell, F; Green, F and Moses, L. Young Children's Understanding of Fact Beliefs versus Value Beliefs. *Child Development*, Vol.61, No.4, pp.915-928, 1990.

31. Moses, L and Flavell, J. Inferring False Beliefs from Actions and Reactions. *Child Development*, Vol.61, No.4, pp.929-945, 1990.

32. Gopnik, A and Astington, Y. Children's Understanding of Representational Change and its relation to the Understanding of False Belief and the appearance/reality divide. *Child Development*, Vol.59, No.1, pp.26-37, 1988.

33. Perner, J. 1987.
Wellman, H. *The Child's Theory of Mind*. Boston, MIT Press, 1990.

Lewis, C and Osborne, A. Three Year Old's Problems with False Belief: Conceptual Deficit or Linguistic Artefact? *Child Development*, Vol.61, No.5, pp.1514-1519, 1990.

34. Beal, C. Children's Knowledge about Representations of Intended Meaning in Ashington et al., op cit., pp.315-325.

35. Goodman, N. *Of Mind and others Matters* Cambridge MA, Harvard University Press, 1984.

36. Murray, L and Trevarthen, C. The Infant's role in Mother-Infant Communications. *Journal of Child Language*, Vol.13, No.1, pp.15-29, 1986.

37. Adler.

38. Seaman, D. *A Geography of the Life World*. London, Croom Helm, 1979.

39. Sixsmith, J and Sixsmith A. Place in Transition: The Impact of Life Events on the Experience of Home, in Putnam, T and Newton, C (eds.). *Household Choices*. London, Futures Publications, pp.20-34, 1990.

40. Mason, J. Reconstructing the Public and the Private: The Home and Marriage in Later Life, in Allen, G and Crow, G (eds.) *Home and Family: Creating the Domestic Sphere*. London, MacMillan, pp.102-121, 1989.

41. Reise. 1987.

42. Perner, J; Ruffman, T and Leekan, S. Theory of Mind is Contagious: You catch it from your sibs. *Child Development*, Vol.65, No.4, pp.1228-1238, 1994.

43. Rowe, D; Rodgers, J and Meseek-Buskey, S. Sibling Delinquency and Family Environment: Shared and Unshared Influence. *Child Development*, Vol.63, No.1, pp.59-67, 1992.

44. Reiss, D. *The Family's Construction of Reality*. Cambridge MA, Harvard University Press, 1981.

45. Furman, N; Buhmeister, D op cit., 1992.

46. cf. Hart R. *Children's Experience of Place*. New York, Irvington, 1979.

47. Titman, N. *Special Places; Special People. The Hidden Curriculum of School Grounds*. Godalming, World Wildlife Fund, 1994.
    Boulton, M. Proximate Causes of Aggressive Fighting in Middle School Children. British Journal of Educational Psychology, Vol.63, No.2, pp.231-244, 1993.
    Cullingford, C. *The Inner World of the School*. London, Cassell, 1991.

48. Cullingford, C. *The Causes of Criminality*. Forthcoming.

49. Male. 19.

50. Female. 21.

51. du Bois Reymond, M; Dickstra, R; Hurrelmann, K and Peters E. *Childhood and Youth in Germany and the Netherlands: Transitions and Coping Strategies of Adolescents*. Berlin, Walter de Gruyter, 1995.

52. Allmacht des Gedankens. The free power of thought.

53. Damon, W. *The Social World of the Child*. San Francisco, Josey Bass, 1977.

54. Turiel, E. The Development of Social-Conventional and Moral Concepts. In Windmuller, M; Lambert, N and Turiel, E. *Moral Development and Socialization*. Boston, Allyn and Boston, 1980.

55. Siegal, M. *Fairness in Children: A Social-cognitive approach to the study of moral development*. London, Academic Press, 1982.

56. Female. 21.

57. Male. 21.

58. cf. Dickens's *Dombey and Son*.

59. Bettelheim, B and Rosenfeld, A. *The Art of the Obvious*. London, Thames and Hudson, 1993.

60. Howe, P and Markman, J. *Marital Quality and Child Functioning: A Longitudinal Investigation. Child Development*, Vol.60, No.5, pp.1044-1051, 1989.

61. Lynn, R; Hampson, S. and Agaki, E. Genetic and Environmental Mechanisms determining Intelligence, Neuroticism, Extraversion and Psychoticism: An analysis of Irish siblings. *British Journal of Psychology*, Vol.80, No.4, pp.499-507, 1989.

62. Grych, J; Seid, M and Fincham, F. Assessing marital Conflict from the Child's Perspective: The Children's perception of Interpersonal Conflict Scale. *Child Development*, Vol.63, No.3, pp.558-572, 1992.

63. Benett, Y. Reflections on Cross-Cultural Familiar Antecedents of Dogmatism. *International Conference on Authoritarianism and Dogmatism*. State University of New York, Potsdam, 1984.

64. Newcomb, T. An approach to the study of Communication Acts. *Psychological Review*, Vol.60, pp.393-404, 1953.

65. Pugh, G; De'Ath, E and Smith, C. *Confident parents, Confident Children: Policy and Practice in Parent Education and Support*. London, National Children's Bureau, 1994.

66. Steinberg, L; Lamborn, S; Darling, N; Mounts, N and Dornbusch, S. Over-time Changes in adjustment and competence among Adolescents from Authoritative, Authoritarian, Indulgent and Neglectful Families. *Child Development*, Vol.65, No.3, pp.754-770.

Steinberg, L; Lamborn, S; Dornbusch, S and Darling, N. Impact of Parenting Practices on Adolescent Achievement: Authoritative Parenting, School Involvement and Encouragement. *Child Development*, Vol.63, No.5, pp.1266-1281, 1992.

67. Seitz, V and Apfel, N. Parent-focused Intervention: Diffusion Effects on Siblings. *Child Development*, Vol.65, No.2, pp.677-683, 1994.

68. Hashima, P and Ainato, P. Poverty, Social Support and Parental Behaviour. *Child Development*, Vol.65, No.2, pp.394-403, 1994.

6 'Lives of quiet desperation?' The world of the school

The family is in itself a microcosm of society. That is how it is from the point of view of young children. It contains all the important elements: rules and authority, individual rights and points of view, harmony and disagreement. It reveals the importance of relationships, and the centrality of dialogue so that individuals can learn how to work in harmony with each other through desire rather than coercion. Parents are experienced not as emotional blankets but as individuals with ideas, and moods, of their own. They represent larger society. They have pasts as well as presents. They go out to earn money. They are invested with the rights of authority. They are also needed as people to explain the bigger world in which children know they will be required to play a part, and from which, even in the earliest years, there is no hiding.

The relationship that children have with their parents is not simply a personal understanding out of context. There are no such things as individuals isolated from society. The dialogue that children need with their parents is not just a pragmatic one of every day decisions: when to get up, what to eat and which television programme to choose. The discourse is about other things, about experiences and opinions, about ideas and about other people. It is when this is lacking - when the only sharing of experience is in watching the same screen - that children have difficulties. They notice how often they talk with their parents. They are aware of when their parents have things to say. They also understand when they are being ignored. Dialogue is not just a matter of a relationship. It is about how two people relate to a third subject. It has to be *about* something other than the two people together.

The expression of an opinion or an idea, and the sharing of information, is what distinguishes the quality of good parenting. This dialogue connects the child to the world outside the home. It shows that there are further relationships to be made. Instead of seeing a world intrude solely through the news or television, or the unexplained experiences of streets, children require a sense in which all must be understood even if not all is all explained. Parents cannot, of course, explain everything but they can demonstrate that they have the willingness to try, or the potential to think about anything which is inexplicable. When children rely on their parents for emotional support they see this not just in terms of physical warmth but in possessing a point of view and enough curiosity to want to communicate that point of view. Understanding society as a whole and in all its manifestations derives, for good or bad, from the parents' ability, or inability, to make some kind of analysis of it. What children will learn, however inarticulate their parents, is the attitude they take; whether this be suspicion of a sense of exclusion, whether it be bitterness and anger, or hope and belief. The faintest nuance of an attitude will be comprehended by children even if it is unexplained.

The expression of an opinion or an idea, and the sharing of information, is what distinguishes the quality of good parenting. This dialogue connects the child to the world outside the home. It shows that there are further relationships to be made. Instead of seeing a world intrude solely through the news or television, or the unexplained experiences of streets, children require a sense in which all must be understood even if not all is all explained. Parents cannot, of course, explain everything but they can demonstrate that they have the willingness to try, or the potential to think about anything which is inexplicable. When children rely on their parents for emotional support they see this not just in terms of physical warmth but in possessing a point of view and enough curiosity to want to communicate that point of view. Understanding society as a whole and in all its manifestations derives, for good or bad, from the parents' ability, or inability, to make some kind of analysis of it. What children will learn, however inarticulate their parents, is the attitude they take; whether this be suspicion of a sense of exclusion, whether it be bitterness and anger, or hope and belief. The faintest nuance of an attitude will be comprehended by children even if it is unexplained.

One of the most important subjects of a dialogue on which parents will have a point of view is the school. This is probably the most important of all social experiences. Children will have met others, and perhaps gone to play-schools and toddler groups. They will have experienced the problems and pleasures associated with playing with other children, with sharing or the refusal to share, with humour and argument. They will also be aware of rules and authority. But schooling is their first significant experience of the workings of society as a whole. Whilst some aspects are exaggerated, the essentials of human behaviour in large crowds are clearly apparent. There are hierarchies of power that seem simple but are in fact very complicated, highly structured but liable to manipulation. There are rules, agreed as necessary but not always carried out or obeyed. There are tensions between small groups and large, between the influence of the individual and the sway of the crowd. There are many signs of chaos as well as organisation, of tedium as well as shared excitement, of justice and injustice, of crime and punishment.

Parents will have experienced schools themselves and will have very clear attitudes towards their experience. This will affect their response to their children's approach to schools. If parents are a microcosm of social arrangements and schools are a public manifestation both of the organisation of groups and the general consensus of what is required of children, it is important that there is some correlation and understanding between the two. When children talk about their futures and their potential careers they are aware of the significance of their parents' thinking. They want to be encouraged and supported in their own ambitions, but they do not want their parents just to say 'whatever happens it will be alright, dear' since this can be a sign of indifference. Children wish to see their parents show a concern for their future, to have ideas, but they do not want their parents to stifle them with their own ambitions. That quality of disinterested concern is a balance of belief and hope.[1] What their children do in school and how well they do should be a central interest.

When parents are out of harmony with the school or with the schooling system this causes a major disruption to children's lives. The lack of connection can happen at two levels; in the degree of actual interest and in the awareness of what the school demands. At one level it is a matter of attitude. At the other it is a matter of discourse.

The implicit or explicit lack of interest in school and all that school represents is a strong influence on children, however easy seems their first transitions into the nursery or reception class. They can learn to adapt to the new demands made on them by the teacher and the ancillary, but they might not yet know what the purpose is. Just as having learned to share books and read at home gives them a significant and long lasting beginning to their academic careers, so does an understanding of why they go to school, not as an alien necessity, but as a route which the parents believe in. Sharing stories and picture books and the idea of reading is just that kind of activity - discussion about something else - that gives children the sense that it is possible to relate to and understand a world outside the confines of the home, a world imagined but more significantly a world on which all imagination rests: every day reality.

When parents have themselves felt alienated from school or when they actually say it is a 'waste of time', children bring with them a strong sense of social disharmony, of disjunction. Schools are difficult enough in themselves and the rites of passage they represent are never easy. But these experiences are almost impossible if they are seen as at best a social no-man's land and at worst enemy territory. Those young people whose experiences have ended them in prison experienced not only their own sense of being excluded but saw their parents caught up in the violent emotional clashes between the school as a system, with its own clear demands, and the desire of the individual to go his or her own way. Seeing their parents argue with the School was as clear an indication of the 'otherness', the exclusivity of the school, as indifference.

> They didn't want me to go to that school. Me mum went to see the headmaster, but me mum didn't know sort of what to do, d'you know what I mean? She was a bit sort of confused.
>
> Me dad used to come to me in the morning ... and I'd lay there and pretend I couldn't hear him ... he used to shout in me earholes and I used to pretend I was asleep.[2]

No real effort is made to do more than shout. But even that bears little conviction from parents who do not really like the school and who feel confused with the system.

There is mounting pressure on schools to exclude children.[3] It is not in their best interests to deal with problematic pupils, but the reasons that some pupils are difficult starts in the home. The analysis of two contrasting and disfunctioning social groups reveals this lack of academic support.

> She was only a cleaner in the school. But every time we used to go home at night she used to get dragged in the office and told about me. They didn't like it ... they hated it always having to go into the office to see about me.[4]

The lack of shared expectations is demonstrated by the tendency to blame each other; the school is aware of the home background, and lays the blame for disruption on it, and the parents see bad behaviour as the school's fault. The sense of exclusion is not just felt by the individual pupil but involves the 'other' smaller society of the home. It is as if two social systems were in battle.

> My mum didn't go up for three months ... She says tough. Like when she did go up, teacher slammed his hand on table and treated her like a kid, so she stood up and give him a mouthful, started accusing him of this, that and t'other and I never went back to school then. Dad just stood there and laughed.[5]

Once the communication between the authority of the system, as represented by the teacher, and the now alternative worlds of home and street breaks down, then the only place that the individual feels he or she belongs is where they are not threatened by discipline - the very discipline they subsequently realise is for their own good. The school is, after all, not seen as a community but as a system, one which needs to put its own interests first. The creation of league tables gives more and more substance to the school not seeing individual difficulties as a necessary part of its brief but as an undermining of the success rate on which it is increasingly judged. It is therefore no surprise that the dislike between the parents of disruptive pupils and the schools is mutual. To the pupil it is as if no 'system', no group of people in the sense of a working community, has any abiding interest in them. The lack of dialogue, the lack of concern is reflected not only in the parent but mirrored in the school.

> They says we don't want you back and slammed the 'phone down ... well, they didn't even bother trying to find a new school. 'Cos I mean it's up to them to sort another school out for you ... all the rest of the schools refused.[6]

The problem for these young people is that 'they' can refer to almost anyone in authority. Sometimes it is their parents, and at other times the teachers. 'They' can quickly turn into social workers and the police. But what has been established much earlier is the indifference. 'They' don't want you ... 'they' don't even bother trying. This is the outcome of a lack of concern. It arises from the lack of true belief that they have any part in the regular social 'system'.

The word 'system' is important, for that is how it appears to young children - not just those who find themselves excluded from it. Social relations are not just cosy, or a matter of negotiation between peers. They are formally organised, and are conducted through agreed rules and procedures. There are dichotomies within every system but the most telling ones are those between two 'systems', like that of home and school. The home consists of many negotiations not always articulated but when there is a disharmony between the outlook of parents and others then the individual pupil tends to reject both, or use both for his or her own purpose. A clash does not produce a choice between one or the other. It might seem that the school's rejection leads to the safety of the return to the family - but this is never enough in itself. Each individual needs some kind of society, regular social regulations and expectations. When the parents' attitudes make it clear that they are not in harmony with the ethos of the school, then some form of society is sought elsewhere.

Parents who are out of emotional sympathy with the way in which schools operate, feeling the weight of academic superciliousness and the barbs of impatience, might nevertheless still wish to 'push' their children. They want them to do well, and might keep on saying that they *ought* to gain qualifications. But this is seen by children not as belief in them but as an emotional force that has far more to do with their parents weight of emotion than their own. It is an expression of their parents ambitions, a desire not to make the same mistakes that they did, or to achieve something in which they can rejoice through their children's success.[7] Such a concern is seen for what it is; the desire to self-fulfilment by one person burdening another. Parents are usually aware of the importance of the role they play, but this does not prevent the influence of their own personal motivations.

The parents who have a real interest in the development of their children strike a delicate emotional balance between concern and pleasure. What really matters for the children, however, goes beyond the attitudes. The harmony between home and school which is so important to children lies not only in attitude but in dialogue. The smooth transition from home to school depends on the uses of language, on the intellectual stimulation of the interchange of ideas.[8] If young children were really intellectually trapped in developmental stages then the uses of language would not matter so much. But that need for extensive intellectual challenges that are reciprocated in others is one that, if fulfilled, guarantees the ability to deal with the demands of school.

The evidence about the connection between the language of home and school is extensive. It has, however, often been misinterpreted as an attack on the socio-economics disabilities and disadvantages of some, or the cultural hegemony of others. That there is a connection between the style of learning and home and demands of school is clear. What exactly this consists of can be subjected to political rather than empirical debate. That children from certain backgrounds do better than others does not mean that there is a need to make negative judgements about 'worse' backgrounds: it does mean that we need to define just what is essential for the development of children.[9] There are certain linguistic characteristics which can be dismissed as irrelevant. Accent, or dialect, the particular ways of speaking according to region or class has absolutely nothing to do with it.[10] The ability to maintain an argument, to listen, and to find the vocabulary to be able to explain, is critical. The style in which this argument is sustained is not important.[11] The emotional warmth and attachment, and the ability to talk is in itself not enough. The sharing of a discourse about something outside the shared relationship is essential.

When all the background factors of academic success and failure are taken into account the connection between home and school in terms of dialogue and the intellectual understanding of relationships are crucial. This reminds us of the importance of the early years; the abilities that are there but that need fostering. To deny their existence is to do a great deal of harm. To be insensitive to the concerns of individual children is a sign of adult self-absorption. Again, this is the reflection of a cycle of intellectual and emotional deprivation. Adaptation to suffering; the means of coming to terms with denial is then translated into making others suffer. This is not manifested in deliberate cruelty so much as in almost casual neglect.

When children of different socio-economic backgrounds are described in their differences of behaviour - some being told to 'shut up and get that telly watched' and others having every detail explained to them, some waiting outside the Headteacher's room in silence and being told 'not to touch the toys', and others having the difference between the word 'chimney' and 'funnel' reinforced - it is difficult to avoid putting intellectual and academic differences down to a class fix.[12] Whilst examples of destructive parenting, intermittent slaps and ice-creams, can seem like the symbols of vulgarity, this is not the point. Class distinctions are crude rather than subtle. The shared experience, and the crucial distinctions are more subtle and significant. When the children who come from the 'wrong side of the tracks' come to school with a different style of language, without an awareness of the demands of academic rhetoric, then it is clear that they will not do so well in school.[13] But to understand this is not to blame the school for being 'academic' nor to blame the child and parents for their 'class'. Every child needs close personal dialogue; the accent in which it is conveyed is as meaningless as the accident of language in itself, the greatest manifestation of human achievement. Every child is capable of critical thinking, of being logical and rational. What every child needs is for this to be recognised.

If young children have been intellectually fostered it is clear that they will have a head start in school. They will know the crucial facts about relationships, between people, between concepts and between words. That they might have come from 'poor' backgrounds in terms of economic difficulties is not a significant factor in itself.[14] Nor is the question of whether they are happy or not significant for success at learning, although one wishes this were so.[15] It is the style of learning at home that needs to be connected with the academic demands of school. Some children arrive at school and obviously clash with the expectations and the ethos. A significant proportion of these express their latent dissatisfaction and unease with aggression. They draw attention to themselves and quarrel. They become unpopular with teachers. But an even more significant number submit quietly. They stay out of the way. They nurse their inner grieving in silence. They remain popular with teachers because they give little trouble. They become invisible, and forgotten.[16]

By the time children enter school they will have either formulated for themselves clear rules of intellectual and social conduct, or they will still be searching for the means to learn about themselves against the existence of other people's points of view. Some will therefore come to school fully equipped to deal with its demands. Others will always be left floundering. The problem is that schools do not know how to cope with those who cannot deal with its demands. Every child carries the consciousness of the connections and the contrasts between home and school. Home has its rules and procedures, the agreements and expectations of people living together, but compared to the school, home will be perceived as less controlling and freer.[17] This is true of all children but for some the contrast will be so wide as to be difficult to overcome. Some children will also have learned the art of providing intellectual stimulation for themselves rather than relying on outside distractions. For these, the inevitable longueurs of school, the tedium that all children experience at one stage or another, can be overcome.[18] Many parents look to school to teach discipline and morality, and this in itself is not just a sign of a culturally idiosyncratic assumption, but one of neglect.[19] Naturally children will learn from any source about the rules of conduct and the nature of morality. This includes the school as well as the home. But to rely just on the school is to deny the fact that the essential rules of discipline and the negotiations of relationships have already been learned, sometimes traumatically, in the home. If the contrast between one milieu and another is too great - if, indeed the parents have assumed that it is the job of the school to teach morality - then there is difficulty.

The 'rite of passage' from home to school is always one fraught with difficulty. Sometimes the problems remain hidden. There are, after all, ways to overcome them, so that some children can hardly wait to get to school. But the potential difficulties remain, especially in those who are intellectually and socially deprived. From a time when children are defined as individual, spontaneous, curious and independent, they are suddenly transposed into pupils, obedient, quiet, self-controlled.[20] For many all thoughts of curiosity and spontaneity wither away with the passing years.

For many educationalists, the answer to the disappointment which afflicts the promise of youth, has been to make schools more sensitive to the children who come to school, forgetting that whatever they do children see schools as monolithic structures, necessarily so.[21] The presentation of freedom of expression, of open-ended play, of avoiding the emphasis on the overtly academic, has been seen as a way of overcoming intellectual atrophy, of retaining the freshness of delight in learning.[22] The problem is that to young children the school will always remain formal, the questions closed. They will still be in groups and in classes, requiring organising and controlling. They might be allowed to do what they want, to pass the time in their own way, but they still recognise that there are facts to be learned and tasks to carry out. Teachers can present topics and themes, but children are aware that there are subjects and 'disciplines'. Teachers might suggest that choice is for the pupils, but the children know they are pupils and that teachers are there to control.

The answer to the disparity between home and school lies not in extending the ethos of home into school but in preparing children earlier. Whether there should be such institutions as schools or not, children seek intellectual stimulation. They need to learn how to be with other people, how to relate themselves to social circumstances, and how to share their curiosity. Their abilities cannot be denied until they enter school. By then whatever 'stage' they are supposed to be at, it is fundamentally too late. From the children's point of view the understanding of the demands that school makes is essential. Whilst they often deny or cover up the difficulties - 'I don't know' - the contrast between their hopes and the expectations of school can be undermining. Children need to be carefully prepared for school.

Schools are in their present form cultural monuments. For this they need not be blamed. They are an unexamined manifestation of societies' assumptions about how best to prepare future generations. From the point of view of children, however, some telling points emerge. Schools present a number of challenges. They are social centres, but they also demonstrate a practice of social control. They are perceived to be the imposition of adult expectations on children. They are assumed to be run in the interests of teachers, governors and the State.[23] Children assume that they have no authority over what goes on and that their wishes are not heeded. They also assume that the only right answers are those which teachers wish to hear. Schools, in fact, present themselves, whether they wish to or not, as the embodiment of society as it will be experienced later in life. Schools are monumental closed systems to which individuals must adapt.

The ways in which schools present a version of society has long been recognised. For some this is a good thing, for others bad. But the sense of an improved system lies at the heart of the interpretation of its effect. Schools are essentially a system of rules and order which dominate not only the behaviour of teachers and pupils, but the curriculum. The purpose of schools is understood as being the maintenance of itself; the lives of teachers and all others attached to them, to sustain the everyday momentum of social being. Some have suggested that this process of self-interest and continuity is the deliberate exploitation of the hegemony of the State.[24] The pupils in school have no such analytical and discussive or political theory. They experience the effect of what is for them essentially a closed and unchanging system, maintaining itself for its own purposes. They imbibe the essential purpose of schools, from their first initiation into them. Schools are there to fit them for the work place, to enable them to do jobs.[25] But schools are also their first taste of wider, organised society; of the experience of groups and hierarchies, of power and its organisation, of the tension between the desires of the individual and the needs of the many.

From the point of view of children schools are monumental closed systems. There are no other institutions quite like them.[26] The memories of the first entry into the formality of rules, of the organisation of a mass of people into groups, sometimes large and sometimes small, and the movement from place to place, linger in the mind for ever. But memories mitigate that full sense of shock when the only place to hide, to be private, is in the mind. However much the school attempts to be welcoming, to overcome the difficulties of entry, it will always be a strange institution. Those children who look forward to going to school and who relish the idea of what schools can offer, like friendships and stimulation, nevertheless soon learn about school as a system within which they can find their own personal place. It is still a system, a monumental and essentially an alien place. Schools might be social centres and used as such by pupils, but this is so despite, not because of, their ethos.

When one studies children's experience of school rather than the curriculum, management or teaching styles, some personal and consistent insights emerge. The essential purpose of schools is never explained or else it is taken for granted as if it were not in question. Children therefore quickly assume that the underlying purpose, seen through the status of certain subjects and skills, is to help them prepare for jobs. And yet the context in which they will find jobs is never fully explained to them.[27] The curriculum is something that is imposed upon them, just as it is imposed upon the teachers. Indeed one of the most fundamental insights that children have of school is of their own powerlessness, their helplessness in the face of a given system. This sense of personal lack of power heavily influences their view of society as a whole, the more so as no-one seems formally to explain it.[28]

What children perceive in schools is a tension between the formal structures, the rules and the hierarchy of decision making, and the social struggles and competitions which take place both within and against these structures. Schools are social centres. Playgrounds are the places where the clashes of personality are most exposed. At the same time children do not perceive schools as being meant for them. Schools are understood to be there for the sake of the teachers.[29] Rules are a necessary imposition, and children assume that without them there would be chaos but they are an imposition nevertheless. The curriculum consists of whatever the teachers want it to be - unquestioned and unexamined. There are then two types of life that take place at the same time; in parallel with the formal curriculum, the organisation of activities, and the roles of teachers are the informal pressures of peer group interactions. On the one hand there is the silence and to many the tedium of work - of 'writing' and arithmetic. On the other there are discussions and arguments about the meaning of life, about all those things that keep children curious but which are not part of the curriculum.

It is no surprise that many observers of schools see them as demonstrating the will of society, as if they were a deliberate imposition of capitalist or socialist values. Children are taught how to adapt, how to understand the hierarchies of authority, not in any deliberate or self-conscious way but by the nature of schooling. The underlying and long-lasting response to the nature of schools, whatever the social system, is the sense that the individual as such does not count for much and to have a voice that is heard is distinctly unlikely, even if a possibility. The whole nature of school is that it is a system which children have to accept. Some would argue that it could not be otherwise. Some suggest that schools are an ideal site for democratic behaviour.[30] Others suggest that they play an essential role in reproducing the forms of society.[31] But the problem is that schools, whatever their hegemony, strike children differently. All agree on the nature of the school, a system to which one needs to adapt. But some children learn how to do so better than others.

The essential ability to adapt to the nature of schools rather than be alienated from them lies not in the nature of the rules or in the hierarchies but in the nature of the discourse. The language of schooling can be in contrast to that of the home. For some children the academic school language remains an arcane discourse, the formality of description being a mystery, not in terms of the words themselves but in the way that they are used. Schools expect children to be adaptable, to accept what is given. At the level of rules, the necessary social organisation, this is no problem. When some children rebel against schooling and question its utility or necessity they do so not because they are expected to adhere to agreed norms of behaviour as much as they feel alienated from the work. They fail to see its purpose. There are certain lessons and certain teachers that they would wish to avoid. The beginnings of truancy can be seen to begin in a number of subtle ways, a sense of psychological aberration, a growing disharmony between the formality of lessons and the tensions of peer relationships, and in the avoidance of mental rather than physical confrontation.[32]

There is a close relationship between what children think of school and what they think of the rest of society, since one mirrors the other, almost as if one were a parody of the other. The relationship consists not in what has been called the correspondence principle - the similarities between the social relations of school and the social relations of production, as in the feelings that children develop of essential personal helplessness.[33] The system, in all its manifestations of control, of battles, of sanctions, rewards and punishments, remains something that is observed rather than participated in. Just as the family faces intense scrutiny, so does the school. Children analyse and begin to understand the complexity of social relationships where there is a battle between authority and personal will, both within the formal structures of the school when a large gang or a year group can realise their latent power of rebellion, and in the smaller power struggles that are maintained throughout the experience of school.[34] Children gain an understanding of the modes of working and the expectations that are not crude representations of one version of society, but of social relationships generally.[35]

Some families subconsciously prepare their children for school. There is a clear overlap between the social or cultural 'capital' that children bring with them and the expectations of teachers.[36] There is no doubt that certain families provide linguistic advantages. Schools draw on the linguistic or cultural backgrounds unevenly. There are particular kinds of discourse used, certain unexplained expectations, commonly held assumptions. And all the time there is that unspoken acceptance of a given: that there are certain subjects to be learned, subjects which have a hierarchy of their own, and that it is the teachers and others 'above' them who decide what these subjects are.[37] Some children learn to adapt to this. They can see what the intention within the given subjects might be. A few children feel more and more out of joint with the system. But many more simply submit to it.

That mixture of helplessness and acceptance is a form of adaptability. Just as children have learned how to adapt to home, so they learn to see how to survive within schools. There is a certain submission in this. Those who know how to question what goes on can take their skills of adaptation further. Those who cannot articulate their questioning make cruder gestures against their need for submission. But the majority keep silent. They keep their thoughts to themselves and remain as invisible as they can.

The need for close intellectual as well as personal relationships is well established. So is the correspondence between the styles of dialogue at home and in the school. But those who then link forms of dialogue solely with class miss the essential point. The temptation to see certain groups as essentially disadvantaged, as always liable to remain outside the 'norms' of the social system can be strong. But this is not necessary. Any parent, once the art has been learned, can convey that curiosity on which children need to feed. Whilst parents hand down to their children their own inadequacies, and the failures of their own parents in turn, there is nothing inevitable about this. The cycle can be broken, since it does not depend on socio-economic circumstances or on 'class'. The disjunction between home and school can come about because of the differences in styles of learning. The school system is geared for the most part to the logical sciences, to linguistics and mathematics. If children do not match this style - if, for instance they are non-verbal thinkers - then they will find school the more difficult.[38] This is why so much emphasis needs to be placed on the explanation of what schooling is for, and why children seek and do not find answers to their questions. The school remains a 'closed' system, with closed questions to which there is only one answer, against which the pupils are being tested. And yet children continue to ask open questions, and the only ones to reply are their peers.

It is only when children enter school that the significance of the peer group emerges. Until then they will have been able to play with other children, or struggle with siblings, but at school the relationships with peers, both singly and in groups becomes very important.[39] There are constant reminders of the ways in which groups function. Until being placed in classes, children will mostly have concentrated on relationships with individuals. There will have been two way dialogues. But in school there are all kinds of arrangements of groups. The idea of a class, whatever its size, is itself significant: the need to accept single commands to generate a collective will, to know when to share and when not to, when to work together and when to compete against each other. There are all kinds of groups; cliques and friendships, people with whom it is easy to work, even if they are disliked, and those who have more or less ability than others. If class sizes are greatly reduced children behave in different ways and find it easier.[40] But the moment a single group of 10 children who have formed links with each other are merged into a more 'normal' class of 30, the group becomes dispersed. Cliques are formed and particular relationships developed from which some are excluded.[41]

The placing of children into classes has all kinds of results, and immediately infers certain expectations. It means, for example, that a lot of time is necessarily spent in waiting, waiting for instructions, waiting to begin, overhearing instructions directed at other people. Children might sometimes have been at a loss about what to do next at home but they will rarely have been actually forced into inaction. Understanding the signals, realising the need for order, knowing how to wait in queues or lining up: the social order of authority is clear. The class also has a collective ethos of its own, within that of the school. It reverberates with the shared relationship between the teacher and the pupils. As this depends both on the personality and the role of the teacher, and on the way in which the pupils fuse either into a whole or break into distinct groups, or both, children experience at first hand a whole range of types of social interaction. It is because of this that children learn to test the teacher, to see how easily his or her will can be broken.

If children test their relationships with teachers, they also do so with each other. They need friendships but they also learn about enmities. What seems like fickleness is part of children's' learning. They are placed in groups, rather than placing themselves. They need to be adaptable to a variety of other people whose learning styles and attitudes are different from theirs. They constantly explore the dynamics of inter-personal relationships, not just observing but testing.[42] They understand the distinction between the role being played and the person within that role. They therefore develop their understanding of the formality of relationships, the need to keep secrets as well as the need to explore, the sense of suspicion as well as openness. These are not always comfortable experiences. One of the crucial social concepts for children is that of fairness. Their morality is very sophisticated. They are able to see 'fairness' in all its lubricious interpretations: what is fair to one is not fair to another, what is fair in one circumstance is not so in another.[43] Their pluralistic understanding of fairness replaces any monolithic view of justice they might have had. Their vision of society emerges not as one which contains some collective sense of virtue and justice but one in which inequality and unfairness abound.

The daily experience of children in schools is however not one in which social difficulties are kept at a distance. There are theoretical rules and the usually accepted manifestation of authority. But there are also a variety of interactions which are stressful and difficult. Some of these stem from relations with teachers: being 'picked on' unfairly, being told off. But most come from the difficulties of interactions with others, being teased or bullied. For many children school is at times a very uncomfortable and at times traumatic experience. All children without exception have experienced some form of bullying, whether overtly physical or the more subtle forms of verbal abuse or ostracism. Those who talk of bullying in terms of percentages define it in terms of deliberate acts of intentional harm. But for children it is the result as much as the intention which matters.[44] Bullying is pervasive, to the extent that children not only talk about it as victims or as witnesses but as perpetrators. Psychological bullying concentrates tellingly on anything that stands out as being 'different'.

The intensity of school lies partly in the complexity of relationships and the feelings of isolation and threat. Whilst the testing of friendships and the forming and re-forming of groups might seem a necessary part of learning it is also fraught with difficulties.

> He's not a very nice boy. He used to be not very nice to me in the Infants. But actually now when we're in the Juniors he's been quite nice to me. I've been playing with him.
>
> Sometimes I push people over by accident and they say I did it on purpose so I get annoyed. And sometimes I get in trouble and I say 'That's not fair' and things like that. And I think I shouldn't do that but I can't stop myself 'cos they push me over as well sometimes. But I still don't swear.
>
> Sometimes this girl at school called Beth; she's nasty but sometimes she's nice. So I can't make up my mind. She sucks her fingers and her friend called K, they're really good friends because they've known each other since they were in nursery and they both suck their fingers and thumbs. Sometimes they don't let me play with them so I don't. And then later she says 'Do you want to play with me?' so I say 'Oh, alright'.   *(girl 7)*

The uncertainties and the ambiguities are apparent. Some people change over time and for some inexplicable reason repair earlier damage to the relationship. Others are unreliable, sometimes being friendly and sometimes not. Particularly close and exclusive friendships are observed, as well as the characteristics that make particular people stand out. And the problems of making the distinction between responsibility and accident, between initiating events and responding to them are clearly spelled out. The ambiguities relate to personal behaviour - 'I push people over by accident' and 'I think I shouldn't do that but I can't stop myself' - and to the behaviour of others, through changes of mind or false blame. All these interactions are complex but also hurtful. There might be a low measure of psychological explanation but this does not distance the actuality of the experience.[45]

School can be an uncomfortable experience because of the strong feelings of being ostracised or left out. This might be as a result of failure at work; there are so many tests that are possible to fail, and children if they take their work and themselves seriously are hurt at failure - until they learn to harden themselves to it by dismissing it as irrelevant. It might be a result of the failure of relationships, of being rejected from the group or from companionship. School encapsulates the possibilities of being rejected, of feeling failure. For all children this almost inevitably happens at one stage or another. Either they overcome the problem or submit to it. But for all children school must include some difficult moments. They learn, if they haven't learned it before, some of the social phobias that are supposed to lie in the province of adults - stress and dread, fear and suspicion. The nostalgia for the good times of school - 'the best days of my life' - either is a commentary on what subsequently happened, or is very partial, the selection of those moments of unselfconscious happiness.[46]

Schools can be rewarding experiences, and there can be a genuine excitement created in them. For the most part, however, children accept the essential duty they have to go to school. It is a laconic routine. It is not to be questioned for if that happens all kinds of other untoward questions are unleashed. Generally they submit to it. They also want to maintain contact with their friends. They know how to make the best of it. But this does not mean that they always enjoy it.

> I don't like going to school and there's loads of other things as well. I like doing maths when I get home from school and I like playing football. I don't like it when people kick around and that. I don't like it when they kick me.
>
> *(girl 8)*

There is a distinction between the rumbustious circumstances of school and work. Many children appreciate the work - they develop a habit where they work at home and go to school to hand it in and see their friends - but do not like the conditions in which they have to do it. They do not always like what they see happening in school and they do not like what happens to them.

The real lesson that is learned from school is about themselves in relation to others. School is a place where confidence is eroded. There are others better or stronger than them. What is learned is how to adapt to this, how to mitigate it, how not to be too 'different'. In the series of volatile relationships, and temperamental changes, the greatest fear is of being ostracised, of being left out. There is a constant desire to have secure friends, to be popular enough to know that there is no chance of being the victim either of bullying or isolation. In the ways that schools are organised, with the choosing of teams and the setting up of groups, there is no opportunity to get on in isolation, just to concentrate on the work. Whilst group work is recognised as a useful teaching device, it can be a difficult arrangement for children to manage.[47] Learning is itself a challenging process; doing so in collaboration or competition with others is even more so. Suppose people do not wish to work with you? There are so many opportunities to convey distaste or dislike. Whether inside or outside the classroom the real fear is not having friends, the sense that 'nobody likes me', or 'I wish I was different'. Being 'left out' is another form of being 'picked on'.

> Some things make me sad like people being horrible and saying 'No, you can't have that' and I say well they mustn't like me or something. Like you say like 'No you can't have that' and then I just feel a bit upset. And say 'Why can't I play?' and I just say 'well you can't play okay' and shouts and things. I get a bit upset 'cos I don't really like it, so I just do the things back. And I really want things like 'Oh please' and they don't let me.   *(boy 8)*

Again we see both the upset and the reaction. The typology of bullies and victims as if they were never the same misses out the essential symbiosis of relationships, provoking and provoked, almost 'begging' for trouble. The reaction to ostracism does not lessen the pain.

There are moments of great security in school of being included in an activity, a sense of safety and routine. But there are also many insecurities. School might seem like a monolithic system but it is not a safe one. The corridors and the playgrounds, the verbal sparring and the accidental pushing are all depicted by pupils as being at the heart of school life. In all the commentaries that children make about school life, the urge to be at least decently successful at work and the desire to be accepted, we see the shadow of rejection or the possibility of rejection. Some try to force themselves on the attention of others. Their urge for a place within the secret and informal hierarchies of the school makes them stop at almost nothing in order to gain an entrance. The sense of rejection, the implacable indifference of others is the more palpable. In it we see the beginnings of social alienation, of truancy and of aggressive behaviour.

Every school experience provides an opportunity for success or failure, of being popular or unpopular. Schools draw attention to those who seem like misfits, who go against the collective norms. Children feel that they want to fit in somewhere, and if one kind of society rejects them they need to find an alternative. Those who do not gain the approval of the teachers - or even one of the teachers - seek to gain approval in their peers. All children seek an audience as well as friends, people who will observe and comment on their behaviour as well as approve it. The testing ground of friendship is one which is expected to provide a commentary, not just an acceptance, an analysis of character as well as a response to it. Children constantly seek definition.

Children also make constant judgements about others. The characteristics of teachers are well known and the messages about them, their styles and mannerisms, are passed from one observer to another. Children are clear-sighted enough not always to maintain the same point of view about a teacher as his or her reputation. They will readily accept and even believe what their peers say about teachers but they will just as readily change their minds according to their judgement about the evidence. The currency of teacher reputation is readily exchanged, but so is that about the reputation and characteristics of children. Again, they can change their minds or be surprised at a change in the relationship, for good or ill. But what they are learning is the fact that some people, for whatever reason, are better than others. They are making distinctions. They realise that their lives can be made a misery by some 'naughty' children. Every school contains them. School then represents the growing realisation that the imperfections of the world, embodied in personal characteristics, is a constant: that some people will always be like that.

Despite all the rules and the pressures to conform, children observe a diversity of behaviour. They see the tensions and the difficulties. They will have observed them at home but now they are translated onto a larger scale. They see people behaving badly and people functioning according to mood. Just as they learn to cope with the temperamental defects of their parents so they learn to manipulate the moods of teachers. They ascertain that there are inexplicable reasons for their behaviour and that there are interpretable signs.[48] They see their peers being 'naughty' to some degree or other, getting away with things, laying blame on others. They see school being contaminated by some children who clearly enjoy the hurt they can inflict on others. That this is a kind of contamination comes about because children are more than just observers. They become caught up in it:

> We are never always good because you have to stick up for yourself.   *(girl 9)*

'Naughtiness' is only partially linked with 'getting into trouble'. A lot of what takes place in school, which affects the inner lives of children, remains out of sight. Sometimes it is deliberately ignored since dealing with it is very hard work. More often it is part of that undercurrent of experience which, since it is not part of the formal structures of the school, remains hidden. Sometimes the private difficulties are linked to the more public admonitions but even then there is a complex interplay between the ways in which the tensions of relationships overlap and affect the ways in which the authorities react. Teachers and others are not just distant observers but are used by the children. They are appealed to, like umpires, cajoled with, like referees. They have the ultimate sanctions. But just as they are invested in authority by the children so they are used to make judgements. Often these are disappointing, but this is because young children at first invest great belief in the true fairness of teachers. The disappointment at being disabused is the more strong; it is a disappointment, an attitude of mind that carries over into their perception of society.

The tensions that children feel between themselves and those that clash with authority can be distinct but can also overlap. It is all a question of who gets the blame; and who is responsible. Getting into trouble seems like an extension of the wilful alternative culture.

> I just don't like the other children. I only like my friends. They pick on me. They're rude. They say naughty things. It's just a habit. I always get told off. The dinner ladies. 'Cos I always get the blame by Johnny. He said I pull his trousers down and go to the Head. I'm the last person to finish.   *(girl 8)*

The 'normal' clashes spill over into the larger social context, and the annoyance of being picked on links the social relationships with work. What seems like a 'habit' is in fact the sense of the habitual. Some people are judged as rude and as naughty, but not in a distant or remote manner. The realisation is that all children are easily affected by those that are around them. They are caught up in the interplay of events, again with a sense of a certain helplessness.

The presence of 'naughty' children is both a threat and a temptation. There is a fascination displayed about what they will get away with and what will happen to them. The intimate tests of relationships are carried out in the context of a larger social sphere. It is when one spills into the other that there is an awareness of more than social turbulence, that children realise some of the consequences.

> My mum wants me to get away from this school really. My mum doesn't want me to talk about it but she might take me away from this school. She doesn't want me to be with Greg. He's the one with black hair. We get in enormous trouble. *(boy 7)*

Children are aware of what their parents think of schools, whether generally or about the particular one they are at, even if they do not want them to talk about it. The effects of children on each other can be so dramatic that the whole attitude to work and to authority can be affected. There is therefore a sense of the contaminating effect of some pupils; one to which no-one is completely immune.

Children all mention bullying in one form or another as part of the routine experience of school. All find themselves to some extent caught up in it. Whilst they rarely claim to be the instigators of bullying they honestly acknowledge that bullying is a complex phenomenon, including retaliation as well as attack, teasing as well as physical abuse, passivity as well as aggression. They also acknowledge that the distinctions between fighting in play and hurting, and between testing or changing friendships and boycotting are very subtle. Those who are most caught up in bullying are often seen to justify themselves as 'sticking up' for themselves. They feel they are provoked into defence. They acknowledge both that they are a tempting target, and that the temptation lies in the very fact that they are easily provoked.

> Some people don't like me probably because, like, if they start kicking me and that I just get hold of them and throw them across the playground or something because I get annoyed. If only people wouldn't come up to me and start kicking me and that. When they start, if I catch them, I just get up and swing them round and make them go spinning round because I get so annoyed with them. They do it to other people and call them names. Really horrible names ...

Sometimes I just walk away but he comes back at you and that, until, like, you just get hold of him and just throw him across the playground, kind of. He just kind of smiles and then because he knows I don't like swearing ... I don't do it back and that's why he can get me back.   *(boy 8)*

Provocation and retaliation. It is sometimes difficult to distinguish between them. This is because of the subtleties of the art of teasing. Children learn to detect weakness and vulnerability and cannot resist the temptation to exploit the fact. The exploitation is a form of exploration, to see what will happen, to test the ways in which people behave and can be made to behave. It is discovering the power that people have over each other, as well as seeing the power that those in authority have over them. It is an extreme form of play, emulating in the microcosm of their relationships what they see being enacted in society as a whole.

The acknowledgement that they can be easily provoked and get 'annoyed' does not lessen the action. Pupils both behave in certain ways and understand it. Their awareness of individual psychology, even if not presented in standard terms, is applied to themselves as well as others, placing their theories of mind into a larger social context. Children see the distinction between the crude forms of 'protecting yourself', through retaliation, and the more subtle art of avoiding these attacks. They know that they should behave differently but that they find it hard to do so. They see that others can detect their vulnerability. What is interesting is that children gradually learn to accept the fact, 'This is the way I am'. This means that they accept their own failures with school work as they accept difficulties with relationships. They grow to submit to their personalities even when they know it is wrong. This is not a failure to understand morality but a realisation that it is far easier to drop 'out' than 'in'.

Fighting, as well as bullying, is a pervasive undercurrent of school life. The distinction between the two lies between a rivalry for power, and a desire to dominate or control others, and also in the sense that fighting can be a form of play as well as rivalry. The bullies are those who think they should have control and who wish to prove it, and who do not like those who 'come back at them', for they are also fully aware of their own weakness. Those who fight see this as a rough form of playing, of showing that they are tough. The most obvious forms of fighting are physical, the rituals on the edge of pain. But fighting includes the subtle forms of teasing or keeping silent, of joining with a particular group so that others notice that they are no longer part of it. It is part of the emotional rough and tumble of the school, the inadvertent part of learning. The fact that it is such a pervasive experience suggests that it is both more influential and harder to control than some of the analyses of bullying might suggest. Schools are arranged to provide the ideal training ground, as if bullying were a natural sport.

Those who are particularly prone to being caught up in bullying are those who stand out by their ability to be provoked, to retaliate. This makes them 'stand out'. This makes them 'different'. They have failed to be invisible, to disappear into the norm. They have failed to cope. Often this is as a direct result of the conditions of the home where anger and inarticulate retaliation prevail. But this is just one form of difference. Anything that stands out, including those physical matters about which children parade such discontent, draws individuals to the attention of others. Being clever or 'brainy' or good at particular sports, having different clothes or simply being from a different ethnic origin from the norm is enough to cause attention.

> My friend ... she's Chinese and people pick on her. They go like that [pulling eyes] and everyone says where's the Wan two or three? I feel quite sorry for her. I still wouldn't really like to be Chinese though. I don't really like their eyes myself really. And I don't like the way they speak really. They speak really fast.   *(girl 7)*

Even sympathy does not prevent the strong collective sense of the prevailing norm making an impact. 'She' might be a friend but she soon turns to 'they'. She might be a person but she is also a bundle of characteristics which are different. Almost anything can be a starting point for discrimination. It demonstrates the power of 'norms', the intense desire not to be seen as different. It explains some of the starting points of racism: the realisation of the potential isolation and vulnerability of others and the desire to be safely anonymous.

The pressure towards conformity and adaptation is a complex phenomenon. It does not mean a lack of sympathy or a lack of understanding. It can be reacted against if pressed too far and if the disjunction between the approach and style of the pupil and that of the school is too great. It is more like an image of the world at large, to discover or to test how the individuals will react. Many think of schools as forcing houses to equip children for the adult world in terms of skills and knowledge. Schools are seen as preparing them for the work place so that what is learned can subsequently be applied. They forget that children are learning an array of other things. They are learning not as many skills as attitudes. They are learning not about employability and industry but about society at large. Schools, inadvertently, by their very concentration on the academic knowledge that is supposed to be relevant, have the effect of making children suspicious of those very industries for which they are supposed to be prepared.[49] Schools do not tend to explain themselves. What children detect is a version of society, where they see conformity, and the avoidance of making too many distinctions, as a central way of coping.

Those children who are 'different' either present obvious physical characteristics or are intellectually distinct - either going too fast or not keeping up with the prevailing academic norms. The pressure to know exactly what is required, not too much and not too little, is squeezed out of the realisation that the result of competition, of targets, can be personal pain and humiliation. It is out of the sense of their own hurt that they have an almost melancholic relish in others being in trouble, of doing badly. They can be unsympathetic to those who are 'different', but they have all the intellectual equipment necessary to understand what it must be like and what it feels like. Children are more easily led than meaning badly and in groups the norms prevail, both within and outside the classroom. Underneath the bullying and victimisation there is a certain sympathy for those who are hurt. For all know what it is like. Even the bullies realise what it is to be a victim, for their turn also comes. Nevertheless 'difference' of whatever kind is an almost irresistible call for teasing or for dislike. Why?

When children come to school they understand the intensity of personal relationships. They all know how to analyse them. Some of them are able to share their understanding through a dialogue which is about other people's lives, both in stories, and about the nature of the physical environment. Their everyday experience is full of curious things which demand explanation. When they come to school it seems as if, far from having the world opened up to them, they see it presented as a closed book. There are tasks to be done. There are patterns of behaviour to be learned. It is as if all knowledge is there to be tested rather than enjoyed. There seem to be two effects of this. One is that the intensity of discovery gradually turns away from knowledge to the exploration of relationships. In place of the struggles of home and the phenomena of negotiation appear the great impassive edifice of an organisational system. It is not the system itself that is then tested, but the relationships within that system. The other effect is that the very intensity of the struggle to understand personal relationships means that the need for some kind of conformity, for shared norms, becomes ever more important. Just as so much intellectual effort is placed into trying to guess what the teacher wants, so is academic effort placed into working out how to do what is necessary, how to fit in. Steering a middle course, not standing out too much, becomes important.

This is certainly true of the academic side, as well as in social relations, avoiding any hint of 'difference'. Young children's intense intellectual gaze, directed at their own and the larger environment, should be fostered by many more social relations and opportunities to learn. But, as is widely acknowledged, the potential of children is rarely fulfilled. To some extent it is because they are assumed not to have these gifts they so amply demonstrate at an early age. The myth of child development in terms of stages holds back attempts to develop their potential. The agencies involved in the years before children enter school do not usually even attempt to help.[50] Their time is spent only with exceptionally difficult cases (when it is often too late) and in defending the bureaucratic demarcation lines between each other. But the lack of the development of such obvious curiosity and excitement in learning is also because children learn how to adapt rather than to learn. Children early on see the tribulations as well as the opportunities of the world. They know that they have to learn survival techniques and they know that one way to do this is not to challenge too much.

In the arena of school children learn about social and academic competition. But they also learn to mitigate it. By the time they are half-way through primary school they have had several crucial facts about learning confirmed. One is that success depends upon pleasing the teacher, submitting to what is required. This might be very proper, but its effects are still seen in students who want to be told rather than to challenge, who wish to get the right answers rather than having to think. The curriculum, after all, is a given that has to be learned, knowledge that is constantly tested. The repetitive practices of schooling constantly stress this.[51] The system is a 'closed' one as in 'closed' questions. There are right and wrong answers rather than an exchange of ideas and opinions. Adapting to this system is the secret of tackling it. Some children find this hard to do. They constantly feel that they are struggling to come to terms.

At first most children ignore the difficulties, which is why observers and teachers of the early years are still aware of their potential. But then children begin to realise the significance of tests and results; the praise of teachers and the expectations of parents. They also realise that there is a dichotomy between hard work and achievement. The two do not automatically go together. Thus their self-esteem, or lack of it, is reinforced not only by the social relations of school but by their ability to deal with the system of assessments. Children begin school with positive perceptions of their own ability. This is because they are most aware of their effort.[52] As they progress through school this belief diminishes. They learn instead to compare themselves to others and rate their own abilities with greater and greater modesty.[53] This is often explained in terms of children's' ill-considered or exaggerated judgements of themselves gradually becoming more realistic. It is as if their faults lay in having high aspirations. But it is more a result of a sub-conscious lowering of standards. One of the constant messages of schools is the comparison of one child with another: it is subtly apparent in the demeanour of the teacher and in the fact that parents wish to know: how is one child doing in comparison with others? Is he or she near the top or the bottom? Children are at first less accurate in their predictions of how they will perform than teachers or parents; but then they have to learn how accurate prediction is valued.[54]

Children's early social relationships concentrate on differences, of beliefs and ideas. They learn about false beliefs and mistakes. There are varieties of ideas, and little uniformity. But in the school this perception of personality and behaviour is joined by a perception of similarity, of people all being judged by the same criteria. At first the criteria children look for are other people's singular abilities compared to their own, concentrating on matters like effort, and style of working, on social reinforcements and mastery of skills.[55] Later they learn to replace these insights with objective and normative information. Sociability is separated from ability. And given these standards, and knowing how much harder tasks could be, since they are aware of the increasing demands to be made on them year by year, without knowing how they will cope, their ratings of their own abilities declines.[56]

The comparison of themselves with others is a significant factor in school life.

If they were first, all the people were first, and I was last I would have to stay in when it's home time and I would actually like to go home. It's just that they're better than me and some day I'll learn more than them. I wouldn't be good at a lot of things and I wouldn't be able to move to seniors very quick and I'd be the last person and things like that. There's, um, two boys I know. They are very good at writing, spelling. One's called Martin and he's a very good runner and things like that as well and he knows virtually about everything.

(girl 7)

The differences of ability are not just a matter of acknowledgement or admiration but also constitute a potential threat. Will she be left behind? Will she have to stay in? How will she ever learn more than them in terms of spelling and writing? The social system of school is significant within the classroom as well as outside it. It might be more covert within lessons, but comparisons in terms of similarities and differences in abilities to master particular demands are constantly being made. The problem is a similar one: how to fit in.

The formal and informal social systems associated with school overlap. This can provide tensions. It is possible to trace the development of truants in the way in which one system - formal schooling - is rendered powerless against the other - the pressure of peers and the forming of groups. The ways in which children 'test' the formal system in their relationship with teachers shows how powerful and influential is the alternative one, and shows how aware all children are of their own culture as well as that of the school. The widespread occurrence of bullying and teasing in all parts of the hidden informal life of a school, although it does not need such obvious symptoms to detect children shying away from the real demands of school.

For children the network of relationships outside as well as within the classroom are an extremely important part of school, and for some the most important. When they describe the experience of school it is the social factors on which they concentrate; on the emotional effects of relationships made the more complex by the competitiveness of which they are all aware. There are, in fact, two overlapping themes that keep emerging from their descriptions of school life - intense relationships including bullying, and self-conscious awareness of their own work performance in relation to others.

There is a constant juxtaposition in the experience of school between the demands of the classroom and the pressures of relationships. When children explore their experience they are far more concerned with the latter than the former, even when they talk about the curriculum. This is why they find it difficult to explain formally what they have been doing in school. Reports might detail tasks undertaken, but the actual experience of children is far more complex than that, and lies in the relationships or in the difficulties, in an argument or the frustration of not understanding, rather than in the task itself. This is why, when parents ask their children what they have been doing they often are deflected by the answer: 'nothing' or 'I don't know'. It is not just because school is a separate world, with its own rules and demands that are left behind, but because children are most aware of the private intensities of the day. The most significant moments are not the formal operations of 'doing English' or 'doing writing', but in the conversations or in the struggles to understand.

Children know about the formal curriculum but they are also aware of undergoing 'topics'. Children suggest that they see this as somewhat arbitrary. It depends of course on the interests (or the whims) of teachers.

> We were talking about different countries and the most countries we were talking about were Germany and India. But this year we're talking about chocolates. *(boy 8)*

It is very difficult for them to record exactly what they have learned. They have their own opinions but the attainment of knowledge is seen as a separate compartment, a task fulfilled which has no subsequent application. Of course if there is a test to be taken the facts will be learned well enough to be regurgitated. Sometimes a particular topic will stand out because it sparks an interest in the teacher or in the pupil.

> At my old school in the last class when I had just become eight my teacher was very interested in green things. And I remember a couple of girls in my class; they set up this jumble type thing and they just gave the money they'd take to Miss C. And also we did projects on like extinct animals. I keep all my exercise books I take home. I've got a massive basket-full at home. And I've still got the project book and I've drawn pictures of dodos and seals and everything. *(boy 9)*

But such enthusiasm is significant for its rarity. When there are signs of excitement they are always as a result of lessons that are singular, or different, outside the usual routines of classroom life. They are the 'one-offs' like setting up a jumble stall, or pursuing an interest at length. For the most part the topics are themselves subsumed in the tasks of writing and arithmetic.

Teachers are the ones who decide what is to be learned, even if there are others who are in control of them. They are also the ones to give rewards and punishments; the centre of the social system of rules and justice. To please the teacher becomes one of the main aims of school. Learning is not its own reward but praise.

> This term I've got the teacher's special award in assembly and quite a few gold stars and quite a few team points. It means they've done good work and they've behaved. Some of the things, Mrs B our Headmistress said about me when I got the class award was that I was helpful. I brought, I produced good work and I did good work and I never gave up doing the good working system.
>
> *(boy 7)*

Adaptability to the school 'system', producing what is required, marks out success and rewards. It implies a shift of emphasis from exploration of ideas out of curiosity to the discovery of what pleases others. Doing good work and behaving, being helpful and 'producing' what is required begin to dominate attitudes to learning. Every child wishes to do well in school but this can also produce a significant strain. What happens if they do not continue to produce good work, when they see others doing better? There is nearly always someone else who finds work easier; and if no-one amongst the peer group then it is the teacher.

All children are self-conscious of their work and worry about it. They fear being told off for producing something 'scruffy' or producing something so neat that it takes them too long to produce it. They feel that they are not very clever.

> If they've got difficulties and they get more right than you, I feel ashamed. Like they sort of like haven't got much, many brains. 'Cos they say if you don't finish it you've got to stay in and do it. And if the person that's not as good as you does it before you, you feel sort of not very good.   *(girl 8)*

Comparisons abound. There are distinctions between having brains and doing the task well. She is aware of who is better or worse, and shame is a widely shared emotion. In the complex syntax lie many jumbled messages, about competition and praise, about the strain, the ability and the pace of work. Children are easily aware of their own academic limitations as they are at home of their own personalities, and their ability to be naughty. They recognise their own faults. The dangerous point comes when they no longer care about them, and give up in terms of behaviour or effort. The temptation is strong because trying to keep up, trying to fulfil the task set and avoiding having to 'do it again', is hard. The finishing of work within an allotted time is the most important factor of all.

> When I do something wrong I have to write it out again and again. Sometimes it's a bit hard 'cos sometimes I don't know how to say something. And it's a bit hard to write it down for me. Sometimes I want to be able to finish it off. If I don't finish it people think that I don't know much things about them.
>
> *(girl 8)*

'Time on task'.[57] Children learn how to pace themselves so that they do not go too fast or too slow. If they are slow they hold up the others and are ashamed. If they go too fast they upset the teacher's calculations, and make extra demands. The relationship between speed and neatness is important. There is a fear of being singled out for attention for scruffy work by the teacher, or being singled out by other pupils for holding up the class. They fear having to repeat work, or copy it out. They would like to have the facility to work fast and well.

> I like doing my work neatly and they do it or not very neatly. I do feel terrible when I'm not the best at something because I always go last. Terrible, because I would never get my work done. It would take me probably all week.   *(boy 6)*

The terror of not going fast enough or of having work rejected is widely shared. Children are constantly making comparisons, for the most part with their own class and the individual relationships with the teacher, just as they are sensitive to their siblings at home. The dread of failure is always centred not on the quality of the work itself - as long as it is neatly presented - but on the speed with which it is done. The fear is of falling behind the general standard, of being the last to finish. The stress is on 'keeping up'. In their comparisons with others the signs of 'cleverness' are the ability to fulfil tasks at speed. But at the same time they mustn't stand out as being *too* clever, or finish their work too quickly.

They just might be a bit cleverer than me. And if they're getting things quicker than me, they're just going to be cleverer than me ... Sometimes when I do my work quickly I'm really bored afterwards. And so if you finish slowly you won't be bored.

Once I did my sums, one of my sums quickly and then another person started going really quickly so then I had to catch up with them. And it was a race. When we were running to the teacher and trying to show her. Sometimes they say that I'm slow at things and that I'm not clever or anything.   *(girl 8)*

Being quicker is related to being cleverer: and the aim is to demonstrate this to the teacher. The sense of competition and comparison is wide-spread. The children compare themselves to others at maths or at reading, but always in terms of keeping up with the others. Getting 'stuck' is to be avoided if at all possible. At the same time children do not wish to be visibly different by being the cleverest. That can lead to boredom. But it can also lead to suspicion, on the grounds that others might be jealous. The middle way, the norm, is what is sought. Clearly that is easiest for those who find the work easy and can pace themselves, far easier not to try too hard than to struggle to keep up.

Because you would be called brainy and perfect. I'd like to be a stage where you're not someone who needs help but someone who's not a brainy but not having difficulties.   *(girl 8)*

Many children are afraid of being found arrogant, or a show-off. They do not therefore wish to be seen as the 'cleverest', but they do wish to avoid the 'embarrassment' of being slow.

There is a close connection between the relationships within the classroom and those outside it; the fear of being found 'different' so that they will be 'picked on'. Children can distract each other from their work, sometimes deliberately. They are also jealous of the extra help a teacher might give to someone else: this, again, is not 'fair'. But children are also aware of the attitudes and expectations of their own families. Just as they have a fair idea of ranks of 'cleverness', even if it is based on a certain typology of achievement, so they see the connections of their present performance with their past and their futures.

> It worries me because my Mum and Dad they're quite clever and my brother's quite clever, so I'd think I'm not the same. I don't like to be the smallest unclever. I like to be thought of as good.
>
> I like to be good at work because I came from a working family really. Everybody does their best in my family. There are certain people who think they're better than me and they don't show it. So when we're in maths and things and we're with the same group doing the same things, they're always going [noise of hurrying] and I say 'I know you're copying me' and they go 'No, No, No, No'.
>
> I know it's a bit boring but ... it's important to learn things. I know it's very boring sometimes.   *(boy 8)*

Finding a place in the world, fulfilling tasks and expectations; the pressure is always there.

The sense of competition and the avoidance of 'standing out' seem to be contradictions but they are both part of coping strategies employed by children. The early awareness of others turns to self-consciousness. The need to fit behaviour into a pattern of expectations demands their attention. This is not a simple matter to achieve since there are so many ambiguities of which they are aware. They know for example that it is important to fulfil set tasks in time, but know that some tasks - like those they will meet in the future - are more difficult than others and that what is easy for one is not easy for another.[58] They also know about ability groups, and the spread of talent, especially as perceived by the teacher, whilst at the same time not wanting to be conspicuous.[59] They find that the tasks set them can be ambiguous or uncertain, especially when they are ambitious. The fear of failure makes them want to do the most predictable, the easiest work. The amount of energy given to avoidance strategies is considerable, even whilst they know the importance of the work.

Children can be teased by their peers for being stupid or for being clever. The latter is seen as a 'show off' and considered to humiliate the others, as if cleverness were a form of bullying in itself. Jealousy is widespread, whether of the ability to do a particular sport or of being 'best at everything'.

> Whoever's the best in the class is usually bossiest and everyone doesn't like you very much because they're jealous of you being the best. And they think you're bossy, like Eve. She used to be in our class and she was the best at everything. And she had loads of boyfriends and everyone hated her because

she, she didn't really care. She was mean to everyone. Bossy, unfair and cruel and well, everyone thought that she was the prettiest in the class and they were so jealous of her, really. So they were all being horrible to her but she didn't care. She's left and now she's gone off to travel round the world.   *(girl 8)*

This portrait of a girl includes not just the effect she has on others but their reactions to her. It demonstrates the volatility, the emotional tensions of the social world of the school. We note bossiness, jealousy, hate, indifference, meanness, unfairness and cruelty. This, under the surface, is the stuff of school life, all controlled by a system of rules and expectations that are themselves a fuel for rivalry.

Whilst children do not aspire to be 'different' enough to attract unwanted attention, they do wish to be at least good enough at something. If all else fails then they can develop the ability of 'protecting myself'. Bullying and teasing are the alternative and concurrent activities in the relationships of school. Physical attacks are the most visible, but the most pervasive results of emotional tensions are more subtle; the teaching, the attacks on anything different. Both at school and at home children can feel themselves to be vulnerable.

Some things make me sad like people being horrible and saying 'No you can't have that' and I say 'well they mustn't like me or somethink'. Like you say 'No you can't have that' and then I just feel a bit upset. And say 'why can't I play?' and just say 'well you can't play, OK?' and shouts and things. I get a bit upset 'cos I don't really like it, so I just do the things back ...

I like a bit of my family as well but sometimes it makes me a bit angry sometimes 'cos nearly everybody like smacks me in the face and stuff. My mum sometimes but she doesn't any more. And my mum smacks me round the mouth and face sometimes. probably because she's French and she doesn't know very much of English. My pretend mum like pulls my ear sometimes.

(boy 8)

There is always an observation about the reasons for other people's behaviour and the causes of their own. Children do not only look at other people in their behaviour but are also critical or disappointed at their own. This gives their feelings, of shame or embarrassment, such power.

Schools might be monolithic systems but, like society, they contain many tensions which cannot be separated from the relationships formed at home. The expectations of teachers and the quality of instruction are not isolated phenomena.[60] Whilst the children perceive schools as dominated by the teachers and what they present to them, unexplained and exacting, children's perceptions themselves add to this state of mind.[61] Children bring with them suspicions and insecurities, the need to accommodate themselves and to cope. The influence of the home and the impact of peers are never far away. Children are aware of the importance of school; and realise that success or failure lies in their own hands.[62] But this very awareness can make them give up.

Attending school gives children their first opportunity to observe a social system in action and to become part of it. They will have already experienced a variety of relationships with other children and with adults, and have some notion of social hierarchies. By the time they attend school, after all, they are aware of the social stereotyping of the adult world as with the association of doctors with men, and nurses with women, so that their expectations will have been primed for the first visit. But school demonstrates two important social phenomena for the first time. Children observe both the need for rules and order, and the dependence on a hierarchy. It is clear that they are aware of the latter; not only the relationships between adults and children, but between adults of differing importance. Not only do they know about the status of the dinner lady against that of the teacher, but that of the teacher against that of the Head. Furthermore, children rapidly become aware that even the Headteacher is not an autonomous power but is answerable to other shadowy figures, like Governors.

Children see school as a formal system, with each person given certain, and different, responsibilities. They also recognise the importance of rules that make the whole system work. They are, indeed, adamant that without clear rules which all obey, the school's internal system would break down. They also apply this observation to society as a whole. It could be argued that this strongly conservative sense of the need for law and order, for the social control of otherwise unruly people derives from their experience of school.

The school is, then, a formal social system. There are rules and expectations, a clear agenda and an attempt to make all pupils and staff share a common purpose and a common morality. There are hidden and implied rules as well as those clearly stated. There is a great deal of emphasis placed on groups and the behaviour of groups, whether these are small, for the purpose of working together, or large, as in assemblies. The system of schooling is clearly laid out.

But the very rigidity of the system, seen as such, causes difficulties and hides the real activities that take place within it. Families are 'systems' too, where personal feelings, however strong, are contained within rules of behaviour. There are analogies between the two systems as well as contrasts. The submission to the shared rules and the recognition of their need is true of both. So is the desire for reward, to be seen to please. Both systems present the means of rejection as well as acceptance. Children experience a tension between inclusion and exclusion, being insiders, knowing where they stand, and being suddenly abandoned. They long for approval. They want to please. They either go on trying or feel that it is not worth it. The possibilities of rejection are always there, and the struggle to remain *within* the system is a hard one.

Children always face a recognition of the threats to personal identity. In the home the threat comes across as an indifference, a lack of dialogue or lack of sharing of values. At school the threats come from the sense that there are certainly some people who hate you. It is as if the self were written large, the more exposed, the more struggling to cope with the rivalries, the unreasonable dislikes, the essential fact of the unfairness, the arbitrariness of life. Schools have many good intentions and the teachers do their utmost, but schools are the way that society initiate children into fear, of being left behind, of being rejected, of being disliked or despised, and into anger, rivalries and jealousy and the sense of injustice. Both are manifestations of the feelings of the home; the fear that is founded on rejection, the anger that is the way of trying to cope. What schools teach so well is the need to submit, to give the self up, to cope, to fit in. Some cannot do so and are rejected. But 'exclusion' is not only the final physical dismissal from school but a psychological state. It pervades the school: all children experience the rejection of friends and the impatience or disapproval of the teacher. If this is also the experience of home, then those feelings of despair or anger are the more reinforced.

There is a constant emotional battle between the desire to belong and the desire to escape. Children naturally wish to be part of the system. They know that their survival depends on their adaptability to it. At the same time adaptability is hard work; it draws on depths of emotional energy that for some are hard to sustain. We need to remind ourselves that it is easy to try to escape, to allow ourselves to find some alternative way, against the formality of blame, and the humiliations of failure, in which to abandon the strain. The anxieties of childhood, the insecurity and the need for support, remain. The strengths of childhood; curiosity and objectivity, tend to fall away. The newer and the more different the circumstances the more there is a sense of helplessness and vulnerability. Schools are adept at this. The constant change, the reformulation of groups, the constantly new challenges all mean that children's desire for the security of the norm is easily undermined. Until, of course, they no longer respond to challenges, no longer even care about the demands.[63]

The experiences of the past are always transferred into new relationships. Just as the early explorations of the world, through story and through observation, tend towards exaggerations, the good and the evil, so these attempts to make sense of the moral basis of the world remain. Schools are not neutral. They might have playgrounds but they encapsulate emotional battlegrounds. The same close and exaggerated relationships - loving and disappointed - that they have with their parents are demonstrated through their peers. The constructive and the destructive impulses - to sympathise and to bully - are constantly at war. The school might seem at first glance a calm and peaceful place where simple learning takes place. But real learning is a personal challenge. It is painful as well as pleasurable. It demands change as well as the accumulation of knowledge. What children learn is the pain of understanding when they long for the security of fact. The irony is that their only security would come from that learning that would connect them with their earliest curiosity. The alternative, whether they survive the system or not, is the insight that gives them access to mediocrity.

Notes

1. It is perhaps telling that the word, even the concept of 'disinterestedness' meaning unselfish and objective, is mistakenly replaced by 'uninterested', which is completely different in meaning.

2. Woman, 21.

3. The competition brought about by market forces and league tables means that there is a conflict between the way schools define their

social role in terms of helping all, and the need to appear to be successful in terms of examination results.
Ball, S. *Education Reform: A Critical and Post-Structural Approach*. Buckingham, Open University Press, 1994.

4. Man, 18.

5. Woman, 20.

6. Man, 16.

7. Summed up in Bettelheim's analysis of the parental phrase "come out", and taken to its most extreme in the parents of would-be sporting successes. *The Good Enough Parents*, op cit.

8. cf. Heath, S. *Ways with Words; Language, Life and Work in Communities and Classrooms*. Cambridge University Press, 1983.

9. Cullingford, C. *The Nature of Learning*. Cassell, 1990.
Wells, G. *Language Development in the Pre-school Years*. Cambridge University Press, 1985.

10. Labov, W. The Study of Language in its Social Context, in Fishman, L (ed.) Advances in the Sociology of Language. The Hague, Monton, pp.152-216, 1971.

11. There is always a temptation to mix-up the two, as if 'formal' language were a particular type of dialogue rather than arising from the need to articulate.
Bernstein, B. *Class Codes and Control*. London, Routledge & Kegan Paul, 1975.

12. Tough, J. *Listening to Children Talking*. London, Ward Lock, 1973.

13. Heath, S, op cit.

14. Not that this helps; on the contrary.

15. Wentzel, K. and Asher, S. The Academic Lives of Neglected, Rejected, Popular and Controversial Children. *Child Development*, Vol.66, No.3, 1995, pp.754-763, 1995.

16. Page, J. *Invisible Children; who are the real losers at school?* Oxford University Press, 1989.

17. Mayall, B. *Negotiating Health: Children at Home and Primary School.* London, Cassell, 1994.

18. Around the age of eight the distinction between effort and reward becomes clear.

19. See The Idea of the School in Cullingford, C. *Parents, Teachers and Schools*. Royce, pp.153-171, 1985.

20. Willes, 1983.

21. Cullingford, C. *Parents, Education and the State*. Aldershot, Arena, 1996.

22. Atley, C. *Extending Thought in Young Children*. London, Paul
    Athey
    Chapman, 1990.
    Barrett, G. *Starting School: An Evaluation of the Experience*. London, AMMA, 1986.
    Drummond, M-J. *Assessing Children's Learning*. London, David Fulton, 1993.

23. Cullingford, C. *Parents, Education and the State*. op cit.
    Cullingford, C. (ed.) *The Politics of Primary Education*. Buckingham, Open University Press, 1997.

24. Gramsci, A. *Selections from Prison Notebooks*. London, Lawrence and Wishart, 1978.

25. Bowles, S and Gintis, H. *Schooling in Capitalist America*. London, Routledge & Kegan Paul, 1976.

26. Cullingford, C. *The Inner World of the School*. London, Cassell, 1991.

27. The social system which can be most easily likened to a school are penal institutions.

28. White, R with Brockington, D. *Tales Out of School: Consumer's Views of British Education*. London, Routledge & Kegan Paul, 1983.

29. Cullingford, C. *Children and Society*. London, Cassell, 1992.

30. Siraz-Blackford, J. Little Citizens: Helping Children to help each other, in Siraz-Blackford, J & I. *Educating the Whole Child: Cross curricular skills, themes and dimensions*. Buckingham, Open University Press, pp.7-18, 1995.

31. eg. Gramsci, Rowles and Guitis.

32. Gramsci, op cit.

33. Cullingford, C and Morrison, J. In Blyth, E and Milner, J. (ed.) *Exclusion from School: Interprofessional issues for policy and practice*. London, Routledge, 1996.

34. Bowles, S and Gintis, H. op cit.

35. Measor, L and Woods, P. *Changing Schools: Pupil Perspectives on Transfer to a Comprehensive*. Milton Keynes, Open University Press, 1984.
    Describes the way in which confrontation can spread throughout a cohort of children, until disobedience rather than school rules, becomes the norm.

36. Alexander, R. In Cullingford, C. *The Politics of Primary Education*. Buckingham, Open University Press, 1997.
    Bronfenbrenner, U. *Two Worlds of Childhood*. London, Allen & Unwin, 1971.

37. Coleman, J. *Foundations of Social Theory*. Cambridge MA, Harvard University Press, 1990.
Bourdieu, P. Cultural Reproduction and Social Reproduction, in Darabel, J and Halsey, A (eds.) *Power and Ideology*, 1977.

38. Burgess, H. The Primary Curriculum: The Example of Mathematics in Cullingford, C. *The Primary Teacher*. London, Cassell, 1989, pp.16-36.

39. Gardner, H. *Multiple Intelligences: The Theory in Practice*. New York, Basic Books, 1993.

40. Furman, W and Bahrmester, D. Ages and Sex Differences in Perceptions of Networks of Personal Relationships. *Child Development*, Vol.63, No.1, pp.103-115, 1992.

41. Blackford, P and Mortimore, P. The Issue of Class Size for Young Children in Schools: What can we learn from research? *Oxford Review of Education*, Vol.20, No.1, pp.411-428, 1994.

42. Smith, P and Connolly, K. Experimental Studies of the Pre-School Environment. *International Journal of Early Childhood*, Vol.10, pp.86-95, 1978.

43. Davies, B. *Life in the Classroom and Playground: The Accounts of Primary School Children*. London, Routledge & Kegan Paul, 1982.

44. Thorkildsen, T. Pluralism in Children's Reasoning about Social Justice. *Child Development*, Vol.60, No.4, pp.965-972, 1989.

45. Olweus, D. *Bullying at School: What we know and what we can do*. Oxford, Basil Blackwell, 1993.
Cullingford, C and Brown, B. Children's Attitudes to Bullying. *Education 3-13*, 1995.

46. Or as Tovey wrote, unfairly but memorably, of Wagner's music - 'Wonderful moments, terrible half hours'.

47. Galton, M and Williamson, J. *Group Work in the Primary Classroom.* London, Routledge and Kegan Paul, 1994.

48. Pollard, A, with A Filer. *The Social Work of Children Learning: Case Studies of Pupils from Four to Seven.* London, Cassell, 1995.

49. See Industry for Education: "Towards Employability", London, 1996.

50. eg. Social Workers who only deal with failure rather than be helped to create success. Temple, B, Hubbard, R and Raynes, N. Parents and the Children Act, in Cullingford, C (ed.) *Parents, Education and the State.* Aldershot, Arena, pp.135-154, 1996.

51. Bennett, N; Desforges, C; Cockburn, A and Wilkinson, B. *The Quality of Pupil Learning Experience.* London, Lawrence Erlbaum, 1984.

52. Stipek, D. Children's Perceptions of their own and their classmates' ability. *Journal of Educational Psychology,* Vol.73, No.3, pp.404-410, 1981.

53. Blackford, P. Academic Self-Assessment at 7 and 11 years: Its accuracy and association with ethnic group and sex. *British Journal of Educational Psychology,* Vol.62, No.1, pp.35-44, 1992.

54. Miller, S and Davies, T. Beliefs about Children: A Comparative Study of Mothers, Teachers, Peers and Self. *Child Development,* Vol.63, No.5, pp.1251-1265, 1992.

55. Stipek, D and MacIver, D. Developmental Changes in Children's Assessment of Intellectual Competence. *Child Development,* Vol.60, No.3, pp.521-538, 1989.

56. Stipek and Tannall, 1984, op cit.

57. This is a much used phrase measuring the amount of time children are *seen* to be quiet, and *seemingly* working. It does not refer to the more difficult to measure learning that is or is not taking place.

58. Kelley, H. Attribution Theory in Social Psychology, in Levine, D (ed.) *Nebraska Symposium or Motivation*. University of Nebraska Press, 1972.

59. King, R. *The Best of Primary Education*. London, Falmer Press, 1989.

60. See Cullingford, C. *The Inner World of the School*, op cit.

61. Marjoribanks, K. Families, Schools and Children's Learning: A Study of Children's Learning Environments. *International Journal of Educational Research*, Vol.21, pp.439-455, 1994.

62. Blatchford, P. op cit., 1992.

63. Salzberger Wittenberg, I. Gianna, H and Osborne, E. *The Emotional Experience of Learning and Teaching*. London, Routledge and Kegan Paul, 1983.

7 Shared insecurities: the context of place

Schools are a symbolic embodiment of society at large. They might be unlike any other kind of institution but they contain in microcosm the two most vital elements in human relationships: order and conflict. The ways in which schools are organised reveal how the interests of different groups are controlled, and how personality and status intertwine. The imposition and submission to rules are never a simple matter for children who constantly witness deliberate disobedience and uncontrolled conflict. Even in the most carefully run regime there are tensions and difficulties in being exactly just or exactly fair.

Rules imply social interaction, their existence dependent on the need to harmonise and stabilise the conflicts that people have with each other. Even if these conflicts do not manifest themselves physically they will be inherent in clashes of personality, as well as in distinctions of temperament and, crucially, in differences of point of view. In the place of some monumental conception of absolute truth and justice, for which human beings always hanker, children witness the frustration of having their own point of view diminished or disbelieved. Rules are never abstract, for children are acutely sensitive to the different ways in which individuals adapt to them and to the variety of temperaments on display, including their own.

Teachers present a clear model of the tensions between personal interests and the need for rules. There is always a balance between them as individual personalities, suddenly discovered by pupils to be human during a school trip, when they are seen and behave out of their natural context and the almost impersonal rôle they inhabit as teachers. Closeness and distance, friendliness and firmness are in a constant tension, between the individual will and the pressure of conformity.[1] Some children, however, demonstrate a more immediate and potentially more significant clash between the order of obedience and the expression of individual choice. They too are bound by rules but this is because they see they need them, not because they are bound by them. Rules are being tested, and the

227

ultimate 'naughtiness' as defined by children, and as applied to their perceptions of themselves, is disobedience.

The analogy between schools and their environments is an important one because children are as aware of the larger community as they are of the schools. They observe and experience the ways in which societies behave. Similar struggles between individuals and between groups are seen to take place. They are aware of the battles for power amongst politicians. They are constantly reminded of domestic and international conflicts. They hear the news about bombs and massacres, murders and rape. They are attentive to the facts of interpersonal conflict, because all these world events, these symbols of pain, are not just distant and conceptually distinct events. When children talk about the news which presents all the pathologies of human nature they reveal how much they understand what it is really like. There is a difference in extremes between the conflicts in the playground and the conflicts depicted on the news but not a difference in kind. The meaning of pain, the shock and the fear, link the two.

When children form their own understanding of society they do so through inference and symbol. They observe the manifestations of difference and conflict, both through secondary media and through personal observation. They then have to make some kind of interpretation of it, to make what they know fit what they understand about their own circumstances. We know about the trauma and the potential trauma of early childhood. Part of this derives from the fact that there is no space between the reality of their own lives and that of others. Whilst they do not 'live' the point of view of others they see the reality of it. They also know the reality of other people's experience.

The children's own environments vary greatly, and they are aware not only of the differences but of the impact of the environment. They know the meaning of space, and are sensitive to the atmosphere of places.[2] Whilst they might live severally in inner cities or in the countryside, in estates or suburbs, they are aware of contrast and differences within their categories. Inner cities can contain shops or tourist haunts, monumental architecture or blighted factory estates. Each is a visual symbol of what people make of the environment, whether there is concern or indifference. The telling messages lie in the contrasts. Why should some seem to care so much about landscape, and why should others allow urban blight. Of course there are not two distinct types of human being. What children see is that society allows contrasts. Whilst some environments are clearly as attractive as an image of a country garden, others promote squalor. The contrast makes an impact.

Whatever their own experience and wherever they live children form a consistent view of towns. Townscapes include a great deal of variety but the word town has a distinct 'gestalt' in the minds of children. 'Town' means the lack of space, it means lots of people living close together. It means noise and crowds, it means the potential of conflict simply as a result of proximity. Towns also mean traffic. At one pragmatic level children realise that roads mean danger. They curtail spontaneous movement. They are part of the warning system given to them by parents and teachers, underlying the justification of fear. But children do not just mimic the views of adults: they experience the reasons for these views.

> The thing is that I don't really like is how much traffic there is. And there's no traffic lights to cross the road. It just makes things a bit awkward 'cos when we're in a rush we try to cross the road and there's no crossings around and there's lots of cars zooming through. So we can't really cross.   *(boy 7)*

Traffic means inconvenience and restriction, but this is because of the underlying dangers: freedom of movement means the danger of being killed. There is a sense of immediate danger as a result of the cars, and children all recognise that at times they will be in a 'rush' and tempted to do something rash.

Heavily trafficked roads can be as much a part of countryside as of towns yet children associate it only with towns. This is because they are not only mindful of danger, but of the constant sense of crowding, of traffic jams and queues, of noise and smoke. It is in towns that cars have the most telling impact.

> You can't really ride a bike there or anything because it's a busy road. And it hasn't got much, well, pavement really. So you can't really do anything.
>
> *(girl 8)*

Traffic is both an inconvenience and a danger. As part of the experience of towns it is held to be a blight on the quality of experience. These children are describing real circumstances. They acknowledge the limitations of where they live just as they understand the home circumstances that are peculiar to them. The dangers of the road are real and are constantly reinforced by the associated noise and smoke.

When children cite the pollution of towns their concern is not the expression of political convention but the result of experience. There is a consistency in their dislike of traffic fumes that proves the fact that they cannot escape it or ignore it. They might try to ignore litter, and whilst objecting to rubbish realise that something can be done about it, but traffic and pollution is inescapable.

> It's always smoky and gassy and the seas are all polluted and things ... make sure that if you drop a piece of, sort of, like litter on the floor you pick it up. And make, you know, those ginormous chimneys that, like, throw out lots and lots and lots of horrible smoke from factories. I'd just try and make the smoke less polluted. It's not a very nice place to live really.   *(boy 8)*

Pollution is a symbol of the negative way in which children see their environment: it's not a very nice place to live. There is no indication that they live in the best of all possible worlds. They volunteer their sense of the limitations of towns, and realise that these limitations are widespread. Factories might be necessary but that does not make them pleasant. Whatever the cause for the litter or the rubbish, whatever lessons learned about what should be done about it, the shared landscape is a disfigured one.

There is a general sense of contamination as if some kind of general cloud had to an extent poisoned their experience of the world, no longer innocent in arcadia, but realising the symbolic limitations of the environment like a general fact rather than an aberration due to some manic or depraved action. But this does not mean that children see pollution as something inevitable and impersonal. They are aware that it is a result of people's actions; dropping litter in the street or dumping it in the sea is the individual act, just as pouring smoke into the air is a collective one. In both cases people are responsible, as responsible as they are for their actions to each other. As they grow older children learn to ignore, or deny the human agencies involved in environmental damage, but at the time when they are forming their own understandings of the world they find it illogical to divorce responsibility from result. This is why any accusation, however false, weighs so heavily. This is what people should not do: and yet they continue to do so.

Children's negative feelings about towns are at one level a result of the associations they have with crowds - whether in the form of queues, shops or traffic. Pollution is a symbolic outcome of this, as well as a reality. The pervasive belief is that the towns they live in are generally unpleasant places. On the one hand they see dog droppings and litter, messes innocent or not but equally unpleasant. On the other hand they see the more general, the more atmospheric contamination of the very air. This is not to suggest that they are unrealistically romantic about what towns could or should be like. Just as schools are centres of social life, so towns contain the conveniences of shops and entertainment.

> It's near the shops, it's near the school, it's near the park. 'Cos where we used to live it was out of the town and you had to go by car or bus to get anywhere. But when you're in the centre of town, you can walk most places.   *(girl 9)*

The fact is that towns are convenient, and necessary. That does not mean that children accept them as pleasant.

The terminology, as ever, that children learn to describe their understanding comes from whatever is closest to hand, but it is a definition of what they already experience.[3] This does not mean that they rely for their reaction on the instincts of environmental correctness. Their general sense of rules that apply to the environment arise from and then transcend local conditions.[4] Their understanding is rooted in their experience of the everyday, but this experience includes a sense of the whole world. They look through the windows of the house, and see where they live. They look out of the window of the televisions and compare. They are always in a context, never in a village stranded in ignorance. They know both the experience and its necessary interpretation.

Children enter social life seeking order amongst the events they experience. They see all the details not as separate but constantly connected into a whole.[5] Their social life in school is never unrelated to the world they both see and know they are supposed to understand. The image of the city is not just a holistic one placed over a mass of experiences but arises from the detailed visual and actual events that seem single and separate and have the impact of singularity, but are pressed into a whole. That sense of the pervasive, that need to generalise, is not a reduction of experience into superficiality. Each moment is intense. But it is a way of coping with as well as understanding that experience, rendering it almost palatable. The general sense of noise and overcrowding emerges from the particular circumstances in which children find themselves, and their realisation of the meanings within them.

> There was a busy road and you had to cross quite a few roads and there were drunks there, too, that lived across the road. Every Sunday and Saturday morning we always got woken up by the noise of drilling and things 'cos next door there's a man and he keeps on drilling and making loads of noise.
>
> *(girl 8)*

The outside world cannot be kept at a psychological distance. Although the art of ignoring events becomes more and more practised, and given the number of tragedies constantly reported on the news some might think necessarily so, there is both a personal insight into the circumstances of others, and a strong sense that this is a reality which affects them. Children have to learn to discriminate, and to distance themselves from what they see. Whilst they do that, the actuality of events nevertheless is close to them, with noise and neighbours.

For very young children there are clear distinctions between people. And yet they react and interact with anyone. Gradually they are taught that some are closer to them and more important than others. This is not just out of familiarity with building relationships but because parents are jealous of their exclusive rights over the love of their children. Children will gaze at anyone and will talk to someone they have not met before about whatever is profoundly on their mind. They see the whole world as social, a network of relationships. It is parents who, at first psychologically, by innuendo, out of their own needs, encourage the suspicion of the occasional visitor and who, later, develop the discrimination between the familiar and the strange into the distinction between the trusted friend and the stranger.

The sense that the world is full of dangers is reinforced by parents and teachers by warnings against 'strangers'. These are the mass of people who could threaten at any time. It is as if no-one is to be trusted. When children talk about 'strangers' they link them with actual events.

> They might be strangers. 'Cos they might take you away with them in the woods and kill you. These two little girls went into the park and he murdered two little kids.
>
> *(boy 6)*

The contrast between a trust in conversation, the openness to anyone, and the fear of the 'stranger' could not be greater, and causes a disjunction of attitude. So much depends on trust, on the sharing of assumptions about rules and fairness, and yet they are taught to develop mistrust, and to think that *anyone* they do not know could have evil intentions. This general warning against the dangers of the street is no mere theoretical maxim, not just a presentation of politically correct attitudes. The warning connects to news stories. It becomes part of children's views of human nature embodied in, in a sense of the everyday that is observed and noted. What children at first see as a unified world, full of people to relate to, even if they have their own point of view, turns into one in which people can be dangerous, can manipulate, or play tricks on them.[6]

Parents, who like to preserve some sense of special relationship within the home, draw on the contrast with the outside world. It is as if the security and warmth of the home were the more distinct if the dangers of the world outside were highlighted. In fact the dangers are intrusive. Children see their own homes not in contrast to but as a mirror of the outside world. They might long for security but know that lack of safety is pervasive and can seek them out anywhere. Home life is, in itself, not thought of as a pure haven of peace. There are few days not punctuated by the heartfelt anguish of pain, anger or disappointment. Children learn to understand the emotions aroused by their experience, but they also look circumspectly at their own particular circumstances. It is true that there is a longing for something stable and secure. We see this in their play. We remember this in our own childhoods, in fantasy worlds of absolute security. But these havens of peace are in contrast to the reality of the world children actually see, and therefore the more important. Security is itself defined by its opposite. The fantasy of space, defined in the countryside, is one born out of the contrasting actualities of proximity to many other people.

There is, in all children, a longing for peaceful security which is sometimes a deliberate escape. There are many signs of children closing down their minds, of seeking to escape their own attention to events. Escapism is not so much a journey to a place made fantastic because of the connecting securities but a hiding from some kind of reality, some kind of test, some kind of threat, whether this be a return to school or a particular lesson. Escapism takes place *within* the home; it is not embodied in it. It forms part of the fabric of the mind, like a daydream in a lesson, or passing the time with a comic in an attempt *not* to think.[7]

Life at home is not associated automatically with peace and stress-free security, even in those homes which are considered the images of perfect bliss. The world of 'Peter and Jane' remains in the minds of all children one that is longed for for its special certainty. The more that the noises of the inner city intrude the more are developed those private mental worlds of sought for security.

The sense of the intrusion of the outside world, whether presented in images or seeping through the window, is a strong one. It is not only when they leave the house that children are made to feel the dangers of crossing the road. There are circumstances when the proximity of other people filters through the walls.

> 'Cos if I'm up there on my own ... 'cos we, out of the flat I hear the telly all the time from the other flats, people being sick and that, 'cos the other night, with my friends, I didn't, um, we didn't go to sleep because we heard John in the next flat being sick and we couldn't go to sleep 'cos we didn't know what it was. 'Cos it was really scary.   *(girl 8)*

The concept of 'space' is not of having just enough room to manoeuvre with siblings but is applied to that sense of not being intruded upon. It does not need strange sounds or a brick being thrown through the window to remind children of the presence of potential danger and the inexplicable. The closer people are to each other - the less space - the more will this sense of threat be highlighted, but it is shared by all whatever the personal circumstances. The dangers and difficulties, as well as the pleasures, of urban life are the material for all the most popular soap operas, and the attempts to convey a less than idyllic reality connect with, and reinforce, children's own direct observations. They talk of their nightmares in terms of the images that encapsulate not just other people's destitution or depravity, but the feelings that what is heard about or seen could be translated into their own circumstances: the roof falling in, a fire, or the stranger coming in.

None of the different parts of children's experience can be separated from each other. The experience of conflict can be observed in the home, in the school, in the streets and in the world at large. The warning against strangers is not theoretical but soon turned into a connection with people they have observed. This in turn is reinforced by the witnessing of bullying, of actual fights involving people they know, so that the physical pain is not some abstract and impersonal charade as in a Hollywood movie of countless gunfights and ritualised slaughter, but something known in its effect.[8] The dangers of the playground are also observed and commented on as taking place in the streets, often with older children 'picking' on younger ones. They observe their neighbours, some of whom they know and some of whom they do not, as 'aggressive' or 'mean' or 'horrible'.

> I'm not allowed out there because I'm not old enough yet. And also, well, people, the person from my school might come along and he might beat me.
> And it can be very hard 'cos if someone - I heard this once - just down the road and along, two people knocked on an old person's door and said 'We're the building people and we're gonna help you with your electricity' and they stole her keys and money in her purse.
> People are being very nasty to one and each other. I think of, like, someone trying to get me ...   *(girl 7)*

The reasons for 'not being allowed out' are clear. Whether it is a general feeling or whether it is supported by evidence, what she has 'heard', the understanding includes people from the school. Nothing could be more everyday than that.

There is a general sense that the world contains many unpleasant and threatening people and that these are close at hand. They include the bullies at school as well as beggars and thieves. The way in which children interpret their world adds the sense of inter-personal conflict and symbols of this to their own negotiated interpretations of inter-personal relationships.[9] Whilst they observe the threats they retain a strong sense of potential involvement - 'someone trying to get me'. This personal connection makes their observations of people the more intense. There are many examples of people behaving badly that are a common sight, as for example, in the case of drunkenness.

> There's one thing I don't like about it. There's too many drunk people. Like we have to, sometimes, I walk back from school and we have to go past the shelter. I'm not quite sure what it's called but there's this shelter and there's a bus stop there, and, like loads and loads of drunk people. It's horrible to see it like that and they've just gone like crazy. I know it sounds silly but they have. And obviously, yeah, it's nice to have a nice drink, obviously, it would be

> nice. I could imagine it. It's nice to go down to the pub and have a nice drink. But it's silly to get drunk 'cos you only need a few beers or lager or whatever that you drink. You don't need actually to get drunk.   *(girl 8)*

The sight of the down and outs, often in a state of inebriation, is part of the experience of every city. Children all talk of the sight of beggars, and of drunks. They might not always understand the reasons for their state, but this makes them the more, rather than less, affecting. For children trying to understand people and their behaviour, these people seem personally threatening. They have not yet been covered by that social patina of explanation, like socio-economic conditions or market-forces. Homelessness can be easily imagined. It does not seem natural for a society to allow it. And yet it does. Does that then mean that the people in the streets have *chosen* to go that way? That is how it seems to children. They try to explain to themselves the 'silliness' of getting drunk, the lack of necessity for it. They have not yet learned the excuses: the shifting of blame from the individual to the impact of circumstances. What children strongly sense is not only the complexity of the 'point of view' but the weight of personal responsibility.

The world is too much with us.[10] It does not lie safely across a threshold that cannot be crossed. Those 'strangers' that are seen in the streets present threats that can also intrude into the supposed safety of the home.

> There's quite a lot of robberies going around. We were robbed once. A few months ago. There's a fire escape leading up to our balcony and they could break open the windows and climb in. But we've got an alarm over there now. I want to live somewhere where you haven't got a fire escape leading up to your balcony. Not very safe when I had the robbery ... safer in school, because lots of people are there. So if a burglary happens, somebody could easily stop them.   *(boy 8)*

There are worries here, beyond the cases of violent intrusion. Safety in numbers seems quite different to the threat of the crowd; but it is a refuge that contrasts with the lack of safety in the home. The moment a burglary is committed, the home cannot be associated with exclusive safety. But burglary is also seen as something pervasive. Where there is money there will be people 'nicking' it. Whilst there is no temptation to quote crime statistics, and still less to make political uses of them, there is a recognition of widespread and endemic crime, especially in terms of burglary.

The sense of threat is illuminated at a number of levels. The streets are unsafe. Nor is there to be found any refuge at home. There might seem to be safety in numbers at school but this in itself causes friction. There are bullies and there are potential killers. All these come together in a sense of profound insecurity. There are many moments when not a thought is given to it, when distractions occupy the mind. But that threat does not wholly go away. The home can itself become the centre of social decay, of a vision of society that contains many elements of fear and threat.

I hear the knocking so I get a bit scared 'cos I think somebody's there. So I, like, sometimes go in my dad's bedroom and say 'do you hear the noise? Well, I did, on my window'. And sometimes I get toothache and I can't sleep at night 'cos I wake up all the time and I don't really like it.

There's this place 'round the back and that's what I sometimes get a bit scared of at night because people can break in from the back, from the old garden door. Because we always leave our door open. Sometimes we leave the key in the door. Or sometimes we forget where we put it and we leave the door open all the time really and you could just climb right over the fence. 'Cos the fence is only this high. And I sometimes sneak 'round there to get 'round the shops and things in the morning.

Because quite a lot of people live 'round our area and these people asked how many bedrooms in next door and things and I thought, like, they were stealing or something. So I thought they're gonna be sneaking in this house and steal something at night.

... flats because sometimes that's even more scarier. With my mum I'm in a flat and sometimes it's a bit scary at night and when you go down in the morning 'cos sometimes I think people are hiding against the walls and stuff. And hiding there, there's places like that and you can't see and things. Sometimes you think, like, someone's gonna get you. And one thing's a bit scary from the top when you look down sometimes you think you're gonna fall. I like just big houses really and a good ... what you can't even break in and a wall against there and a wall against the side and stuff. I'm living in a flat now. It's a bit scary.

One bit about rich is sometimes you should be careful because sometimes people can steal it off you. Like if friends come to your house or go to the toilet they can, like, look around your house sometimes. And so you put it in a really secret place what's got an alarm or something.

Like grown-ups sometimes, and sometimes children can sneak, because children know where they put their things, don't they, because they live with them, so they sometimes can steal fifty pound notes without letting the adults know, so they can buy computer games without letting you know.

They probably tell them off and say 'Where did you get those computer games?' and I said 'I swapped it' and they say 'what for?' and I say 'nothink'. And they think, like, he must have gone a thief and got them.

Sometimes it makes me a bit scared at night, like banging on the windows and stuff and things outside. I feel a bit worried. I think, like, they keep a spying on me.
(boy 8)

This is not a world of childhood innocence. The sense of threat is translated into a personal understanding of crime. On the one hand the world is 'scary'. People could suddenly appear from the shadows and 'get you'. On the other hand the techniques of burglary - checking the house, pretending that goods have been acquired legally, ignoring suspicion or guilt - are also understood. In place of trust we see suspicion even of friends. They 'sneak'. In the place of a sense of security are all the implementations of artificial aids - burglar alarms, high walls and secret hiding places. Anything 'rich', worth stealing, is under threat. All sounds become suspicious. The sense of being scared is joined by being worried and then by the sense of profound insecurity. 'I think, like, they keep spying on me'.

The world that children experience contains many contrasts, between fear and trust, threat and security. But it also quite clearly contains not just those who turn the violence of school bullying into something larger, but an even greater number who have forsaken normal society - the beggars and the drunks. They are part of a visible stratum of the very poor. They remind children of the contrasts between the way people live, and the possibility of suffering that could confront any of them. There are many visual symbols of poverty. A succession of pictures on television presents the starving in Africa; advertisements for charitable agencies hammer home the association of certain countries with abject poverty.[11] But these images of distant countries, however real, are important because they link so closely to children's personal experience. This plays a major part in children's understanding of poverty. They see the edges of society in city streets; the homeless and the hungry. It is this extreme that defines poverty for them, rather than some socio-economic definition against averages. Poverty is a profound experience as well as something that children have to account for. There might be haunting images from television but what makes the question of poverty palpable for the children is the fact that they have *seen* it. Having seen poverty they also wish to define why it exists. Personal confrontations with the symbols of poverty, like homelessness and cardboard boxes, are linked to attempts to justify or explain it in terms of personal actuality and responsibility. The general state of poverty, the secondary sources of information, are constantly linked to personal experience, the general statement to the particular.

> Some people haven't got homes. I've seen some people who are tramps, without homes. I have seen them in the park sometimes. Once in the news there was someone but she died then. I see her everywhere on the streets, she goes in the road walking along. She's very old. *(boy 8)*

There is both an understanding of the widespread nature of poverty and the impact of the personal encounter. Faces are more easily associated with occupations than with names.[12] Some faces that are so personal and yet anonymous remain the particular vision that defines the whole. The children talk of a 'somebody'. They cite seeing people in sleeping bags, pushing their belongings on shopping trolleys, wearing plastic bags for shoes, and sleeping in cardboard boxes. But these images are also actual and particular people. They have their 'point of view' and are remembered as 'he' or 'she'. They might remain anonymous but they reflect not only a social problem but something about the society in which they find themselves.

> 'Cos once I bumped into a poor person, me and Daddy, walking home from this furniture shop. We walked out of the garage and we sort of walked and we saw this old, poor man. He had a beard and a hat and we've seen him around quite a while. And he asked if we could go and get him a cup of tea. So we did and he had some money to buy it. But the people in the shop, he'd been in there loads of times and they just won't let him buy a drink or a cup of tea. 'Cos they might think that he might disturb all the customers and make them go out. Or they don't like him or something. He might because he's well, he was a bit smelly 'cos he hadn't washed for a while, 'cos he didn't have a sink, really. And he's, well, he was quite dirty and he wore ragged clothes. The only part of posh clothing that I saw on him was some blue like posh trousers that you wear to a wedding or something. He had a light blue pair. And he had black scruffy shoes with all holes in them. And he had a hat on. *(girl 8)*

The children who witness the poor with such detailed intensity have not yet learned how to walk on the other side, to dismiss responsiveness to their plight as a form of encouragement. But they see the logic of other people's reactions: distaste at the smell, a threat to economic livelihood.

The poor are individuals, but they are also pervasive. Whilst they cite the particular and the proximity - 'down my road' - they also assume that these are not unique cases. They expect to see the same kinds of people anywhere in any large town, just as they would expect their television images of Africa to be confirmed. The marks of poverty are clear - 'they look in dustbins'. 'They've got loads of bags'. 'They're dirty'. 'They have trolleys'. 'They live in cardboard boxes' - they are consistent and assumed to be seen everywhere - 'In the streets, everywhere in Britain. Everywhere really'.

With such a consistent vision of the very poor, detailed and personal, what effect do they have on the thinking of children? How are they affected by them? How do they explain them? The effect works through the profound importance of personal relationships in terms of dialogue and mutual understanding and the realisation of the 'point of view'. These two necessities for learning, which encapsulate the experience of young children, are only slowly eroded by the studied artificialities of indifference. The superficial social gestures that are the diurnal necessities for survival have not yet completely formed the attitudes of children.[13] There is still the alert realisation of what people are like - insisted upon by the peer group. Those who are poor are not the faceless background to a society, but also the individuals within it. They remain people.

Whilst the home is no comfortable refuge it is still a necessity. 'Homelessness' defines itself. People need a place to stay, a place where they belong. Children clearly look at poverty with some measure of shock. They know what it would be like. They do not like what they see but taking people as individuals they both see how preventable it should be and how inevitable it seems to be. The poor are always with us. Children see the poor as being marked out by some personal crisis or affliction: poverty is eventually a personal, individual matter just as suffering is personal. Children do not have social theories to explain the facts away, and are not bolstered by political or sociological commentary. The reasons for poverty are personal. People are 'kicked out of home'. They sense that poverty is a mixture of misfortune and personal choice. This does not mean that they blame the person. They see poverty not purely as personal choice but personal misfortune. But they also connect the two.

> It's like poor people may need help and some people 'cos they're poor. They just can't get around and that. People like grow up and go out of their homes 'cos they don't want their mum and dad to look after them any more and they become poor and they just lie on the streets with a blanket or two. Because they don't want to live with their mum or dad.   *(boy 8)*

Home is seen as a refuge, but also as a place that can be rejected. Home is a kind of essential economic fact, a stability. Those who are homeless are assumed to have chosen to be so, to have deliberately removed themselves. Falling out with parents is one explanation; the other is the desire to go to a different town like London, hoping for a 'big job' and then failing to find one. In both cases social dysfunction, individual choice and individual failure are cited.

Poverty is defined by the children as a result of not having enough money or somewhere to stay, or as being rejected, being 'chucked out' or choosing to go. They know what lack of money means but such a complete absence of it, such a sense of dislocation is almost like social ostracism. It is an image of living on the edge of society. No-one can be outside it, for 'alienation' from the very society of which a person is part is impossible. Aliens are from another planet. Children cannot see the poor in this way, for they still have compassion. But they are profoundly disturbed by what they see and have to find ways of mitigating their understanding. Somewhere there has to be blame, but this lies in the interaction between the individual and the circumstance.

> He can't find a job anywhere 'cos people don't normally give jobs to people that can't have good clothes. They start off rich, they leave, they forget about getting a job, and they can't get a job, then, and they can't get in. It's probably their fault. It's more their fault than anyone else's and it might be their fault.
> *(boy 8)*

The sense of an explanation - the author of blame - is also accompanied by pity. They know that poverty is 'really sad' and that something should be done to alleviate it. But it is a personal matter. There are still individuals with personal choices and personal responsibilities. The poor are a part of society and a part of children's experience. They are representative of one extreme possibility in their own personal futures. In so far as the individual suffers it is so deeply felt that it is like a 'fulat', a personal responsibility.

When children see the very poor and try to explain them to themselves they realise both how symbolic of the realities of the world they are and how difficult to explain. The difficulties of the explanation lie in the fact that this is both raw data, unpolitical in the narrow sense, and actuality. The explanations that children have to find for themselves are complex, always involving factors of personality and variables of circumstances. Poverty is not a personal choice but it is embued with personality. It is a matter of chance, but felt acutely whether sought or not. Poverty is part of the human condition.

> Some of them are drunk and some of them are drug dealers. They're just, well, some of them are drug dealers and some just tramps. Sometimes we see them in the park, sitting on benches. They are the places I know. Some people aren't, um, having got enough money to make a business or get a job. And they can't make money to spend on things and for food then you obviously just have to find things for yourself. Just get things.
>
> When it gets cold weather you haven't really got anything to keep you warm. It wouldn't be very warm at night in the rain when you just have plastic covers to keep you dry.   *(boy 7)*

Observation and explanation; personal empathy and a grasp of what economic necessity is like and what could be done about it. But the effect of personal knowledge is deep, and cannot be isolated entirely from the daily happenings in children's own lives. The future - of jobs they hope for, and security - could easily be one of not having enough money, or failing at business. And the sense of having to 'find things for yourself' goes deep. There might be personal self-belief in that, but little security.

Poverty is not an abstract concept. Just as children see the limitations of their own home and its environment, so they acknowledge the fact that they themselves could be either relatively or absolutely poor. They see the visible signs of 'absolute poverty' as they experience 'relative poverty'. They know that society contains extremes. Whilst they do not know how to place themselves in the hierarchies of financial aggrandisement, they know that one extreme, of destitution, is not just a theoretical idea. It afflicts their sense of themselves. Poverty is a complex notion, caught up between subsistence which might seem plentiful to some, and the subjective experience that suggests that limited access to expensive entertainment is deprivation.[14] For children of all backgrounds it is, however, a real phenomenon, and they understand themselves, and their futures, in relation to it.

Images of the poor, however responsible the individual, are not abstract or second hand. Whilst they understand the chance and the relativity which surrounds the fact of their birth - they always realise that they *could* have been born somewhere else - children's understanding of the importance of not being poor transcends that. Children can acknowledge that had they been born elsewhere to other parents then they would have a different language and different outlook: but what matters most to them is not to be born poor.

> I don't mind really what I would be, but I wouldn't like to be a poor person. I wouldn't mind what country I come from but I wouldn't like to be poor.
>
> *(boy 9)*

The poor are seen to struggle and to suffer. They are at the margins of, but never outside, their local communities. They are deprived of the essential necessities, like a choice of food or freedom of manoeuvre. Children develop a strong fear of poverty.

Economic understanding derives fundamentally from children's unsupported attempts to understand the workings of society. They are driven not by images but personal experience; their parents having jobs, or being 'out of' a job, worries about paying bills and the difficulty of acquiring what they need. They might not understand the workings of money, but they understand what money does. They know they need it to buy the necessities of life. The amount of money of the world might be of a constant quantity and abstract meaning but it becomes palpable in the need for food, clothing and housing.[15] These are seen as the vital commodities that make life possible. Outside lies the reality of deprivation. The transactions of capital remain arcane. Their effects are immediate.

Given children's attitudes to home it might seem surprising that of all aspects of deprivation living in the street is the most significant. They yearn for the security of a place to stay. Home might not be emotionally comfortable, and it might contain amounts of argument and stress that set them on edge. But whilst they acknowledge that some children have deliberately left home, and whilst there remain major dissatisfactions, the sense of a place; warmth, light and at least a degree of security behind locked doors, remains an essential. The pragmatism of life is that people have to look after themselves, that they will struggle to find their own sense of purpose - is all centred on a place to live. There will always be relationships of a kind. But children want a place of their own. The homeless are therefore symbols of a greater displacement than the absence of a home. They represent the alien, the person who, seeing all, has not come to terms with it. They are what children most fear in themselves. They know the pain, but have not learned how to accommodate themselves to it.

Most children have seen people, like strangers, living in the streets. If they have not personally witnessed it they will have known about those accumulating images of deprivation. Beggars, like burglars, are a part of the social world. But whilst these might be the part of the pathology of the extreme, they are also a constant reminder of what could be. The home might not be perfect but it is there. The lack of money which leads to not having enough food to live on might seem theoretical. Being driven out of the home for lack of ability to pay the rent is not.

> If you wanna pay your rent because if you can't, if you haven't got enough money to pay the rent and you really want something and you haven't got it and you haven't got enough money and can't get it that would be kind of poor. Horrible, 'cos you haven't got any money to buy food or anythink. You got to work for money. You got to pay a rent and you've got to own all the money ...
>
> *(girl 8)*

It sometimes seems as if that legal requirement to have a place of residence which at once makes a person eligible for support, and liable for tax, were an instinctive claim on social coherence. Once you have enough money you can pay the rent. That is the ultimate 'possession', not the acquisition of goods.[16] Beyond the burglary of goods lies the terror of the loss of place, whatever the place might be like.

Poverty and homelessness are linked in children's minds for a number of reasons. The sense of wanting to 'belong', whether to a peer group or a larger and more lubricious manifestation of people together, runs very deep. The need is for other people, but these can be almost anyone provided they are willing to make a relationship. At the same time there is the recognition of the place, ideally 'safe and warm'. Poverty, as symbolised in the homeless is ultimate insecurity. There is no place to call one's own. The idea of being 'chucked out', of having no central physical place is like losing all sense of purpose. This is not because there is a lack of purpose or identity. On the contrary. The human experience is essentially very lonely. The dependency on relationships is both the means of learning and of distraction. Young children instinctively know that there will always be others, new people, different kinds of relationships. At the same time they are instinctively aware that they should guard themselves, that they should be careful, that they should not give themselves away. All the conflicting voices they hear are 'be careful: go on, avoid strangers: make friends'. In such a jumble of voices and contrasting rules of behaviour they try to find their way. Where, then, do they find their centre?

They need a place to be. 'Place' is, of course, a term so vague as to be almost geographical. Place is the parameters that imply at least the groundwork for personal security: safety and warmth, but more significantly, enough of the physical reliabilities to let emotional and intellectual exploration take place. Each child remains and feels individual. Those images of the old or of the 'down and out' are also individual people. Society contains them all. Before they have acquired that self-absorption of philosophers, the world presents itself as a mass of actuality. The poor are not a theoretical construct, but a personal possibility. Such possibilities are easily translated into, and connected to, personal circumstances.

> I don't want to be a different person, like a person like, um, richer than I am. Because it's my mum can't, like a few weeks ago she got paid and she, she got her water cut off. And she went to a place where you pay for your water and she had to give them all her ... all of it. And they started laughing or things and they started saying 'we've had so many, many people just wanting to give, um, just pay their water'. Very hard to, like, get new clothes and things like that. I've had this rugby shirt for about four years. My mum bought it when you could just see the top of my finger.
> If I turn out to be poor, I'll be sad.   *(boy 8)*

The fear of poverty runs deep. Poverty is humiliating as well as sad. The constant deprivations, through which they compare themselves to others, is a daily reality for some. But the threat of poverty, the possibility of losing whatever they have, affects them all. It is as if they know that this aspect of their lives has a strong effect on the quality of their individual achievements. It is as if they connected, painfully, the actual circumstance and the personality; the outcomes of experience and the feelings that both led to and resulted from them.[17]

Children's understanding of the economic system is sometimes characterised as being naive. This is a misinterpretation of what is a commonly held view of society which is encapsulated in political debate. It is true that children do not express interest in or knowledge of the capitalist system, of interest rates and investment, of competition and profits. But the necessity for money and its effects, if not its operations, are clear. When children analyse the effects of the social system on the very poor they continue the debating points between nature and nurture, between the effects of the environment and personal responsibility. They do not make a simple distinction since they know that both play a part. Their view of the responsibility of the down and out for his or her own position is based on an acknowledgement of the power of the will. This comes about from the development of their own determination. They know it is always a possibility to 'drop out', not to bother to get up in the morning, to play truant. Instead they are determined to go on doing what is difficult and unrewarding. They keep attending lessons which humiliate them and take tests which expose them.

When children explain beggars it can sound as if they are taking a very conservative view - that it is the responsibility of the individual to do something about it, and that one cannot simply blame society. This does not mean that children are unaware of the socio-economic facts, the cycles of deprivation which afflict so many. They have a firm grasp of the underlying realities of a monetary system, the contrasts between the rich and the poor. They might not have the sophisticated explanations of economists, but like all others, know the effects of economics. They also have a view of social circumstances which is not abstract, or a matter of general policy. They see the people in society as individuals, needing money, wanting a voice, needing control and restraint. They see the people eventually as having their own points of view and their wills. This does not mean that their concept of mind connects with achievement. There is a distinction to be made between individual efforts and success. They know that it is harder for some to achieve what they want than others. Children therefore have a firm grasp of the mixture of helplessness and submission to circumstances and personal will that makes up the lives of people in society. What young children have not grasped is self-abnegation, the indulgence of completely giving in.

Children do understand the essentials of the economy and they also understand the importance of money. Much has been made of children's 'subjective' view of money and of their difficulties in understanding currencies and rates of exchange. It is supposed that there must be 'stages' when they do not possess and interpret systems, when they confuse personal and social roles and do not recognise the function of money.[18] Whilst the sophistication with which the economic system is explained remains obscure to anyone but academics, and complicated to anyone but politicians it is hard to detect any time when the basic functions of money and its effects are not understood by children. In parallel to the context of their own lives children see the contrasts in the style of living and the amounts of possession in others. We must not confuse the understanding of values - what is a 'good' income - with the understanding of functions. Money is after all both a reality and a symbolic system, both as lubricious as inflation and as multifaceted as rates of exchange. Those who have tried to detect stages of thought have under-emphasised children's grasp of the concepts of power, possessions, equality and inequality.[19]

These studies of children's ability to explain financial transactions have suggested that children at first do not recognise the basic function of money, as if it were freely available.[20] But from children's point of view, money *is* available, even if in small amounts. What they do not understand is what a symbolic £50 or £500 or $50 or $500 actually amounts to. But they see the monetary transactions, they see shops. More to the point they see the effects. This gives money a very important place in their understanding. Children might be subjective in their view of money, and not be able to recognise coins, and they might express a lack of interest, but they do understand the essential financial functions and their importance.[21] Money is for them not an abstract concept, although there are few of them who have been actively taught about it.[22] Those children who have the experience of trading or bartering very quickly grasp the concept of 'profit'.

Whilst children do not understand clearly the symbolic terms of finance they know about values, about poverty and riches, about possessions and the power of money. The centrality of money is emphasised in their description of where they stand in relation to the circumstances of others.

I think that we are rich and poor. Other people are rich and some are poor, but most of the time we're all quite happy the way we are. I think we're both because I'm quite poor and my sister's poor, but my mum, but every day we get a little tiny bit richer because my daddy goes to work. But if we do get too rich, we give some of our money to charities. So we're in between I should think.   *(girl 7)*

The extremes of the rich and poor are well known, but all children suggest that their own circumstances are somewhere in the middle. Indeed, that is where they would prefer to be. They dread being poor. But they recognise that being rich carries responsibilities as well as dangers. They assume that money needs to be spread, as it affects all, and they feel that the rich are obliged to help the poor. Money *is* after all, available.

Many children do not feel they *need* a lot of money. They know they must have the essential necessities, like food and warmth and clothing. They know that they need money to buy or rent a home. They also know that money is what buys presents. They see the immediate effects of having more money as well as the essential support of having enough. Money makes desirable toys and other possessions available.

You can get what you want, like you can get two bikes, like two gear ones and a BMX or something. And you can get the toys you really want. And shoes you really want.   *(boy 8)*

Children make an important distinction between adequacy and greed. Whilst they know it is better to be modest they are still tempted by greed. Of *course* they would like to have all the toys they dream of. Of course they are cajoled by advertisements into desiring the latest fashionable Christmas present.[23] The peer group puts added pressure on keeping pace with collective trends. But children also recognise that some of this is an example of being greedy. They might be disappointed on birthdays not to get what they had hoped but are equally clear about the dangers of being spoiled - a psychological explanation they often give for bad behaviour. Their sense of relativity makes them balance the actuality of their own circumstances with those of others. Riches are attractive. Countries contrast with each other, and some which are the most attractive present themselves as full of good things. The United States is the symbol of desirable possessions and desirable activities.

People say it's really quite a rich place and say that it's a healthy area. And they say you get loads of brilliant trainers there like Nike and Reebok that I've got at the moment. I'm going to get Reebok pumps. They say it's quite good there and they got, you know, all the T-shirts you get like Surf Lords. I've got some of them and Hot Tunes and Ocean Pacific. You get all those. I've got all those. They make really good things, you know.   *(boy 9)*

Marketing succeeds, and its success depends on people having money to spend.

Possessions are desirable. Some children think of the desirability of having money because it can be expressed in terms of large houses with swimming pools. Others think of the symbolic gestures of gold watches and designer labels. They are also constantly reminded of the power of money, or its lack, through the medium of presents. They all report their parents explaining that they cannot afford a particular item, or other members of the family stepping in to make up the shortfall. What they do not do is to work out weekly budgets. They do not know what a good income consists of in terms of amounts. They do not know, beyond their pocket money, what things actually *cost*.

I know one man and he's really rich. He's a friend of ours. And he gave me a ten pound note for my birthday. And he gives it to our, to my mum as well. But he gave her a fifty or a twenty. I can't remember. He tells us and he's got two really good cars. One about two thousand or fifty thousand pounds.
                                        (boy 8)

Large amounts of money, beyond those that they deal with tend to confuse children. They confess to not knowing much about money and not having a great deal of interest in it. But this lack of interest is in the abstract concepts. They do not know how much you need to live on for a week, and speculate that perhaps £200, or $300, or £10 a week might be enough. What they do know is the effects of money. They know about rents and about bills. They also know about not having enough.

The underlying concern is the possibility of falling into poverty, of not being able to pay the bills.

So that I would be, well, not poor but so I can stash some money somewhere if ever I need it for emergencies and I would be short of money really. You need money to pay the gas bills so you can still have your light or electricity or

> something. If there's no electricity and you have no money you could not have
> fires because you would not have the money to make fires or you would not
> have the money to buy the coal to light the fires.   *(girl 8)*

Not knowing how much a ton of coal would cost is not as significant as the
awareness that money is needed - for all the services as well as food and
clothing. The fact that children do not explain the intricacies of interest
rates and investment serves to draw attention to the more immediate
personal effects of money.

Children are aware of the poor at the margins of society and do not
assume that they might end up like that. But they are also aware of the
reality of more prosaic poverty, of having not enough to live on, of not
finding a job, or not having a place to stay. That cycle of dispossession, of
having no fixed abode, and therefore not being able to claim benefits,
which means having nowhere to live, is well understood. There is little
theoretical about poverty. The rich are a different matter. All children are
aware that there are some people who are very rich.[24] Their views about
them are a mixture of faint jealousy and spite. Having possessions is real
enough, having space to live. At the same time the rich are symbolic,
images of greed. They are only seen in glimpses and do not carry the same
immediacy as those on the streets.

Part of the imagery of the seriously rich comes from television. That is
where the fabulously wealthy, whom they never meet, parade their goods
and lifestyles, taking the concept of designer labels to almost unbelievable
lengths. But at a more prosaic level the rich are symbolised by particular
possessions, like a 'mansion' or a Rolls-Royce. Those glimpses into the
material power of money are shared by all children. The very rich are like a
distant tribe, snobbish and selfish, associated with being 'posh'. But there
are also people that they know, who also are recognised by what they wear
and what they drive.

> They wear really smart clothes and they got tons of new things. I know one
> person who's rich. He's got everything. He wears these smart jeans and things
> like that.   *(boy 8)*

Riches mean possessions, and large houses.

They're very rich. They've got three dogs and they've got an absolutely massive home with five bathrooms, four bedrooms, three living rooms and a kitchen and they've got a wood and they've got three fields for the dogs and stuff. *(girl 8)*

These are not symbolic. There is no doubting the attractions of possessions. But there is also a shared feeling that wealth can be overdone. Those that are what they describe as 'telly rich' are also described as having 'posh' things. They are also seen to be careless with money, being able to 'burn it', or buy a 'Ferrari F40'. They are seen as extravagant and having power over other people, having servants to run their large homes. There is a definite distaste that runs through the children's accounts. There is an assumption that there is something corrupting in being rich. That some responsibility for one's own destiny that are seen in the poor also explain the rich: children assume that they have become so out of greed, out of sheer desire. They assume that the rich are not very popular - and not very nice.

Children know the power of money but despise extravagance. They assert that they would not like to be too rich themselves. Greed, snobbery, bossiness and selfishness are all associated with the very rich as if there were something wrong in such wealth. The rich *ought* to give more to the poor so that they wouldn't go on being so rich. Children do not like their fellow pupils in school standing out from the crowd. They despise the haughty or the 'show-offs'. They also think that being rich is to be spoiled.

I know one called J. 'Cos he goes to this school now. He used to go to P. Juniors. And he used to fight a lot as well. And he's spoilt. He's got three cars. He's got a garage and he's got five computers. He's got a Wendy house. He's got five pounds and two swimming pools. I don't really want him to be spoilt 'cos it's not really fair on the other people. *(boy 8)*

Since they associated the rich with so many defects children vow that they would not like to be rich - or spoilt - themselves. They seek the middle way.

Children are very aware of the contrasts between the rich and the poor. They see a vast distinction between the ways that people live.[25] They have a tendency to see the rich and poor as different *kinds* of people.[26] They are aware of class distinctions particularly in terms of possessions rather than behaviour.[27] They see the social and economic realities of contrasts which depend on money. But they also have a distaste for the exaggerations of the extreme differences: they fear one and they despise the other. When children see their circumstances they seek to make some kind of order out of it. They are aware of enormous distinctions and great inequalities. They see themselves as being comparatively ordinary and not at all unusual. They are absolutely clear that they could be in richer circumstances, that their own homes, even when not threatened with burglary, are imperfect, that their towns are polluted and the streets dangerous. This is the accepted case. They might long for something different but have to accommodate themselves to what is.

One of the consequences of a society of such contrasts is children's underlying sense of injustice. The sense of relativity in their own circumstances, the resentment of unfairness in school are compounded by the reflections on communities and society as a whole. Why should some have so much and others so little? There is a strong feeling that there is an unequal distribution of money.

> Some people are rich and some aren't. Well, I like watching these films about Robin Hood and that because they say 'rob from the rich and feed the poor'. And I think that the rich should give money to the poor to help them live and that. 'Cos they've got a lot of money but the poor people haven't.   *(boy 8)*

> I think that rich people ought to give about a hundred a year to the poor people 'cos it's sad for the poor and it's happy for the rich people. I wouldn't like to be rich because you've got everything. Like you'd be sent to private school and things like that. They've got a big mansion. And they've got about four cars. I don't think it's nice to be rich. Because you feel sorry for the poor. 'Cos you're well off and they're not and it's just generally that I don't like rich people much because it's the person that counts and not how rich and poor they are.   *(girl 8)*

It is the person that counts. And the person is either rich or poor. It might not be 'nice' to be rich but it is distinctly unpleasant to be poor. Since the whole social system consists of so many individual people, with their own points of view and their own feelings, children try to create an order of understanding which takes in both personal feeling and responsibility and a system of rules and arrangements that should cater for all. The unequal distribution of wealth is both a fact and an injustice. That each person is responsible, or they feel responsible for themselves, is accepted; but so is the arbitrariness of fate. Children find themselves where they are. They know they are locked into their own outlook. But they still acknowledge the chance that brought them there.

In adjusting to their conception of the world children seek to accommodate themselves as they do to the home and to the school. They must adapt. They must submit, for the alternative has dire consequences. They see those who do not keep going within the system. They understand the consequences for those who take what seems an easy way out by not bothering. The punishment for those who do not find a modus vivendi are clear. The temptations for those who wish to take a short cut to possessions are apparent. What children are learning to do is to find their own middle way. This is done subconsciously by pruning any extravagant thoughts or ambitions, by accepting standardised and received wisdoms, by not thinking so much. It is done consciously by adhering to standards, by avoiding differences.

There is much speculation about how young people are moulded into a cultural system. But this assumes that they are pliable and that they can be dealt with as the collective will wishes. It leaves out their clear intelligence, their emotional drives and their own rationalities. What is clear is that it is children themselves, given all their insights and experiences, who strive for adaptation. Whether this is a good thing or not, it is part of the human experience. Sometimes this middle way, this avoidance of the dangers of the extreme, can seem almost like an idyll.

> I see myself in a lovely little cottage and not much to eat but having a happy life. Having to work quite hard for it. But I think I'd rather have quite a lot of money but living in ... I'd rather be poor than rich but I really don't know, 'cos rich you'd be able to see lots of things but poor, you would, like, I think, you would be more content if you were poor. Because you wouldn't have so much to ask for. You'd be alright with what you've got. I think poor people are nice because they don't want everything.
>
> If you're a person that doesn't like loads of stuff I'd be quite content being poor. Whereas I'd be, I don't think I'd be quite so content being rich because you know that you have the money to buy things more. Then you'd want things.   *(boy 8)*

On the face of it, this yearning for the middle way, sounds like the advice of an 18th century poet.

Who moves within the middle region shares
The least disquiets, and the smallest cares.[28]

But children's fear of extremes is born of trauma rather than rationality. Their sense of the conventional is an anguished response to what they find their lives to be, with conflict and no immediate resolution, with complexity and no bland explanation.

Poverty and riches are both the forming and the result of desire, or contentment. Do people really acquire what they deserve? The sense of both personal desire and responsibility, and the forces of destiny combine in the minds of children, forming their dissatisfactions and contents, their attempts to understand and the essential incomprehensible nature of life. In forming their own individual ways children are struck by the binary divides; good and bad, rich and poor. Their sense of being in the middle does not derive just from a desire for complacency but from the opposing forces in which they find themselves. There is a constant interplay of different kinds of experience and different types of understanding. There is information that they need being presented to them; but some of this is false. They long for an understood and accepted framework of rules; but they see the constant intensities of personal relations. The rich and the poor are groups, are definitions. They are also people. Behind every abstract idea is a personal reality. The middle way that children seek is survival.

Notes

1. cf. The idea of 'charisma'; the tension between sure and approachability, between distance and friendliness. Cullingford, C. *The Effective Teacher*. London, Carnell, 1995.

2. Hart, R. *Children's Experience of Place*. New York, Irvington, 1979.

3. Vygotsky, L. *Mind in Society*. Cambridge MA, Harvard University Press, 1978. *Thought and Language*. Cambridge MA, MIT Press, 1962.

4. Haste, H. *Growing into Rules*, in Bruner, J. and Haste, H. (eds.). Making Sense. London, Methuen, 1987.

5. Yonuiss, J. and Volpe, J. A Relational Analysis of Children's Friendships, in Damon, W. (ed.). *Social Cognition*. Washington, Jossey-Bass, 1978.

6. cf. Rosengren, K and Hickling, A. Seeing is Believing: Children's Explanations of Commonplace, Magical and Extraordinary Transformations. *Child Development*, Vol.65, No.6, pp.1605-1626, 1994.
   Four year olds tend to talk about the inexplicable in terms of 'magic', five year olds already in terms of 'tricks'.

7. Cullingford, C. Children and Comics. *Research in Education*.

8. Children quickly distinguish between reality and fantasy on television; accepting the mass violence of thrillers as part of the drama whilst being genuinely upset by a single, sudden physical attack in the studio. Cullingford, C. *Children and Television*. Aldershot, Gower, 1984.

9. Haste, H, op cit.

10. 'Getting and spending we lay waste our powers'.
    Wordsworth, W. *The World* (is too much with us).

11. Cullingford, C. Children's Attitudes to Developing Countries. *Primary Practice*, 1996.

12. Cohen, G. Why is it difficult to put Names to Faces? *British Journal of Psychology*, Vol.81, No.3, pp.287-297, 1990.

13. Or some notable fictional misfits who try to see the world as it is, like Prince Myschkin in Dostoyevsky's *The Idiot*.

14. Huston, A; McLoyd, V and Coll, C. Children and Poverty: Issues in Contemporary Research. *Child Development*, Vol.65, No.2, pp.275-282, 1994.

15. As Beckett says in *Waiting for Godot*; "The Tears of the world are of a constant quantity".

16. Furnham, A and Jones, S. Children's Views Regarding Possessions and their Theft. *Journal of Moral Education*, Vol.16, No.1, pp.18-30, 1987.

17. Garrett, P; Ng'andu, N and Ferron, J. Poverty Experiences in Young Children and the Quality of the their Home Environments. *Child Development*, Vol.65, No.2, pp.331-345, 1994.

18. Furth, H. *The World of Grown-Ups: Children's Conceptions of Society*. New York, Elsevier, 1980.

19. Lea, S; Tarpy, R and Webley P. *The Individual in the Economy: A Survey of Economic Psychology*. Cambridge University Press, 1987.

20. Furnham, A and Stacey B. *Young People's Understanding of Society*. London, Routledge, 1991.

21. Bruner, J and Goodman, C. Value and Need as Organizing Factors in Perception. *Journal of Abnormal and Social Psychology*, No.42, pp.33-42, 1941.
    Berti, A and Bombi, A. The Development of the Concept of Money and its Value: A Longitudinal Study. *Child Development*, Vol.52, No.6, pp.1179-1182, 1981.

22. Furnham, A and Weissman, D. *Estimating the Value of British Coins. A Development and Cross Cultural Perspective*. Unpublished. Cited in Furnham, A and Stacey, B, op cit.

23. Ward, S, Robertson, T. and Brown, R. (eds.). *Commercial Television and European Children*. Aldershot, Gower, 1986.

24. cf. The famous, if apocryphal, exchange between Fitzgerald and Hemingway:

    'The very rich are not like you and me'.
    'No. They have more money'.

25. Townsend, P and Corrigan, P. *Poverty and Labour in London*. London, Low Pay Unit, 1987.

26. Leahy, R. The Development of the conception of Economic Inequality: Descriptions and comparisons of rich and poor people. *Child Development*, Vol.52, No.2, pp.523-532, 1991.

27. Short, G. Perceptions of Inequality: Primary School Children's Discourse on Social Class. *Educational Studies* Vol.17, No.1, pp.89-106, 1991.

28. Pomfret. On his Friend Inclined to Marry.
    Tomkins, E (ed.) p.238. 'Do not aspire to riches in excess'. Poems on various subjects: selected to enforce the practice of virtue and to comprise in one volume the Beauties of English Poetry. London, Crosby and Co, 1804.

8　Face to face: understanding the human condition

There are many rites of passage in our lives, and certain experiences that leave their mark, but there is no period as significant as the early years. What happens to us then helps form what we become. If we really took seriously the potential and real traumas of those years we would be far more sensitive to children and we would know far better how to nurture and develop human talents, as well as overcome the unnecessary tendencies towards disaffection. The problem is that we, as our children will probably do in their turn, have learned to ignore much of the information and have created a kind of mythology of the past. The rites are what we remember rather than the trauma of the passage.

Each person is unique in personality and experience. But we all share a common humanity, and all bring into the world with us both intellectual capacity and emotional vulnerability. We need to be able to celebrate the individual but we also need to understand the nature of the human experience, how the mind and heart cope with what they find. Between the individual and humanity lies that middle ground, the chance that places a person in a language and a culture that so clearly influence the way he or she thinks and feels. This book is, however, not about the ways in which particular environments produce prejudice and stereotyping, but about the way that individuals deal with their experiences, whatever they are.

Children possess clear intellectual capacity, often, if not always, unfulfilled, and exhibit great sensitivity to the surroundings on which they gaze. Their ways of learning are therefore dependent on their cultural surroundings. It is almost impossible to separate a notion of abstract intelligence or the processing of information from the circumstances in which it takes place. Intelligence is exhibited in a context in which it can communicate itself. It is impossible to demonstrate the process of thought without using information that is intrinsic to it. On the other hand each individual makes something different of the information that is presented. It is important to distinguish completely between the effect a speaker intends to have on the mind of the listener and the actual effect of the message. The speaker cannot ever be sure that he is saying even what he intends to say.[1] All analysis of response shows the subjective nature of the reading of any text. But the very fact that the text can be read underlies that these are shared as well as distinct interpretations, that there are cultural as well as individual understandings.[2]

The unique nature of each person's interpretation is not as much a matter of genetic make-up as a matter of chance, of what kind of information is presented to them. There could be twins who are completely different. The difference cannot be simply put down to birth, since no two people's actual experience will be alike. One might have overheard a particular remark, or interpreted it in a particular way. Sometimes it is possible to remember years later the comment that someone made. 'You're the caring one'. Labels are freely or inadvertently given. 'She's messy'. 'Here comes fatso'. Even if they are well intentioned, these comments leave their reverberating effects and can become the groundwork for later emotional difficulties or a lack of self-belief. It is no wonder that people learn to protect themselves from their own sensitivity.

Children receive many different types and levels of information which are all tangled up. These include the immediate interaction with their parents and siblings, a microcosm of the world. They undergo strenuous relations with their peers and in the social control of larger groups. And at the same time they receive direct information about the macro-world, about news and about society at large. Children interpret one level of experience in the light of another. They cannot fail to be aware of those issues that dominate all peoples lives. They cannot be physically or emotionally withdrawn from the realities of the world, which is why they have to learn how to cope with it themselves, psychologically. The kinds of information they receive are many and varied. They include the mixtures of fact and fantasy, dialogue and story, explanation and overheard remarks, experience and the imagery of the outside. They hear truths and falsehoods, misinterpretations and insights. They need to make all this coherent for themselves.

Children are not born stupid even if some appear to wish they were. Even what seems as simple a term as 'attitude' contains a variety of complexities.[3] An attitude can denote a fixed point of view, or a neutral one, it can be a search for something new, and an emotional readiness, or a subconscious indifference. For all the desire to form a rigid habit of mind, a mental set, the inadvertent always has an opportunity to creep in. Whilst young children are busy forming concepts, and understanding the classifications of the world, even these are never simple but contain both intellectual properties and emotional ones. With every conceptual configuration arrives the possibility of a stereotype. Attempts to see similarities and differences are a necessity for comprehending the physical world and the world of ideas but can also depend on prejudice.

The problem with understanding the nature of children's experience, as presented by the nature/nurture divide, is a problem faced by the children themselves. They are trying to understand phenomena, like the fact that different types of bird have similar beaks, in terms of both analogy and homology. The beak might be efficient for certain conditions and the birds might originate from the same genetic stock. Both are sensible explanations.[4] Similarly children look at a variety of species to find out distinctions and parallels. They learn both the ontogenetic - those traits and parallels *within* individuals - and the ethnogenetic: parallels between individuals. There is a constant searching for a number of understandings, all of which overlap.

The processes of thinking and interpretation are complex. They include imaging and associating as well as criticism. When scrutinising new material like a story, there will be elements of all three responses even when one of them dominates. To image is to confine the conception into some ikon that makes it seem real. To associate is to draw on personal experience, to bring the reality close to home. To criticise is to maintain objectivity and self-awareness, to be able to distance oneself from what is perceived. All three forms of response are constantly present and each have their strengths and limitations. To be too critical is not to understand, since it is impossible to enter in to the presented contextual world. To be too associative is to be idiosyncratically inventive in interpretation, to pick on minor or irrelevant details, or to distort by amplification and to interpret impulsively - in other words to be inaccurate.

Children are constantly 'reading' their environment as they read stories. This is done at a number of different levels rather than in one consistent way. When presented in terms of reading, there is so much evidence of the processing of interpretation including imaging and associating that there is no question of doubting the complexity of the experience. There are constant juxtapositions between fact and fantasy, parallel realisations that it is a 'story' and that it presents truths, constant lapses into and out of concentration. When children are studied through their interpretation of real events, like real tasks, there is a tendency to try to create a simple model of information processing as if people were like computers. Such mechanistic accounts of intelligence remains attractive for those who wish to simplify and isolate the behaviouristic functions of the brain. The problem is that such models leave all emotions out of the account, together with reactions *against* concentrating. Even the most demanding intellectual task will not elicit such purity of logical thought for which philosophers or mathematicians yearn. The actual skills involved are more complex and more intuitive.

That 'purity' of intellect, likened to serial thinking, analytical, logical and single-minded, presents the mind as if it were like a machine, scientific, mechanical and relentless. But real thought runs at a number of different levels; often taking in many more than one idea at a time. Most ideas cannot be singled out; there are multiple simultaneous thought processes that make the human mind unique.[5] Thinking is like a complex social behaviour. Whatever the attempts to break it down into a series of isolated and distinct competencies, real quality of understanding will be excluded. Quality of thought can be recognised but not easily measured. The difficulty about accounts of the mind is that the means - the experiment, the isolation of variables - has completely dominated the end, which should be understanding. The desire to measure and to prove deductively a particular hypothesis has overcome the recognition of the different dimensions of the mind and the motivations which direct it - including that of the researcher himself.

For all its potential logic the mind is receptive to the influence of details. Certain remarks, ideas, or experience stand out. Not everything is processed with ruthless and exclusive logic. Thinking, therefore, cannot be explained simply in terms of words. There are a host of perceptual images, that are far less easy to control and measure than verbal understanding but which, like words, form their own network of meanings.[6] The picture, the idea, the ikon, or the image cannot be reduced to a word. Images and verbal processes run together and intertwine. Images themselves can come in a variety of forms.[7] They can be directly or inadvertently aroused, they can derive from or promote associations or be triggered by and produce other verbal connections. Either images or words can produce chains of symbolic transformations. All these forms of imaging, enactive, ikonic or symbolic, the first to do with behaviour, the second with the types of imagery and the third with language, are constantly employed.[8] What seems like an abstract idea can never be purely abstract.

If the interpretation of the world depends so clearly on the mind of the individual there can be no simple notion that tasks can be abstracted from their context. Clearly there are many who would like to think that the information being didactically presented is automatically the information being taken in, just as there are many who long for setting up particular intellectual tasks that could, like a learning machine, automatically have an effect.[9] Sometimes it seems as if we have not come a long way from Pavlov; but then this too is a sign of the way in which the alert mind is formed, trailing with it as much weakness as glory. Every new experience is bound to be interpreted in the light of what has happened previously. It is impossible to make any situation so pure that there are no other 'contaminating' associations. New knowledge will always form up against old knowledge. The operation of mental acts, interpreting the world, the 'epistemic', coming to know, operates in parallel with the 'antic', the means by which a situation is construed and represented, made into an inner reality.[10] When a new piece of information or a new circumstance is encountered then the framework, a previous way of dealing with something similar, is inevitably drawn from the memory, even if it interferes. New knowledge must fit into the old, even if this is an uncomfortable fit. As a result categories of information do not carry with them distinct boundaries, self-contained and distinct. We are dealing with a haze of information and response, with intuition as much as with order, with parallels of interpretation rather than the cold manipulation of tasks.

This suggests something of the vulnerability as well as the power of the mind, its individual strength and the significance of context. New knowledge floods in, but needs channelling. There is always a balance between the freshness of the information and the canals of experience that are already formed. It is difficult to distinguish how the two habits of learning, prejudgement and reception, interact since even to young children something they have just learned feels as if it had always been known.[11] Furthermore they assume that knowledge is not exclusive to them. They think that it is shared by all rather than a secret. They are not resistant to new information nor are they jealous of it. For them it has the properties of excitement and availability. Later knowledge becomes power - something that you use to get the better of other people.

New information nevertheless fits into as well as helps form, what is already in existence. Children need to learn how to connect ideas, how to make structures of information, how to categorise and how to perceive hierarchies of knowledge. Each of them does so in his or her own way. New information does not come readily packaged and explained. The constant acquisition of knowledge means that children's theories of mind and understanding are continually undergoing change. There are times when they will come to a particular perceptual and emotional conclusion which might be wrong, and might influence them for some time. It then is either re-examined in the light of later experience and modified and adjusted or stays latent in the back of the mind. Certain misconceptions can last for years and then be suddenly revealed. New knowledge is absorbed, and becomes part of an already existing structure even if that structure is unsound.

There is always something inadvertent in learning because of the interpretative activity of the mind. No information is received as something neutral. It carries a meaning, and meaning implies structure. The irony is that the very desire for order, for categorisation, leads to arbitrary interpretations.[12] Subconscious influences come to bear and inferences are made without a complete knowledge of their effect. Perception and memory are constructive processes. They depend on the creation of schemata. There are no such things as stimuli devoid of a place in a hierarchy and structure of interpretation. What children look for are the significant features of new information, that is, what is significant to them. Perception needs to be categorised for it to make sense, as in the learning what particular phonemes are necessary and meaningful in speech.

The interpretation of experience is not, however, utterly individual. It is, as in the case of language, dependent on the sharing of agreed meanings according to the particular circumstances and codes of the environment. Perception might depend on categorisation but is formed by what is commonly agreed to be significant.[13] The young child interprets. This can be idiosyncratic. But he or she is also taught, to some extent, how to interpret. What is difficult is that the distinction between the two sometimes appears arbitrary, if it is detected at all. Information and interpretation, facts and attitudes, unsullied experience and the expectations of it are all part of a tangled web.

In the centre of this mass of influences, both personal and external, is the steady gaze of human intelligence. Nothing escapes. All is observed. When we recognise and acknowledge this fact we need to rethink some of our misconceptions of the experience of being human. Most of these false interpretations of childhood are in themselves a result of the experience, a result of denial, of deliberate forgetfulness, or the need to justify all the compromises of existence. Perhaps the disappointments of the real against all the unfulfilled hopes and expectations are too great.

The recreation of the myth of childhood rests on a nostalgia for simplicity and irresponsibility; and is shared by children themselves. It is an assumption of an essential stupidity, which was never there, and a longing for a previous time of undiluted happiness. There are many moments of happiness in childhood and times of extreme and unmitigated joy. But these are not the only emotions that children carry with them. We all know the effects of abuse on subsequent lives, and how traumatic incidents mar forever the emotional well-being of people. We all know those who seek counselling trying to trace the pain that now afflicts them to where it began. There are all kinds of therapists delving into the psychological bases for subsequent feelings of pain and inadequacy. That there is a connection between mental difficulties and childhood is clear. But we have assumed that such connections only belong to the mentally unstable, that there are signs of comparatively rare failure. It makes the myth of a normal childhood the more powerful to isolate the unhappy exceptions.

When we begin to explore the realities of childhood with the mythologies of development and optimism stripped away we realise that for all children the early years contain trauma. We do not discover this in our own memories, since we have, as the evidence here demonstrates, all learned the coping strategies of adaptability, of conservation, of ignorance. If there were in our own inner lives traces of the difficulties of the early years we would be the first to deny it, for we are relatively successful in wiping them away. It is when we look objectively at the experience of children, with that same clarity that they bring, and when we hear what they have to say that we see what a fragile state childhood is for everyone.[14]

Children's experience is varied and complicated. But with the moments of happiness there are moments of trauma. These are not necessarily obvious, nor are they the result of deliberate attempts to inflict pain. They are the strain of attempts to understand. The word 'trauma' might sound extreme, but taking its Greek then Latin root it does cover a measure of complexity, even ambiguity.[15] It contains the sense of a wound, or an injury or a shock. It suggests something either caused by or 'pertaining to' the experience. Wounds can heal. One can recover from injury. But the marks are still there, however small, and the memories do not entirely fade away however controlled.[16] The child's entry into the world is traumatic. Whilst this can be mitigated, it firstly needs to be understood. The inadvertent can play an important part.

The gaze of the child is one that is constantly making discriminations, seeing categories, learning what to interpret and what to ignore. Listening to the particular human voice, for example, entails not only concentrating on it and not being distracted by the background sounds like a passing bus, the hum of the refrigerator or barking, but knowing exactly which phonemes are the ones which carry meaning and which units of sound can be ignored.[17] But the physical categories are not the only ones which are in operation. Whilst it might seem that there are different layers of perception, from the immediately physical, through concepts, to refinements of moral action, these actually are pressed on the child's consciousness at once.

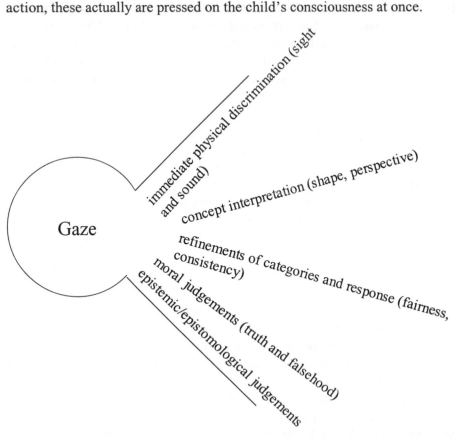

These cannot be depicted as so many layers, circles that spread out like the effects of a stone on still water, since all of the choices of response are being made at once. The most immediate physical responses include the concepts of perspective, and long before the words that define the concepts are learned - up, down, before, behind - the concepts are used. And primary matters of human interaction - consistency and variability - are making their mark.

It is not possible to cut off the child from his or her ability to see and the need to interpret. 'Well wadded with stupidity' we might become but we do not start that way.[18] Nor are these perceptual discriminations purely cerebral. They carry with them all the emotional weight that we observe in young children's almost pathological extremes of joy and pain. Their response is unmitigated by control. Their very reactions seem simple but the feelings are real. Their outcries are not just physical, but a result of interpretations. They do not cry, like birds, automatically when near food, but cry because they understand a want.

The passions, the extreme feelings of childhood, stem from their difficulty in making new experiences fit. They have not yet learned how to create such a framework that there is a place for every raw event. But 'framework' is too architectural a term to suggest the organic growth of understanding, the constant networking of a series of discriminations and categories. The mind is both powerful and fragile. Like the body it is prone to damage, to bruising, to scars and to renewing of tissue. The structures of the mind are constantly changing and whilst we become less and less aware of this, the early years in all their vulnerability demonstrate the effects of events on a constant and steady alertness of thinking and feeling.

As we grow older we know better which experiences and ideas to allow into our awareness. We know what to avoid, and what to ignore through what becomes an almost automatic interpretation. There are many subconscious choices and deliberate directions. But for young children all events will force their way into their consciousness, bidden or unbidden. Some experiences will bruise and affect their vulnerability to the next. The only real difference between the young and the old is experience. There is no difference in intelligence sensitivity or in rudimentary capacity and understanding. Experience is all. Would we do the same again? The answer, with hindsight, is often no, never. That much we know and we regret. But we did at the time make certain decisions, and in the same condition, without hindsight, would do so again. For young children the immediacy of the events and the consequences are far closer together. They might not have to make such large decisions but they feel their effect the more quickly.

Each individual is uniquely affected by circumstances. There is an essential fragility and vulnerability, as well as mental strength, in the early years. There is also an essential instability. The natural tendency is not to be stable but to fly off course, to veer wildly away. It takes all the effort to hold a steady course.[19] In this way trauma is a normal state. It deserves all kinds of sensitivity and support to overcome this. The idea that the young come into the world innocent and good and that it takes extreme cruelty or mismanagement to throw them off course is the opposite of the truth. Given the nature of early experience it is the more amazing how many adapt, develop strategies for survival and become healthy 'normal' human beings.

The very old differ from the young in their experience but also have a lot in common. They understand the significance of events, of the big defining moment. An old actress tracing her life will recollect the overarching event together with the still immediate feelings it aroused - 'he left me'. They know the hurt remains, and understand the emotional significance of such moments. They also relish the alternative joys that are the more important for being ellusive. Significant and defining events are like traumas. Young children are closer to them every day. The old pick out these significant moments; the very good and very bad. The young have them thrust upon them every day.

The essential feelings of the self do not change. Adults feel about themselves not as developing entities but also as essentially the same. 'I feel the same as I did as a child'. The child is as likely to say 'I feel I am a grown up'. Self-feelings do not change, although attitudes towards other people, trust and mistrust, do. In all there is the essential egotism of the subjective. However kindly towards others, however full of missionary instincts, it is the inner self looking out even if it learns to choose and interpret what it sees. The essential egotism, the vulnerability, the sensitivity to events and their manipulation to avoid pain is not the same as self-love. It is more a conscious identity which is permanent whereas self-love is love for something transient and superficial and which can be taken up or dropped at will.[20]

The essential feelings of the individual self remain, but we learn how to interpret and misinterpret events, to make them, if possible, more distant.

All learning includes the use of deliberate ignorance so that the new has less of an impact. We also manage to take what are traumatic events and make them appear normal, or part of a system. There are many examples of this. Being bullied is an intensely painful experience, whether it comes in the form of teasing or physical abuse. And yet there are still those who think of it as a normal and inevitable part of childhood experience. From the point of view of the 'system' in which it takes place there need to be typologies of victims and bullies and definitions of bullying as an intentional act. But the inadvertent can hurt as much as the deliberate. All children feel themselves to be victims at one time or another. Until we accept and understand this nothing fundamental in the way of policy can be done to alleviate the problem.

But the first sign of avoidance of a problem is a denial of its existence. If something is kept hidden or if something is explained as nothing more than an ordinary part of life, then nothing needs to be done about it. Difficulties can be more easily denied than explained. When, for example, certain pupils of normal or marked ability were having difficulties with reading it took a long time, despite all the psycholinguistic evidence, to accept that there is such a phenomena as dyslexia. It was easier to put down failures to read as stupidity or backwardness. But we know how complex is the mind and how easily concepts which draw on odd correspondences can be misconstrued, just as we know how difficult it can be to match the learning style of individual children to the tasks set. Knowing more about dyslexia, having accepted its existence, gives a greater insight into the complexities of the brain.

Another example of the human tendency to dismiss difficulties as part of the normal, or as a sign of inadequacy, is the struggle for recognition for what is called social phobia. The very fact that all people have an understanding of what it feels like leads ironically to its dismissal. Instead of gaining insight into the causes of the fear of being in public or making presentations, the assumption is made that it is but an extreme form of shyness. Like bullying it is supposed to be part of normal life. We have all been shy. We need to overcome that even if we do not develop the brazenness of politicians. But if we are sensitive to feelings we will remember how often children go through the traumas of exposure. They are shown up. They are 'picked on'. Traces of this remain.

All these social emotions deserve greater attention. The problem is that people are so caught up in systems that they forget the individuals in them.

It is sometimes easier not to give too much thought to things but to carry on with the practical. One analogy of this are personality inventories, questionnaires that demand an instant and automatic response. They are deemed to work - to pick out the extrovert and the introvert, the self-confident and the shy - but no-one knows exactly why.[21] The more a question is pondered over - as a child so aptly might - the more difficult it is to answer. To take one example

All in all I'm inclined to feel I am a failure.

This has been carefully tested for reliability. It seems bland enough. But who, out of poor self-esteem, or self-knowledge would be inclined to disagree? Failure against some vast ambition, or even failure against the hopes and expectations of childhood, is easily possible. But if you compare yourself to others, when you acknowledge, with that same self-knowledge what you have achieved, your inclination changes. What you are left with is a concept of self-esteem or confidence which is unexamined and untrammelled by the reality of experiences. It is as if the individual were to be no more than part of an inventory, a factor in a typology. Thus, in a practical way, do we learn to survive psychologically.

There is a difference in thinking between seeing 'types' in a 'system', a structure and an order, and in thinking about the thoughts and feelings of the individual. One example of this is the concept of alienation. On the face of it the term is contradictory. Whilst it is possible to be alien from another planet and whilst children might feel themselves like aliens, it is strictly impossible to be an alien within the society of which everyone is a part. But the *feelings* of alienation persist. The attractions of the term lie in the edge it gives to the sense of being excluded from, or outside a system.[22] From the point of view of the system there are all kinds of formal means of excluding people - from unauthorised truancy to formal and permanent exclusion. But by the time policies are in place the sense of personal alienation, a psychological exclusion has been long established. The feeling of being an outsider, of being discounted, are shared by all. It starts with classes or with peer groups, with friendship and enmity. It then becomes enshrined in more subtle and more formal manifestations, class or 'exclusive' clubs. The desire to belong, to a tribe or religion, to a political party or to a group is the reversal of that sense of distinction that makes other people beyond the pale.

The establishment of what is inclusive or exclusive is but a social example of strong personal feelings, of the desire to some semblance of collective security. The fear of not belonging, of being ostracised, makes the desire to be a member of a group or a gang the stronger. If one does not fit into the formal system there will be other alternatives to adhere to. What is longed for is the familiar. There are a number of studies of people, wrapped up in their own cultures, who enter 'alien' territory. This is supposed to be a 'shock', a sudden confrontation with the unfamiliar.[23] But what is disturbing is not so much the strange and the new, which can be exotic, but the absence of their own familiar everyday routines. These can be carried with them and are the more strongly defined when there are other habits to be compared. For children their early years are a deep culture shock. They have to adapt to particular expectations and habits. They obviously learn the particular language and expressions of wherever they happen to be, become 'branded on the tongue'.[24]

The familiar becomes defined against the alternative. People near borders literally or metaphorically are far more antipathetic to their neighbours when daily confronted by their differences. Familiarity here does not necessarily breed understanding. Rather than seeing the underlying experiences of being human, they prefer to identify themselves within the elaborations of the group. Young children are initiated into the sense of membership and the understanding of alienation subtly, automatically and undeliberately. But it becomes an established and powerful tradition because of the experience of threats to the autonomy of the individual. Other people are a protective bastion. They are another form of establishing shared norms as a protection against too much of the new breaking in. It is easier to deal with new information if the reaction to it is understood even before it is received.

The development of cultural stereotypes is an inevitable part of growing up. At its worst it can develop into extreme forms of prejudice. The traumas of childhood can form themselves into both a fierce loyalty to a gang, defined against what is seen as a threatening and 'alien' society, involving alternative uniforms, just as repressive if not more so but coming into being because of feelings of rejection. Or they can develop into the pathological end of self-definition, in having unquestioned prejudices against others. Both are signs of the scars of insecurity. The traumatic events of childhood lead to both 'psychotic' and 'neurotic' reactions.[25] Adaptability means submitting to shared norms, and suppressing differences. The pressure to do this, especially in schools, is strong. There are internal barriers to escaping from the norm. But there are also strong pressures on self-definition against what is seen as other people's cultural attitudes. The conflicting and joint cognitive and emotional pressures of self-identity and definition against the differences of others are strong and develop early. Long before we experience the outcome of tribal and religious conflict, the seeds have been planted early through the experiences of children. One way of dealing with the traumatic events of home and school, of self and others is not only to conform to expectations but to stifle the self in supposed conformity.

Children adapting to prejudice and stereotyping can easily be blamed on their parents and society. But children must be understood to have a need for such defining attributes. It is one of their ways of coming to terms, of adapting. Until we understand the nature of this experience and their needs we will never tackle the results of tribal conflict. Children look critically at what they see. They do not simply imbibe it. But they know when it is worth their while to submit to it. And it is true that the experiences they are presented with do not help them to find their own means of remaining autonomous. The security that children seek does not come easily. There is no such experience as 'ontological security': that confidence in the consistency, constancy and reliability of their environment.[26] Their experience is more full of underminings, of misunderstandings, of alternative interpretations. They see and understand the unreliability and the insecurity of the world around them.

Children continually relate what they objectively see to their own feelings.[27] The news that flashes on the screen is neither of addictive interest, nor does it mediate risk and danger.[28] On the contrary, it is a constant reminder of what happens and can happen. It might be defined later in their lives as the inevitable outcome of the behaviour of others - of other cultures and habits - but in their early years they have not yet built their cultural defences. Their first experiences are all directed at them, at their questioning minds and their exploratory emotions. They live in a state of eternal temporality. They receive each new item of experience as new and fresh. For them everything is the first time, subjective as well as objective.[29] They learn how to deal with new events by adapting them to themselves, for better or worse, as they get older.

The development from early childhood to maturity is usually described as the acquisition of new knowledge paralleled by the growth of intelligence and ability. It could be better described as the means by which intelligence adapts to new knowledge. Adaptation does not mean the accumulation of unrelated new insights, nor the acquisition of a succession of theories. It implies the strenuous efforts made to fit in, to play an anonymous individual part in the larger scheme of things. There is something of denial in the submission to events, a necessary one but a denial nonetheless. Adaptation can be positive and it can be limiting.

One of the results of this adaptability is the way that adults view their own pasts. They have learned to see childhood from their own perspectives. They also find themselves in the roles of parents and teachers which bring automatic responsibilities and clear difficulties faced with the, to them, 'alien' world of childhood. It is easier to come to terms through sentimentalising rather than by taking what is going on seriously. It is, in itself, a survival technique. There is, after all, a burden of responsibility in being a parent that is psychologically unbearable, but is therefore the more casually denied. It is much easier to transform the fragile experience of the young into naiveté. It is an adult tendency to place their fantasies on the young. The literature that is written for young children assumes that they live in a world of peculiar fantasy. The ways that adults talk to young infants displays an extraordinary range of the absurd that bears no real relationship to the actual matters of intelligence. It can be amusing but it is clearly a joke that children feel they like to play along with: for the infantile style of address is above all an attempt to make a reciprocal relationship. That is crucial. But it is also a manifestation of the placing of adult superiority - another form of a 'club' - over children.

One problem with adults listening to children is that even if they *do* listen, they do not necessarily like what they hear. And if they do understand they do not know what to do about it. We have likened young children to intelligent if unsophisticated creatures, burdened by the expectations of those whom they are confronted with, entering an alien world. But human adaptability itself concludes with the defensive fog that surrounds what seems to them as indeed alien. Childhood is an alien territory, another world. Most people will ensure it stays that way, for their own sake. But that does not help us understand it.

Knowing how to adapt and how much to deny is not just a sign of a fall from grace, or the assertion of self-interest. Nor is it just a result of the conditions of early socialisation. Knowing what to leave out, how to limit oneself is at the heart of the socially based learning process. No process of learning is entirely out of context. The language and the style of writing clearly is varied, and whilst the human mind always displays that alert, objective and bewildered intelligence, it has to adapt according to the circumstances in which it finds itself. One example of this is learning to read. For many people this seems like a simple matter, or one that will inevitably be acquired in time. But at its heart lies one of the complexities of learning; how to pick out the salient clue from a mass of alternatives. The secret lies not in the accumulation of new information but in the discarding of it, in knowing how to discriminate against the relevant. Spoken language depends on phonemes: those sounds that carry meaning from one voice to another despite the dialect, despite the ideolect. Each persons voice is, after all, so different that each has his or her unique speech pattern. Every word can be sounded in many different ways; and yet the word 'book' is understood in Newcastle, Liverpool, Birmingham, East London, Suffolk and Buckingham Palace let alone Alabama, California and New York. The secret lies in knowing how many clues to leave out. It is as if categorisation were a matter of rejection, of discarding the irrelevant for the purpose.

Dyslexia (referring only to reading rather than the many other potential dislocations of information) is a result of not knowing how to reject information rather than not knowing how to imbibe it. Recognising the distinctive features of sound is like recognising patterns, the underlying significance from a great deal of detail. It is like concentrating on one voice at a party in the middle of a babble of conversation, something that gets more, not less, difficult. The ability to extract the significant information from the background is a sophisticated one, not shared by computers, since it means an intuitive sense of the irrelevant, of knowing what to ignore. It should be easier for a machine than the human mind to extract the significant items of information but somehow the recognition of patterns is one of the necessary facets of the mind. By analogy, think of reading anyone's hand-writing where the letter 'A', even in print, can be written in various ways.

A a A ɑ *A a* A a ﬁA a *A* ɑ A ɑ A ɑ **A a**

Learning what is significant in sight and sound is a sign of adaptability. It can be construed as understanding the significant detail. But it is also knowing what to ignore. Those who do best can see quickly what is necessary. No-one would disagree with that. But it also implies not exploring those other issues that might not seem the point at the time. It implies that in the closed world of questions and right answers adaptability means the rejection of the alternative answer. Learning then entails not the richness of complexity, but the habitual adaptation to the necessary. For many, learning is a balance between the two, but for most, learning means veering sharply to one end or the other, the explosion of matter or the constraint of a formula. The details are all important, but demand order. But the details should accumulate first before order is imposed upon them.

At one extreme and pathological end of learning is the ability to be so heavily directed towards the interpretation and adaptation of new fact into an existing framework, or point of view, or prejudice, that evidence has little chance of survival. It is as if what had been learned was a hatred of learning, of understanding anything new. This might sound extreme if we did not have the daily demonstration of politicians on this side of human pathology. It is always useful to remind ourselves of the defensiveness of an established order - against a new idea or new theory. This is not only the cynical attachment to wealth and power, or a deliberate implementation of the fact that knowledge can be power and should be responsibility, but a manifestation of the limits of human learning. Rejection of the unwanted becomes as important as the accumulation of new awareness. This is not an inevitable process but a natural one, not one that brings out the best in people but one we have imposed on ourselves. It is 'natural' in the circumstances.

It must be recognised that people learn to become impervious to new ideas and information. They know how to dismiss the challenging, since it is uncomfortable, on the grounds that it is either obvious or irrelevant. To fight anything as untrue is to engage in a dialogue which presupposes an alternative truth. The more sophisticated unlearning game that human beings demonstrate is the undermining strategies of saying that whatever is presented is already known. The art of genius might lie in making the obvious fresh or the clearly true newly apparent, but the art of human defensiveness lies in the rejection without forethought on the grounds that it is not necessary to know. Either it is so obvious that we can continue in our ways imperviously or it is so irrelevant that nothing is disturbed in the modus vivendi.

This belief in the familiar of the status quo, in the cult of fashion, is not only felt as a necessary comfort, but is a great protection. It means that belonging to a group, a self-definition as part of a society, can be extended beyond an immediate milieu. The presentations of the insecurities and discomforts of being human are translated from the peer group in the school to their manifestations in society at large. Nothing on the face of it could seem more absurd than the kinds of snobbery felt in the superiority of being seen driving a certain kind of car. However anonymous the onlookers, there is a thrill accompanied by an unacknowledged wave of the ridiculous in seeming, for a moment, superior. But this snobbery is shared by children. Their exquisite embarrassment at their own parents' possessions, their self-consciousness about what their parents say or what they wear, the constant competition about what labels their clothes represent, says something about the shared insecurities and defensiveness of the social world. The mixture of the real - 'it is more comfortable to be in a larger car' - and the absurd - 'I wouldn't be seen dead in that' - shows how far into the mind sets of children do the social snobberies and etiquette penetrate.

One has to ask: is that culture? Or is it the inhibitions of social learning, which afflict all children? It is not just the moderately wealthy who are aware of power and status. They might present themselves in terms of snobbery and embarrassment. But all children know about the distinctions between riches and poverty. If these differences are not presented in terms of snobbery or inferiority they emerge fiercely in terms of envy or resentment. In whatever sphere these social distinctions enter in they affect the lives and minds of children. They might not be dominant but they already demonstrate the seepage of the adult world into the reality of children's experience. They also represent those social forces that wound what are supposed to be the unsullied minds of children.

Every experience has its impact, whatever the attempts to mitigate the fact. Experience is denied rather than forgotten, suppressed rather than ineffective. There is a telling phrase 'he has forgotten more about the subject than you've ever known'. Apart from the obvious put down and the reverence for the accumulation of knowledge, this assertion in fact suggests inadvertently a truth that is important for all. What is *known* is dependent on what seems to be forgotten. What is worth expressing is embedded in discarded facts. It is sometimes impossible to know where one ends and another begins. That ability to explain complexities in simple and lucid terms emerges out of a morass of information, disorganised and at times seemingly impossible to comprehend. But whilst the experience of learning a new subject has its distinct phases, so does the experience of all learning, and learning the most important subject of all. Nothing is, in fact, completely forgotten. Every fact shapes what the individual mind ultimately makes of its relationship to other facts. Even the discarded make their mark.

But what do we mean by forgetting? If the forgotten is that coastal shelf of accumulated experience, invisible and seemingly uninfluential, how does one account for the detritus that creates its make-up? Forgetting is, after all, of more than one type. In the same way that there are different approaches to new information, those which cope with the requirements of a problem and are engaged with it, and those which defend themselves against entry into a problem, so there are different processes involving forgetting.[30] For every tide of mental energy trying to enter into an idea there is at least another which retreats from it. Learning to seek out exactly what is wanted, and limiting itself to that is much an art as the uninhibited embracing of the fact. What children cannot do is to inhibit their own learning of the immediate, of human behaviour and its interpretation. They can hide from the official subjects of the curriculum and they can defend themselves from knowledge of that kind. They cannot do the same from their understandings of the everyday. A fact like a date may easily be forgotten. But an idea, personally concluded, never is, however obscure.

Remembering and forgetting are both shaped by desire, by conscious effort, and by the indeterminate effects of chance, the subjective connections of associations. This balance means it is possible to retain more than one belief at the same time, even if they are contradictory. We cannot think of the human experience without its paradoxes. There are always conflicting forces of good intentions, of cultural values and of curious behaviour. There is always a strong chance of the individual being diverted into the most anti-social or even the most inhuman behaviour, especially when there is a strong social group to enforce it. Obedience to a norm is what is culturally presented to the clear minds of young children. Their attempts to survive traumas make them vulnerable to the calls to conformity and to not standing out too much. What therefore seems as a socially acceptable stance becomes easy to conform to.[31]

This does not mean, however, that they can be moulded into whatever form that society wishes. The desire not to stand out or be too different does not altogether overcome the individual spirit. The result is the ability to believe two things at once, even if they are contradictory.[32] Far from being a kind of logical machine, the mind is able to contain parallel as well as serial ideas, to live with contradictions. In the desire to adapt, as well as in its clear intelligence, the mind learns to know both to adhere to a particular belief and know that it is absurd. The trauma of the early years can result in all kinds of limitations as well as strengths, with beliefs that are a result of wishful thinking as well as beliefs based on knowledge. Coming to terms with the realities of the world also reveals that self-deception pays. The examples laid before children are many and often contradictory. Having to extract those which lead to stability from those examples which can mislead remains difficult.

Just as the mind learns how to make order out of perception through categories, especially through words, so is the social order internalised through common interests and connections. Sometimes there are mistakes clearly made as in mixing up the word 'dog' with all four-legged animals, or in assuming 'bear' is just one toy and no other. This mismatching of categories and objects is not just a sign of the 'sweet' fallibility of children but of their need to bring order out of what would otherwise be, and seems like, chaos. Categories overlap. They contradict each other. But in each cluster of events, objects or behaviours, the power of the mind lies in placing meaning on them, seeing wherever possible the connections which hold them together. This is not just a matter of order being imposed on the mind but the mind asserting its strength in perceiving and creating order. It is the mind that creates order out of chaos.

Or, in a refinement of this principle, orders. Whilst in the subjective mind there might seem to be just one all-embracing meaning that holds all in inner thrall, such an idea does not describe the actual workings of thought. The mind has the ability but not the advantage of philosophy and logic. It accepts many points of view, it sympathises with different illogical positions. It asserts its own beliefs however implausible. It cries out for external help knowing that there is nothing there to answer the call. In fact the mind contradicts itself, just as the person behaves in ways that do not make sense. The behaviour of some is frustrating because it can be so variable, responding not just to a new circumstance but a new set of beliefs. At its most extreme this is put down to hypocrisy, as if it were a deliberate and knowing deception. But this is self-deception. Hypocrisy is an example of this tendency of the mind to have multiple standards, often contradictory. They all arise from one immutable desire: to understand by constructing an order of assumptions into which all experiences fit.

Experience is complex. There are some who manage the limitation of having just a single point of view, so there are others who have so many that they seem to lack all scruples.[33] Either is an unnatural extreme. But it should be no surprise to discover that the common human condition contains contradictions as well as guilt, the ability to act against principle as well as remorse. It all stems from the desire for conformity in an ambiguous and complicated world.

That thirst for belonging, both inner and outer, both social and personal, is so deep that it even overrides contradictions. People act according to the example of their peers not just out of weakness or fear, but because there are such pressures on them that they cannot resist that part in themselves that wants to play a part in a collective agreed will. Conformity is often despised but rarely explained. It is not just the weakness of others but an innate drive as strong as some obscure and hidden symbolic urge. How else do we explain those terrifying and inhuman acts perpetrated by people ostensibly civilised. The ache for obedience to a coherent code is often praised as a sign of 'shared values'. Loyalty to a political party, not 'fouling one's own nest'; being nationalistic, all these are constantly praised as virtues. But 'values' were shared by the National Socialists, where the lust for conformity was made a parody of a virtue in itself. But examples do not have to be so spectacular. Those people volunteering to carry out an experiment for the white coated scientists in authority were willing to electrocute their fellow citizens to death because they wanted to conform.[34] They assumed that this was what, in the circumstances, they were supposed to do. They knew they were not supposed to kill. This idea remained intact. But they also knew they had been told to, and that this seemed to be the standard norm in the laboratory in which they found themselves. Thus were their contradictions made clear. They were generally sorry for what they did whilst doing it.

For young children trying to make their own order of the world they see there is a need to make what they can of it, even if it is wrong. They cannot and do not keep an open mind until all the evidence is there on which they can make a judgement. Thinking is itself making a judgement. It is a choice. It is choosing to make a connection with one idea and not another. Whilst no-one would still cite young children as empty vessels into which all the facts are poured, they are still treated as if they were, as if they did not have a mind, in the true sense, until such time as enough evidence had accumulated in order for them to make decisions. Over and under extensions of categories, mistakes and misapprehensions, are all signs of the cerebral guessing game that is the mind at work.[35]

Children are not born with security but with a strong need for security. They are not born good but have an urgent desire to be good. Despite their awareness of their own limitations and their acknowledgement of the rewards of selfishness, there is an urge to do what is justifiable to themselves. The problem is that they are faced with such a mass of contradictions. They are both easily influenced and easily motivated, both at the same time. Their fragility is not a result of innocence or naivity but of that very urgency towards finding their own way. They wish to fit and they know it is difficult. Against the temptations of giving up or giving in, they wish to have a sense of moral security, a steadiness of judgement, a sense of self-mastery. The problem is that self-mastery involves relating to other people and their expectations. It cannot be separated from it. Children wish to conform with the collective expectations of others, with shared moral judgements and with rules. These are a result of *their* desires, rather than something forced upon them.

The desire to find their own place in society or in societies in at least one group is set against the constant awareness of the power of groups in both inclusion and exclusion. Their own most difficult and despairing moments are those when they feel themselves to be outside the normal spheres of activity and affection. That psychological alienation can be felt at home, with the sense of being abandoned by the parents, of being cast into an oblivion of indifference. This is then translated into the peer group or peer groups of school, reiterated in the approval or disapproval of the teacher, and then writ large in the sense of exclusion from the 'shared values' of the school. The sheer loneliness of rejection leaves a wound for which bandages are sought in the form of conforming. By then it does not particularly matter with what group that sense of belonging arrives; and that is the danger. For most, these matters are dealt with in the everyday absurdities of snobbery and superciliousness, those who are 'in' or 'out' of our particular exclusivity or taste. For a few the idea of a gang is the only refuge.

The developing understanding of human relationships is as much influenced by their difficulties as by their successes. One of the themes that links their personal experience with what they see of society at large is injustice. The unfairness of what people do to each other; the bomb in an aircraft 'accidentally' murdering the clearly innocent is repeated in large or small forms day by day. Children's striving for order is a longing for fairness, for equality of treatment by their parents by their friends and by teachers. But they soon recognise the arbitrariness of mood and circumstances, the hidden forces that drive people to make decisions which are clearly wrong. They also see how easily people can 'get away' with doing things which are wrong. Whilst they are themselves testing the limits of the system they are in they are doing so in order to make sure it is working. Their testing rests on the expectation that they will be kept in order, not on the hope that they will escape order.

The world that children see is an angry one, full of injustice and inexplicable suffering. They cannot ignore this. They feel easily threatened by it. What they try to do, their way of habituation, is to learn how to put it into perspective. This does not mean being able to ignore what goes on altogether but to make such disorder somehow conform with their understanding. Before they have learned to harden themselves they have learned that such daily dislocations of fairness need to be taken into account. On the one hand it does not make sense. On the other hand it has to make sense because it is there. The examples of the pathology of human nature make them long the more for a kind of security. And this can be a false one.

The balance between a desire for conventions, for harmony and order, and a realisation of unfairness and injustice is struck in the setting up of rules. Children are quick to seize on the agreed rules of a game, the discipline of action which is neither moral or immoral. Rules are the more important because they are held to be both essential and the only safeguard against chaos. Children are quick to negotiate conventions and sometimes even quicker to change or bend them. They are striking up bargains, making new pacts, seeing what they can do to manipulate the rules to their benefit. But, like born diplomats, they have a strong sense of the importance of rules, however much they try to bend them. They have a Confucian respect for convention for they see it as the only social alternative to conflict.

Children's early explorations of theories of mind, of points of view, quickly reveals contradiction and conflicts. This is not just an objective neutral stance. It is a realisation that there is a fundamental unfairness possible in life, not so much in the contrasts of birth and circumstances but in the very systems that people set up. For young children unfairness wounds. It is like being in a court case where the majesty and dignity of the law is being held up, and everyone, even the lawyers, know that on a legal technicality injustice is being done. Such an experience has a deep effect. What everyone agrees should not happen does, with everyone's connivance. Without the plastic surgery of cynicism, another form of self-deception, children are presented with a very troubling idea of the world - which remains bewildering. For them glimpses of such injustice can be an almost diurnal occurrence. Looking for some ultimate authority they find it is not there.

Of course such disappointment cannot be articulated because it has no ready relationship to the carefully structured frameworks of agreed positions; scaffolding serves to 'hide' what goes on. It is not as if children, however unsullied, could remain for long essentially different. They bring their damage like their intelligences with them until we do not know whether one is distinct from the other. The idea of being like an alien from another planet at least conveys the possibility of objectivity and intelligence. It also conveys the sense of horror, the absence of the familiar, the difficulty of finding some moral and logical substance in what is seen. But it does not convey that countering ontological fact of similarity. They do not see, like a god, within indifferent distance. They see, objectively, what they must surely join. They have, in fact, no choice, however succulent the inner fantasies of a better world and however necessary the possibilities of an alternative reality. What they see is what they will also become.

Learning to adapt is, therefore, a plangent reminder to them that they have no real choice. What then is the best way? In the absence of the proper discourse and explanation that helps each individual to become a real him or her, the answer lies in parody. To some extent parody is the way in which people learn, unselfconsciously, how to behave. They cannot truly imitate. Even the most meticulous actors cannot do that. But children are their own individual beings trying to adapt. They have their own ideas, their own visions. They wish to fit in. They do this by taking on the gestures of the adults, those means of learning how others order their lives and cope with them. Sometimes these would-be imitations can seem vicious, with those terrible gestures of violent assertion and obscene experiment. Sometimes they can be intended copies of what ought to be, almost as formulaic as a practised dance. But children try to emulate in their own way those strategies used by others, those means of coping for which they always seek. The examples given them are not powerful because children are weak and malleable but because children constantly seek out example. They need to learn. Often what they learn is to their detriment.

The essential difference between the experience of being young and old is not the greater accumulation of knowledge but the greater ability to discriminate against certain types of new knowledge. The time when the most rapid advances in accumulating intelligence are made is that of language acquisition, when such rapid advances are being made that the capacity of all minds is clear. This is not theoretical knowledge, the definition of words, but practical. Words are not just acquired but acquired by being used. A new concept is placed within the familiar context and makes a slight difference to it. If that development were continued the vocabulary in use, and by implication the conceptions and ideas unleashed by it, would be massive.[36] But as we know such an expansion does not take place. This is not because of a lack of capacity, some kind of withering of the mind as the brain stops growing, but the result of choice and experience.

No-one makes a conscious effort not to learn, even if it almost appears to be the case with some. Once the familiar boundaries of the mind are set, once some kind of personal identity, like a personal version of a nation, with borders and beliefs, is established, any new encroachments, of idea or vocabulary, take their place. What experience teaches is what to ignore, what to leave out and what to guard against. That same social phenomenon of being safe, of belonging, of not standing out, is also a mental and emotional one. It is possible to learn how to acquire what is necessary. It is equally possible to anticipate what is wanted.

One of the difficulties in school, when faced with new demands, is that there is always a temptation, or even an urge, not to concentrate. Take that young child being asked to read who looks anywhere else for an answer, who wishes to be told it, and who can no longer apply the mind to the page, even to detect the simplest of words. Think of the closure of the mind against a subject where all the clues seem to have disappeared and the feeling is as if one were innumerate. When the direction is lost, or the explanation not given, the mind seizes up, it withdraws from contention. This is not to be dismissed as sheer stupidity. It is more a failure of application, a lapse from effort. Thus the sense of accommodation to not learning is reinforced by experience. The desire to fit new information into what already exists with ease contrasts more and more greatly with what is seen as too demanding.

Conflicts of demands can work at a number of levels, from those made on the mind when the threat of failure, of not passing an arcane test, or getting the answer right, to those made by the wider perception of themselves in the world. Children are always confronted both by alternatives - the 'clever' and the 'stupid', the rich and poor, the unhappy and the contented - that their discriminations have wider outcomes than their mental agility. When children are confronted with a demand or an experience that they cannot accept there is a *refusal* to think. With psychiatric patients this is characterised by fixation, but the inability to see any possibility of change, but it is an experience that all share.[37] At its most extreme the individual feeling threatened clings to past happenings and stops thinking. But at the level of the every day, as children confronted with Piagetism tests demonstrate, there is also a *refusal* to answer even what seems the simple questions. When a demand is context free, when there are no connections to be made with what is already known, when there is no possibility of it fitting in, there is an almost automatic psychological rejection. One of the first abilities (and potential disabilities) that children learn is information management. They understand their own process of learning which rests on the secure ground of the familiar as well as their powers of absorption. They also understand the management of information as a means of helping or hindering the efforts of others. This makes them the more bewildered when confronted with the inexplicable by others.[38]

No-one, alas, is born with hindsight. That gives everyone an awareness of, and a potential, regret for the past. Nothing that happens fails to leave an effect, and this is understood by young children. Even they look back on their infancies and express regrets or nostalgia. At first these regrets are about their own personalities or temperament. They wish they would find life as easy as others seem to do. Unhappiness is a lonely emotion. At its most extreme it becomes the self-absorption of depression. But the individual sees him or herself at moments isolated from others. At those moments that sense of being 'outside' social relationships or even 'outside' knowledge throw them in on themselves as if there is no obvious escape.

Children can often seem distracted. They appear to dream but they are listening to some of those inner conflicts that are so loud and so inarticulate that no-one seems to be able to help them with. It is not just the moment of birth that is defined as a trauma, but subsequent moments of understanding. Young children's thirst for connection, attachment, responses and encouragements are often rewarded. It might seem that some have nothing to mar their optimism. But this is not the full condition of early childhood. It also contains awareness of the discriminations, the anomalies and the rejections. Children are not self-centred. That is something that has to be learned. Children are constantly gazing at what they see, coming to terms with it, relating to it. They see other points of view and are very sensitive to their relationships. They can be selfish but that is quite another matter. The sense of the self arises out of experience.

Young children can be likened to anthropologists studying the mysteries of behaviour. But they do not bring with them a ready made alternative to compare to what they see. Their study is the study of absorption. This can lead to juxtapositions of their intelligence and their circumstances. The child who has great mental gifts (which is the normal rather than exceptional) can become frustrated or bored unless there is understanding and support. A constant urge for attention and stimulation which is denied soon leads them to avoid anger or annoyance, and to adapt, since they cannot change their circumstances, by changing themselves. The way to survive is to diminish the demands. When children are kept limited they learn to limit themselves.

It is children's hunger for understanding that makes discourse with adults so important. The process of learning is never a purely academic matter. It is bound up with the emotional and the subjective, with understandings and misunderstandings, clues which are false as well as the seemingly self-evident. This constant interpretation and reinterpretation needs to be shared. Children see others in different types of social relationships but they also need them themselves, at a number of levels. The quality of conversation depends on recognising the child as a thinking being and not simply as an object for love. After all real relationships include all the levels of real friendship: an exchange of ideas, a curiosity about points of view and a willingness to discuss differences of opinion. True emotional engagement is only possible when the other person is real rather than the construct of imagination.

In learning about the self and others there is always a balance between innovation and adaptability. To make clear decisions and reach a true understanding there is a need to adapt to new problems; but if adaptation dominates, or is taken too far any real creative sense of self is lost. Similarly an innovatory spirit which does not take into account the actualities of the context will find itself clashing helplessly. These conflicting tendencies do not always balance. Everyone has made the mistake of falling too far into one side or the other. Children's learning depends on what they learn from their mistakes and from their experience, whether they survive by losing their identities - the fitting in - or whether they think their escape is through rejection. The interplay between the mind and the environment, between actions and perceptions, beliefs and desires is so constant that one cannot understand one without the other.[39]

The struggle for young children in society is to know what is expected of them and what they expect of themselves. They are not moulded by circumstance, and yet they can be burdened by expectations as well as need them. It is as if children define themselves against what they are intended to become. They do not want the hopes to be too high for they are constantly reminded of the possibilities of failure. But they equally resent a lack of expectation. It is better to hope too much than not at all.

We sometimes forget the temptation and the pressure to give up. Given the traumas of early life, inescapable and profound, human beings' continuing motivated struggle to succeed is the more remarkable. But it is not an easy process. Naked come children into the world, emotionally as well as physically. They cannot escape the pain, however much cosseted. They see the Emperor in new clothes, they tell the truth, even as the adult is capable of weaving such a garment of self-deceptions that he believes himself fully covered. Seeing the difficulties as well as the joys of the world means being often reminded of the barriers of difficult tasks. The temptation is to say 'why bother'?

Not that there is any real escape, except in the pathological extremes. But the pathologies of being human are acquired early and go deep. Early childhood is a time of extremes. It is a time of great fragility. It needs to be understood and nurtured. Only if we take it seriously can we learn to be fully human.

Notes

1.   Beal, C. Children's knowledge about representations of Intended Meaning, in Astington, J; Harris, P and Olson, D (ed.) *Developing Theories of Mind*. Cambridge University Press, pp.315-325, 1988.
     Iser, W. *The Act of Reading: A theory of the Aesthetic Response*. London, Routledge and Kegan Paul, 1976.

2. This should not be taken to suggest that anything said is meaningless or 'absurd'; nor that intentions do not matter. After all the motive for saying something is part of the message, and whatever the difficulties caused by the attitude of the listener, meaning well matters.

3. Fishbein, M and Ajzen, I. *Belief, Attitude, Intention and Behaviour*. Reading MA, Addison-Wesley, 1975.

4. Bates, E. *The Emergence of Symbols: Cognition and Communication in Infancy*. New York, Academic Press, 1979.

5. Gilhooly, K. Thinking: Directed, Undirected and Creative. London, Academic Press, 1982.
    Neisner, U. *Cognition and Reality*. New York, Appleton-Century Crofts, 1976.

6. Paivio, A. Mental Imagery in Associative Learning and Memory. *Psychological Review*. No.76, pp.241-263, 1969.
    Deese, J. *The Structure of Associations in Language and Thought*. Baltimore, John Hopkins Press, 1965.

7. Horowitz, M. *Image Formation and Cognition*. New York, Appleton-Century Crofts, 1978.

8. Bruner, J. *Beyond the Information Given: Studies in the Psychology of Knowing*. London, Allen and Unwin, 1974.

9. Or they try to believe that 'Mensch ist was er isst'.

10. Feldman, C. Thought from Language: The Linguistic Construction of cognitive representations, in Bruner, J and Haste, H (eds.). *Making Sense*. London, Methuen, pp.131-146, 1987.

11. Taylor, M; Esbensen, B and Bennett, R. Children's Understanding of Knowledge Acquisition: The Tendency for Children to Report that they have always known what they have just learned. *Child Development*, Vol.65, No.6, pp.1581-1604, 1994.

12. Brunswick, W. *Perception and the Representative Design of Psychological Experiments*. Berkeley, University of California Press, 1956.
Bartlett, F. *Remembering: A Study in Experimental and Social Psychology*. Cambridge University Press, 1932.

13. Ornstein, R. *The Psychology of Consciousness*. New York, Harcourt Brace-Javonovich, 1977.

14. Just as the defence against a new idea will be to say that the author speaks entirely from his unique experience (which is not the case).

15. Oxford English Dictionary: It originates from the Greek: 'wound'.

16. Underwood, G. *Attention and Memory*. Oxford Pergamon, 1976.

17. Every language has its distinct phonemes. In Chinese, for example, 'R' and 'L' are the same. Hence 'Flied Lice'.

18. George Eliot. *Middlemarch*.

19. Hence the analogy with the 'Eurofighter'; an aircraft designed to be inherently unstable but kept on course by computer controlled correctives.

20. James, W. *The Principles of Psychology*. New York, H Holt, p.323, 1890.

21. Eysenck, H. *Readings in Extroversion and Introversion*. London, Staples Press, 1971.
Omacbus Personality Inventory.

22. Williamson, I and Cullingford, C. The Uses and Misuses of 'Alienation' in the Social Sciences and Education. *British Journal of Educational Studies*, Vol.45, No.3, pp.263-275, 1997.

23. Habermas, J. *The Structural Transformation of the Public Sphere: An Inquiry into a Category of Bourgeois Culture*. Cambridge Polity Press, 1989.

24. Wharf, B. *Language, Thought and Reality*. Cambridge MA, MIT Press, 1956.

25. Eysenck, H. op cit.

26. Giddens, A. *The Consequence of Modernity*. Cambridge Polity Press, 1990.

27. Winnicott, D. *Through Paediatrics to Psycho-Analysis*. London, Hogarth Press, 1975.

28. Silverstone, R. *Television and Everyday Life*. London, Routledge, p.17, 1994.

29. McGinn, C. *The Subjective Views, Secondary Qualities and Indexical Thoughts*. Oxford, Clarendon Press, 1983.

30. Bruner, J. *Beyond the Information Given: Studies in the Psychology of Knowing*. London, G Allen & Unwin, 1974.

31. Milgram, S. *Obedience to Authority: An experimental view*. London, Tavistock, 1974.

32. Pears, S. *Motivated Irrationality*. London, Allen and Unwin, 1984.

33. cf. Musil's *Der Mann Ohne Eigenschaften*.

34. Milgram, S. op cit.
Latané, B and Darley, J. *The Unresponsive Bystander: Why doesn't he help?* New York, Appleton, 1970.
Arendt, H. *The Trial of Adolf Eichmann*. London, Seeker and Warburg, 1969.

35. cf. Goodman, K. *Language and Literacy*. Boston, Routledge and Kegan Paul, 1982.

36. Miller, G. *Spontaneous Apprentices. Children and Language*. New York, Seabury Press, 1977.

37. Shands, H. The Hinting of the Self: Toward a Genetic Affectology, in Modgil, S. and Modgil, C. (eds.) *Towards a Theory of Psychological Development*. Windsor, NFER, pp.61-89, 1980.

38. Hala, S; Chandler, M and Fritz, A. Fledgling Theories of Mind: Deception as a Marker of Three Years Olds Understanding of False Belief. *Child Development*, Vol.62, No.1, pp.83-97, 1991.

39. Johnson, C. Theory of Mind and the Structure of Conscious Experience, in Astington, J; Harris, P and Olson, D (eds.) *Developing Theories of Mind*. Cambridge University Press, 1988.

Conclusions

The acute attention paid to the world in which babies suddenly find themselves is the first sign of a critical, and not just responsive intelligence. Some find the thoughts of such intellectual scrutiny rather disturbing. It is easier to respond to the lack of experience that manifests itself in idiosyncratic ways by dismissing it as the informed expression of the genuinely naive than to ponder on all the consequences of such early intelligence. And yet, all the studies that so interestingly delve into the early years of children demonstrate that as early as can be observed - the limitations lie as much in the difficulties for researchers as their subjects lack of a developed language - the very young observe, note and respond with a degree of sophistication of mind that is both telling and vulnerable.

Young children not only respond to stimulation but seek it out. They like to be able to observe complex, even puzzling phenomena. When, in the experiment cited in the Introduction, very young children looked at visual games being played, they demonstrated not just the ability to count. When the hand took away one of the three figures and left two that was logical and commonplace, and the children soon lost interest. But when the hand that took away one of the three figures and left four *that* was a surprise, a game, an aberration that commanded the children's attention. They were not only counting but puzzling how such a trick could be carried out.

The young children, however, also demonstrated, by their lack of interest in the ordinary and the everyday desire for intellectual stimulation. Lying in a bare room or bland cot they miss the visual excitement that makes up their observed world. So they can easily become bored. Their very desire to share information, even before they can articulate it, is often denied by default. This seeking for intellectual challenge can lead them to develop strategies for boredom. We know how often older children are 'bored' or seek distractions. Part of this lies in their habit of having to cope without stimulation, of longing for some kind of intervention, however rare. This, ironically enough, leads them to look for passive distraction rather than developing their own internal curiosity.

The other part of the phenomenon of being 'bored' is a sign of looking for some kind of alternative world away from the threats and the shadows that they see covering their present and their future lives. Boredom is

291

manifested in distraction, in seeking something to do, something to alleviate worries. It is associated with doing those things that have the least demands on the mind, the watching of television, or the reading of comics. Being distracted is a means of coping.

The fact that young children are vulnerable intellectually as well as physically suggests that we should be far more sensitive and careful about their needs. Even if all is not complete by the age of eight there are many indications by then how the individual will subsequently respond to, and deal with, experience. The crucial point is that their early intellectual vulnerability is manifested in their *need* for stimulation and the advance of curiosity. Far from taking a Jesuitical assumption about forming the basis of a mind, we are learning about the way the mind has difficulty in developing *without* some kind of intense cultural dialogue long before religion has any meaning. Neglecting rather than trying to form the young mind has dire consequences.

The problem with such acute and raw intelligence is that what happens to it is not always intended. Parents do not *wish* to damage their children. There is no conspiracy to make life difficult. The problem is that such vulnerable young minds can be hurt inadvertently. In schools bullying is often defined as *intentional* hurt. But there is no child who has never *felt* hurt. An inadvertent remark can cause long term difficulty. An overheard quarrel between parents can be long reinterpreted. That tendency to take everything personally starts very young. The fact that someone else is making random remarks does not present the sense that we are, individually, somehow singled out.

Just as young children try to make sense of a mass of information and apply their critical scrutiny to it, so they also do so emotionally. There is no piece of evidence that does not affect them personally. Every bit matters, and it matters not only *now*, at this moment, but in the back of the mind, over time.

Certain formative moments stay in the mind, often as a level too deep and complex to be easily recalled. We must remind ourselves that not all these are traumatic. We are not dealing just with the pathological end of the human experience but with the every day. For *all* children their experience is intense. They have great and immediate excitements as well as intense pains. Because of the immediacy of their experience we tend, as observers, to assume that nothing is lasting, but this is mistaken. The emotions and the intellect are nervously exposed and the vulnerability is immediate. But whilst one feeling replaces another the inward impressions and their interpretations remain.

Such intensity is difficult to bear. What we have learned as adults is how to deal with it, and young children, without much help learn to deal with it in their own way. One central way of doing so is by categorising, an early form of stereotyping. Just as they compartmentalise their observed world they stereotype themselves, into a position or a role. The other means of coping is to observe how others create their shared stereotypes and then find a means of not being too individual, discovering how to adapt and fit in. On the one hand new information is made to fit in to the existing intellectual framework. On the other the individual strives to fit in to what is perceived as a shared habit of thought.

Critics' scrutiny of the environment leads to responsiveness. Response leads to adaptability. Whilst all new information can be made to fit into previously accepted habits of thought, the process of fitting in to other people's perceived points of view is just as powerful. There is a safety in the middle way, a cultural acceptance of what seem to be the most powerful, influential and potent forces around, whatever they are like. The pressure of adapting is very strong. The question of what is adapted to remains open and often arbitrary. Those who think they can do anything with moulding young minds miss the point. Young minds wish to mould themselves and wish to find something into which to be moulded, both at the same time. It is a personal choice to adapt.

The subtle 'choice' that each person has is between self-awareness and self absorption, between respect for a diversity of materials and points of view and a narrowing into strong and simple prejudices. The process of learning depends on creating categories and this includes stereotyping. Stereotypes are normally perceived in negative terms but they are necessary as well as powerful. There would be little humour without stereotypes. The question is whether stereotypes are understood as such or whether they retain all the perceived weight of fact. The movement of early learning is either to the embracing of the richness and the ironies of cultural stereotypes and perceiving them for what they are, or the narrowing down of the point of view to a fixed and permanent position. Young people either learn to develop a relationship, a dialogue and a tension between themselves and their environment, with self-awareness, or they merely take in, or absorb, those parts of information that suit them.

So much depends on the early years, or when the habits of mind are formed. That safety of the middle way of avoiding rather than embracing new and challenging points of view is a result of the vulnerability of early experience. There is something inherently unstable about these years. We should not think of childhood as an untroubled and settled fairytale which only the most violent or difficult circumstances would upset or harm, but as a period during which every effort, intellectual as well as emotional, needs to be made to help preserve equilibrium.

We know much more about human abilities and feelings than we do about their consequences. What are the implications of young children displaying highly developed if unformed intelligence, observing not just physical phenomena but understanding the vagaries of human behaviour? We also know that some of the influential theories of human development are misleading, especially in the way they are generalised; but we have not yet replaced them. In the middle of all the developments and distractions of the new technology we need to place a similar amount of time and energy into understanding the human experience in a fresh and open minded way. There are calls for urgent action, more punishments or better rewards, anything for an instant palliative that will transform society. But we need to have an empirical base on which to plan policies.

The more we contemplate the temporary solutions however well-meaning, the more we realise how far off the mark they are, since they are never based firmly on empirical evidence. There are genuine solutions to the growing number of crimes and the increasingly angry and disorderly behaviour that affects so many people's lives. And there are answers to the misery felt by so many. But the first step is the most difficult, and as this book makes clear, it is not a 'Normal' part of human nature to face up to anything difficult.

If there is a plea that arises from the evidence it is that we try to *understand*. Why should this be so difficult? One reason is that people like what is familiar even if it is mistaken and hate to change their point of view. The assumptions about human nature are so deeply ingrained that any challenge to it will meet with quick dismissal on the grounds that it is flawed because ... because some excuse will always be found to dismiss it.

Another reason for the difficulty in trying to understand is the political one of trying to conjure up answers before the question has been understood. The urgency of action and the desire to be seen implementing it quite undermines the evidence. Indeed, politicians, who, we must remind ourselves are also human, have an almost pathological dislike of new evidence that would challenge their position. For them evidence has two major faults. It is complicated and cannot be reduced to a slogan, and if understood makes them responsible for taking long-term action. When they want all the credit for themselves they cannot wait for years to see the results of their policies. There is accumulated evidence about the causes of criminality - far deeper than socio-economic circumstances or natural depravity - so that we *could* deal with crime. But does anyone want to? It seems not. Cynics have described the political mind as acting before thinking or as speaking rather than thinking and then refusing to change once the act is complete or the thought altered. It is noteworthy that the greatest political insult is the 'U-turn' as if a change of mind as a result of evidence is a political sin.

These glimpses into some examples of everyday shared human pathology serve to remind us of the difficulties of the circumstances in which all young human beings find themselves. We know that there is a natural tendency to rely on familiar networks - of ideas as well as people. It is no surprise that there should be a desire to remain comfortable in the shared assumptions of the unchallenged and dogmatic... It is difficult to teach old dogmas new tricks.[1]

The human instinct to reject evidence which is disturbing and to seek a middle way of mediocrity, to surround ourselves with the familiar and easy and to avoid understanding is a result not of limitation but ability. There lies the irony. The giftedness of young people in their grasp of language is clear. But this very ability has clear consequences. They receive a mass of uncensored and uncontrolled information, about themselves, about other people and about the society at large. All of this they have to make into a structure, a theory of their own.

The result is that the early years are at one level or another traumatic. There are wounds as one set of attitudes conflicts with another, as alternative systems grate. There are extremes of emotion, disappointments, anger and grief. The early years are inherently unstable.

This is, of course, quite a contrast to the more widely held belief about the simple and unaffected joys of childhood. But it arises from the evidence. It is only when we understand the nature of the human experience in the early years that we can begin to address all those issues that cause so much public concern, and will continue to do so as unabated as the problems that lead to the concern, whilst we ignore the essential cause.

When we study the actual experience of childhood unblinkered by the set dogmas we not only see the abilities and difficulties that are associated with those years but the remarkable human achievement it is to survive them. It is a marvel how many people do not fall away but do their best, to do their duty to each other and themselves when it would be easier to give up. That striving for good is a remarkable human achievement. Of course it can be easily upset, as in the behaviour of protagonists in a civil war. But the desire to succeed *despite* all the temptations not to, and despite the constant cajolements of others that put up even more possibilities of failure, says a great deal for the human spirit: not born good but striving to become better.

We need to turn away from a sentimental view of childhood as all sweetness and light and acknowledge the complexities of the experience. Otherwise we make rose-coloured spectacles of ourselves. Understanding the determination to succeed *despite* the difficulties, acknowledging the extreme sensitivities and fragilities of childhood and realising how inadvertent are some influences and how obviously wrong are others which damage gives us a start in putting forward policies to help. The remarkable achievement of every human being is the determination to succeed against difficulties. The most traumatised of young grow up at once, tired but not satisfied.[2]

There are any number of policy implications that arise from the evidence of the human experience. The most important one of all is to learn to base policy on evidence. We are all witnesses to the squandering of money on vast projects that make no difference to the problems they are designed to address, although they do pay a lot of money to the people that run them. The problem is that real change is long-term. It is slow, and complex. It depends on complex factors which involve many people. Real change cannot be imposed.

Some conclusions in terms of action arise naturally and inevitably from the evidence. The fact that different government agencies do not work with each other - another sign of human jealousy and exclusivity - does not help. The fact that all the attention is on the failures, with social workers only burdened with the increasing numbers of people who need a cure, when what they could be doing in the way of prevention could be far more effective, suggests an indifference or insensitivity to all people's needs.

Parents deserve support since parenting is a difficult task - especially to those who themselves suffered from it. The importance of the first few years is often acknowledged theoretically, but if it were really accepted, all manner of provisions would change. And schools? The teachers do their best in the face of great difficulty.[3] But how often do we really stop to look at the nature and purpose of schooling?

There are three main issues that need to be addressed although this is not the place to suggest a new education policy, whatever the temptation. The first, most significant one is how we approach the early years, including parents. It would not imply an interfering state if the community, including all agencies, from health to social welfare were involved, with all parents, in the nurturing and developing of young children, especially intellectually. The second issue is the nature of schools as institutions. They can be places that are not only under-resourced but giving an impression of institutions whose only close parallel is the prison service. And they are places where petty crime, like bullying can thrive. The third issue is that of the curriculum. We witness the learning of facts and the increase in assessment. But what is the real purpose of the curriculum? Should it not be concerned with what a civilised human being should understand about the world in which he or she is placed? Should the fundamentals not be understanding of oneself, of others, and of society as a whole? To children in school the purpose of what they are learning is rarely if ever explained to them. Instead they assume that English and Maths which dominate the timetable, are an end in themselves when they should be at the *service* of rather than centre of the real curriculum. And what about the skills of thinking?[4]

There is a great deal to be done. But the concluding plea of this book is that we should try to understand, that we at least attempt to understand the questions that arise from each day's stories of human depravity, whether those that involve many victims that are so extreme that they stir the public conscience, or whether they are the almost routine everyday occurrences or 'incidents' that fill the inside pages of the newspapers. For the readers they might be peripheral but not for those involved.

But these occurrences are in themselves the extreme. From the point of view of the individual the suffering of being a victim is intense, even if to others no more than a statistic. The actual case is that all people have been through, and go through traumatic events. Grief and shock are a part of the human experience, just as are joy and reconciliation. They are also part of the experience of the early years, rather than saved up for later. Many of these feelings are at their most intense in childhood before we have learned how to manage them. Often they are suppressed. Usually they are forgotten. But their effect remains.

But in the end, when we have understood the clever misreadings of the human condition and the psychological impulses that cause them, when we understand the nature of childhood and its effects, when we acknowledge the complexities of experience, we are left not with a sense of despair, but of wonder. How do human beings usually survive all this? What great capacity is there that leads them through what seems like alien territory until they are absorbed into the shared landscape? What great desire maintains some form of equilibrium in the face of so much that is difficult and contrary?

Oh brave new world, that has such people in it ...

Notes

1.   According to Dorothy Parker.

2.   Juvenal Satire 6. "Lassata Nondum Satiata". Literally "wearied but not sated", used by Thackerey in *Vanity Fair*.

3.   No-one should underrate the complexities of teaching; infinitely more difficult than the most intricate of medical or surgical practice, but not recognised as such.

4.   Quinn, A. *Critical Thinking in Young Minds*. London, David Fulton, 1997.